Second Edition

GREAT JOBS

FOR

Sociology Majors

Stephen Lambert

VGM Career Books

Chicago   New York   San Francisco   Lisbon   London   Madrid   Mexico City
Milan   New Delhi   San Juan   Seoul   Singapore   Sydney   Toronto

The *McGraw·Hill* Companies

Library of Congress Cataloging-in-Publication Data

Lambert, Stephen E.
    Great jobs for sociology majors / Stephen Lambert. — 2nd ed. / revised by Julie Rigby.
        p.   cm. — (Great jobs for)
    Includes bibliographical references and index.
    ISBN 0-07-140301-9
    1. Sociology—Vocational guidance—United States.   I. Rigby, Julie.   II. Title.   III. Series.

    HM585 .L24   2002
    301'.023'73—dc21   2002069048

1 2 3 4 5 6 7 8 9 0   LBM/LBM   1 0 9 8 7 6 5 4 3 2

ISBN 0-07-140301-9

McGraw-Hill books are available at special quantity discounts to use as premiums and sales promotions, or for use in corporate training programs. For more information, please write to the Director of Special Sales, Professional Publishing, McGraw-Hill, Two Penn Plaza, New York, NY 10121-2298. Or contact your local bookstore.

This book is printed on acid-free paper.

This book is dedicated to my long-term colleagues at Plymouth State College. As I approach my twentieth year on this beautiful campus, I want to express my deep gratitude for the pleasure of working alongside Steve Bamford, Diane Brandon, Gene Fahey, Michael Fischler, Dick and Pat Hage, Tim Keefe, Jim McLaughlin, Merryl Reichbach, and Bob Tuveson—my colleagues in the division of Student Affairs.

Writing this book, with its emphasis on the sociologist's fascination with how people and organizations function, has renewed my appreciation for the fine group of colleagues I have an opportunity to work with day in and day out on my campus.

Contents

Introduction

The Value of a Degree in Sociology

As a busy career counselor I have spoken with many, many sociology majors throughout the years. Sociology has always been one of the more popular declared majors, and in recent years the number of students graduating with degrees in sociology and related social sciences is on the rise. It is striking how many of the students I talk with describe sociology as a "perfect fit" with who they are and what they want to learn. Sociology is such an appealing field for several reasons, but perhaps one of the most compelling is that as a sociology major you are not just permitted but actively encouraged to pursue your questions about the social life of people. Few subjects could be as interesting, and few have a laboratory that encompasses every site of human interaction. We are social beings, and therefore it follows that we would be intrigued by questions regarding our social relations, social structure and change, and the causes and consequences of human behavior.

Because sociology is the study of people in their social context, it calls for observing and studying the behavior of people as members of a group, rather than as individuals. If you're fascinated by groups and the behavior of people as social animals, the sociology major provides a deeply fulfilling course of study.

Sociology as a social science is a fairly recent development, growing out of a need to explain humankind's social behavior in a manner that was not addressed by other social sciences, such as history, economics, and political science. Economics studies the production and distribution of wealth. History addresses the problem of telling a factual, accurate story of what has happened in the past. And political science wrestles with questions regarding the distribution of power in society. Each examines human actions but from within their own discipline's framework. Sociology borrows some from each of these fields but focuses on the study of people in social relationships. During the course of acquiring your degree in sociology, you develop a sense of history, as well as a good working knowledge of economics.

Sociology also touches closely upon the work of other disciplines. One of the closest working relationships is that between sociologists and statisticians who analyze the significance of sociological data. You'll examine the importance of this professional relationship when you study methods of social research.

Psychology and sociology have been so closely tied together that a specialization that incorporates both fields has evolved: social psychology. Social psychologists also acknowledge the contributions of both cultural anthropology and psychiatry. Psychologists attempt to understand individual human behavior, while sociologists try to discover basic truths about groups. When these two social sciences are combined, the focus is the study of persons as members of groups. Social psychologists study how individual behavior affects group behavior and the ways in which groups influence individual behavior. Sociologists and psychiatrists have also contributed to the efforts of the medical community.

Ethnology and ethnography, social sciences that treat the subdivisions of mankind and their description and classification, are other fields with which sociologists work closely. Problems in racial understanding and cooperation, in failures of communication, and in differences of belief and behavior are all concerns of the sociologist who studies underlying reasons for group conduct.

I don't hesitate to recommend that students who are undecided about their choice of major or career explore sociology as a possible alternative. With all its strong ties to other fields of study, sociology is a very strong undergraduate preparation for many other careers: research, law, business, nursing, travel and tourism, and anthropology. It not only can provide a strong liberal arts background, but can also foster an understanding of the human condition that can be brought to bear in many, many areas of employment or further education.

Some of the particular ways in which sociology develops you academically is through the synthesizing and generalizing that sociology does as it borrows from other disciplines.

In sum, as a sociology major you have received an extremely strong foundation on which to build the career of your choice. With your understanding of social change and your well-developed research and communication skills, the real challenge ahead lies in deciding where you are most eager to apply your many talents.

Sociology Offers Unlimited Possibilities

The sociological inquiry focuses mainly on two areas: the social relationships or interactions of people in groups and the role expectations or common beliefs and values people are likely to have about themselves and others within what they regard as "their" group.

As individuals, we often describe ourselves by letting others know what groups we belong to. Hence, part of our identity may be made up by our membership in a community safety board, a cross-country ski team, a sorority or fraternity, or a book club. It is an interesting exercise for sociology majors to put the groups we ourselves belong to under the microscope to examine how they work, who is friendly and who is not, and who is cooperative and who is competitive within the group. And while we may have a sense of why some individuals are singled out as leaders, how cliques form within a group, or how leaders treat members of the group, a rigorous sociological examination could reveal some elements that we had not yet taken into account. Do these exercises sound frivolous or unrelated to the pursuit of sociological knowledge? Not to a sociology major, who knows that these and many similar questions are what sociology is made of.

Another focus is to investigate the realm of values and beliefs. The attitudes and opinions that are held in common by groups are what bind them together and create the many smaller divisions within society as people cluster around commonly held beliefs. This can be quite complex, when ten members of a political party may belong to ten different religious organizations or have widely varying views on racial tolerance, birth control, education, or any number of subjects which they support through affiliation in other groups, with either active participation or simple identification with the aims of those groups.

Let's look at a standard description for an Introduction to Sociology course. At hundreds of colleges and universities around the country, new sociology students are registered in a class that covers something like this.

An introduction to the study of society which is an overview that includes an examination of the issues of socialization, human interaction, social class, social inequality, human diversity, and social institutions.

This introductory course will paint, in broad brush strokes, the canvas of sociological study. You will probably begin by looking at the human world in the largest sense. You will become familiar with the sociological perspective on culture, society, how we "fit" in society (socialization), and the elements of personality.

You'll examine populations and how they move and why. Within those populations, you'll examine structures of class and hierarchies of esteem. You'll also examine communities, minorities, and the division of labor.

Much of your time will be spent looking at the social institutions of family, marriage, education, religion, and politics. You'll study social problems of child and spouse abuse, juvenile delinquency, and unemployment.

Each of the topics outlined in this introductory course is but the merest tip of an iceberg of information, study, and research and even subspecialties that are the life's work of sociologists around the world. Sociologists specialize in an array of focused areas. The following is a partial list of these:

- **Penologists** may specialize in research on the control and prevention of crime, punishment for crime and management of penal institutions, and rehabilitation of criminal offenders.
- **Criminologists** specialize in research on relationships between criminal law and social order in causes of crime and behavior of criminals.
- **Industrial sociologists** may specialize in research on group relationships and processes in an industrial organization.
- **Rural sociologists** may specialize in research on rural communities in contrast with urban communities and special problems occasioned by the impact of scientific and industrial revolutions on a rural way of life.
- **Social ecologists** specialize in research on interrelations between physical environment and technology in spatial distribution of people and their activities.
- **Social problems specialists** may specialize in research on social problems arising from individual or group deviation from commonly accepted standards of conduct, such as crime and delinquency, or social problems and racial discrimination rooted in failure of society to achieve its collective purposes.
- **Urban sociologists** focus on research on the origin, growth, structure, and demographic characteristics of cities and social patterns and distinctive problems that result from an urban environment.
- **Demographers** are population specialists who collect and analyze vital statistics related to population changes, such as birth, marriages, and death. Demographers plan and conduct demographic research, surveys, and experiments to study human populations and affecting trends.

- **Clinical sociologists** are concerned with group dysfunction and work with individuals and groups to identify and alleviate problems related to factors such as group organization, authority relationships, and role conflicts.
- **Social pathologists** specialize in investigation of group behavior that is considered detrimental to the proper functioning of society.
- **Social welfare research workers** conduct research that is used as a tool for planning and carrying out social welfare programs.

This list hardly makes a dent in the possible fields of study that can engage or will engage the sociologist of the future. The sociologist is in the very middle of our culture. Those who enjoy analyzing the meaning of current trends should enjoy thoroughly the professional experiences of sociology.

Many of these specialties demand an advanced degree. And in times of economic recession, those with a master's degree or Ph.D. will be more likely to get job offers than those with B.A. degrees, because employers can secure graduates with greater skill and knowledge for the same salary they might have paid B.A. holders. Nevertheless, possibilities for entering the field still exist for the persistent applicant. For example, one can start with a job in a research organization as an interviewer—a typical entry-level position. Or you might assist in other ways with the collection of data. Begin immediately to acquire as many of those "portable skills" offered in your workplace as you can, including computer applications, training, leadership opportunities, and writing assignments. Use any educational benefits offered to begin acquiring the educational background you feel will move you forward in your career.

If you've selected sociology simply because you want a degree that promises the most mileage from your investment in a college education, sociology delivers! Many new graduates will be hired as trainees and assistants in business, industry, and government, where once again, the outlook is best for those with training in quantitative research methods. Some with a bachelor's degree may obtain work in social welfare agencies.

A sociology major is also a fantastic way to launch yourself into other related careers. Many people choose to major in sociology because of the strong preparation it gives you for fields such as journalism, law, business, social work, recreation, and counseling. With the proper state certification, some may teach sociology in high schools.

Sociologists also have a noticeable role in a number of federal government agencies, a career path that is discussed in detail in this guide. While many government sociologists work in research, others are active in administering a number of federal programs, while another whole subset function in an advisory capacity. And in the private sphere, some individuals may be employed by private research organizations while others contribute their sociological expertise to management consultant firms.

Whether you are determined to enter the workforce right away or considering a graduate degree in sociology, it will be immensely helpful to your own self-awareness and for your résumé to think about doing an internship. Whether you are still in college or pursuing an internship upon graduation, the intern experience will allow you to try on for "fit" a potential career. Though many internships do not pay, the dividends can still be enormous, as they increase your chances of admission to graduate school (should that be your destination) as well as your ability to get the next job. As you may well know, entry-level positions are often advertised for those who have both a degree as well as a year or two of actual work experience. An internship not only allows you to fine-tune your own career search, but also opens doors that might otherwise remain closed.

Thoreau's *Walden* remains a popular book though written between 1846 and 1847. Part of its attractiveness is probably our yearning to live in a simpler, less complex society. The reality is that we do not. In fact, many would argue that society is becoming bewilderingly complex. All of us, no matter what our major, would do well to learn a great deal about the society and world we live in. It is the only antidote to prejudice or sentiment. Sociology's promise is to replace blind sentiment and thoughtless prejudice with sociological knowledge. This is especially important in a democratic country such as ours where there are so many choices and legal protections for those choices.

All of our major adjustments in life, including the important transitions into and out of college, are far easier if we understand and appreciate how society and its trends work. How are organizations structured and how can you make your own way in them? What is the current dialogue on privacy and freedom of choice and what impact does that have on your role as a worker? Are societal shifts temporary or is there some long-term trend occurring? The answers don't lie in this book, but for the student embarking on a study of sociology, these and many other questions will provide the beginnings of a wonderful, possibly lifelong dialogue. Sociology will fulfill the promise of a lifetime of excitement, discovery, and satisfaction.

PART ONE

THE JOB SEARCH

The Self-Assessment

Self-assessment is the process by which you begin to acknowledge your own particular blend of education, experiences, values, needs, and goals. It provides the foundation for career planning and the entire job search process. Self-assessment involves looking inward and asking yourself what can sometimes prove to be difficult questions. This self-examination should lead to an intimate understanding of your personal traits, your personal values, your consumption patterns and economic needs, your longer-term goals, your skill base, your preferred skills, and your underdeveloped skills.

You come to the self-assessment process knowing yourself well in some of these areas, but you may still be uncertain about other aspects. You may be well aware of your consumption patterns, but have you spent much time specifically identifying your longer-term goals or your personal values as they relate to work? No matter what level of self-assessment you have undertaken to date, it is now time to clarify all of these issues and questions as they relate to the job search.

The knowledge you gain in the self-assessment process will guide the rest of your job search. In this book, you will learn about all of the following tasks:

- Writing résumés
- Exploring possible job titles
- Identifying employment sites
- Networking
- Interviewing
- Following up
- Evaluating job offers

In each of these steps, you will rely on and often return to the understanding gained through your self-assessment. Any individual seeking employment must be able and willing to express these facets of his or her personality to recruiters and interviewers throughout the job search. This communication allows you to show the world who you are so that together with employers you can determine whether there will be a workable match with a given job or career path.

How to Conduct a Self-Assessment

The self-assessment process goes on naturally all the time. People ask you to clarify what you mean, you make a purchasing decision, or you begin a new relationship. You react to the world and the world reacts to you. How you understand these interactions and any changes you might make because of them are part of the natural process of self-discovery. There is, however, a more comprehensive and efficient way to approach self-assessment with regard to employment.

Because self-assessment can become a complex exercise, we have distilled it into a seven-step process that provides an effective basis for undertaking a job search. The seven steps include the following:

1. Understanding your personal traits
2. Identifying your personal values
3. Calculating your economic needs
4. Exploring your longer-term goals
5. Enumerating your skill base
6. Recognizing your preferred skills
7. Assessing skills needing further development

As you work through your self-assessment, you might want to create a worksheet similar to the one shown in Exhibit 1.1, starting on the following page. Or you might want to keep a journal of the thoughts you have as you undergo this process. There will be many opportunities to revise your self-assessment as you start down the path of seeking a career.

Step I   Understanding Your Personal Traits
Each person has a unique personality that he or she brings to the job search process. Gaining a better understanding of your personal traits can help you evaluate job and career choices. Identifying these traits and then finding

Exhibit 1.1
SELF-ASSESSMENT WORKSHEET

Step 1. Understand Your Personal Traits
The personal traits that describe me are:
(Include all of the words that describe you.)
The ten personal traits that most accurately describe me are:
(List these ten traits.)

Step 2. Identify Your Personal Values
Working conditions that are important to me include:
(List working conditions that would have to exist for you to accept a position.)
The values that go along with my working conditions are:
(Write down the values that correspond to each working condition.)
Some additional values I've decided to include are:
(List those values you identify as you conduct this job search.)

Step 3. Calculate Your Economic Needs
My estimated minimum annual salary requirement is:
(Write the salary you have calculated based on your budget.)
Starting salaries for the positions I'm considering are:
(List the name of each job you are considering and the associated starting salary.)

Step 4. Explore Your Longer-Term Goals
My thoughts on longer-term goals right now are:
(Jot down some of your longer-term goals as you know them right now.)

Step 5. Enumerate Your Skill Base
The general skills I possess are:
(List the skills that underlie tasks you are able to complete.)
The specific skills I possess are:
(List more technical or specific skills that you possess, and indicate your level of expertise.)
General and specific skills that I want to promote to employers for the jobs I'm considering are:
(List general and specific skills for each type of job you are considering.)

continued

Step 6. Recognize Your Preferred Skills
Skills that I would like to use on the job include:
(List skills that you hope to use on the job, and indicate how often you'd like to use them.)

Step 7. Assess Skills Needing Further Development
Some skills that I'll need to acquire for the jobs I'm considering include:
(Write down skills listed in job advertisements or job descriptions that you don't currently possess.)
I believe I can build these skills by:
(Describe how you plan to acquire these skills.)

employment that allows you to draw on at least some of them can create a rewarding and fulfilling work experience. If potential employment doesn't allow you to use these preferred traits, it is important to decide whether you can find other ways to express them or whether you would be better off not considering this type of job. Interests and hobbies pursued outside of work hours can be one way to use personal traits you don't have an opportunity to draw on in your work. For example, if you consider yourself an outgoing person and the kinds of jobs you are examining allow little contact with other people, you may be able to achieve the level of interaction that is comfortable for you outside of your work setting. If such a compromise seems impractical or otherwise unsatisfactory, you probably should explore only jobs that provide the interaction you want and need on the job.

Many young adults who are not very confident about their attractiveness to employers will downplay their need for income. They will say, "Money is not all that important if I love my work." But if you begin to document exactly what you need for housing, transportation, insurance, clothing, food, and utilities, you will begin to understand that some jobs cannot meet your financial needs and it doesn't matter how wonderful the job is. If you have to worry each payday about bills and other financial obligations, you won't be very effective on the job. Begin now to be honest with yourself about your needs.

Inventorying Your Personal Traits. Begin the self-assessment process by creating an inventory of your personal traits. Using the list in Exhibit 1.2, decide which of these personal traits describe you.

Exhibit 1.2
PERSONAL TRAITS

Accurate	Eager	Inventive
Active	Easygoing	Jovial
Adaptable	Efficient	Just
Adventurous	Emotional	Kind
Affectionate	Empathetic	Liberal
Ambitious	Energetic	Likable
Analytical	Excitable	Logical
Appreciative	Expressive	Loyal
Artistic	Extroverted	Mature
Brave	Fair-minded	Methodical
Businesslike	Farsighted	Meticulous
Calm	Feeling	Mistrustful
Capable	Firm	Modest
Caring	Flexible	Motivated
Cautious	Formal	Objective
Cheerful	Friendly	Observant
Clean	Future-oriented	Open-minded
Competent	Generous	Opportunistic
Confident	Gentle	Optimistic
Conscientious	Good-natured	Organized
Conservative	Helpful	Original
Considerate	Honest	Outgoing
Cool	Humorous	Patient
Cooperative	Idealistic	Peaceful
Courageous	Imaginative	Personable
Creative	Impersonal	Persuasive
Critical	Independent	Pleasant
Curious	Individualistic	Poised
Daring	Industrious	Polite
Decisive	Informal	Practical
Deliberate	Innovative	Precise
Detail-oriented	Intellectual	Principled
Determined	Intelligent	Private
Discreet	Introverted	Productive
Dominant	Intuitive	Progressive

continued

Problem solver	Sedentary	Tactful
Quick	Self-confident	Thorough
Quiet	Self-controlled	Thoughtful
Rational	Self-disciplined	Tolerant
Realistic	Sensible	Trusting
Receptive	Serious	Trustworthy
Reflective	Sincere	Truthful
Relaxed	Sociable	Understanding
Reliable	Spontaneous	Unexcitable
Reserved	Strong	Uninhibited
Resourceful	Strong-minded	Verbal
Responsible	Structured	Versatile
Reverent	Subjective	Wise

Focusing on Selected Personal Traits. Of all the traits you identified from the list in Exhibit 1.2, select the ten you believe most accurately describe you. If you are having a difficult time deciding, think about which words people who know you well would use to describe you. Keep track of these ten traits.

Considering Your Personal Traits in the Job Search Process. As you begin exploring jobs and careers, watch for matches between your personal traits and the job descriptions you read. Some jobs will require many personal traits you know you possess, and others will not seem to match those traits.

A job overseas as an international human resources manager calls for a person who is adventurous, empathetic, flexible, and open-minded. Working closely with individuals from another culture also requires tolerance and the ability to tackle new challenges, such as learning a foreign language. Human resources positions, both at home and abroad, are best filled by those who are organized, thoughtful, and discreet.

Your ability to respond to changing conditions, your decision-making ability, productivity, creativity, and verbal skills all have a bearing on your success in and enjoyment of your work life. To better guarantee success, be sure to take the time needed to understand these traits in yourself.

Step 2   Identifying Your Personal Values

Your personal values affect every aspect of your life, including employment, and they develop and change as you move through life. Values can be defined as principles that we hold in high regard, qualities that are important and desirable to us. Some values aren't ordinarily connected to work (love, beauty, color, light, relationships, family, or religion), and others are (autonomy, cooperation, effectiveness, achievement, knowledge, and security). Our values determine, in part, the level of satisfaction we feel in a particular job.

Defining Acceptable Working Conditions.   One facet of employment is the set of working conditions that must exist for someone to consider taking a job.

Each of us would probably create a unique list of acceptable working conditions, but items that might be included on many people's lists are the amount of money you would need to be paid, how far you are willing to drive or travel, the amount of freedom you want in determining your own schedule, whether you would be working with people or data or things, and the types of tasks you would be willing to do. Your conditions might include statements of working conditions you will *not* accept; for example, you might not be willing to work at night or on weekends or holidays.

If you were offered a job tomorrow, what conditions would have to exist for you to realistically consider accepting the position? Take some time and make a list of these conditions.

Realizing Associated Values.   Your list of working conditions can be used to create an inventory of your values relating to jobs and careers you are exploring. For example, if one of your conditions stated that you wanted to earn at least $30,000 per year, the associated value would be financial gain. If another condition was that you wanted to work with a friendly group of people, the value that went along with that might be belonging or interaction with people. Exhibit 1.3 provides a list of commonly held values that relate to the work environment; use it to create your own list of personal values.

Relating Your Values to the World of Work.   As you read the job descriptions in this book and in other suggested resources, think about the values associated with each position.

For example, working as an affirmative action coordinator might complement one's own personal values, such as a need for moral fulfillment in a fast-paced and challenging workplace.

Exhibit 1.3
WORK VALUES

Achievement	Effectiveness	Precision
Advancement	Excitement	Prestige
Adventure	Fast pace	Privacy
Attainment	Financial gain	Profit
Authority	Helping	Recognition
Autonomy	Humor	Responsiblity
Belonging	Improvisation	Risk
Challenge	Independence	Security
Change	Influencing others	Self-expression
Communication	Intellectual stimulation	Solitude
Community	Interaction	Stability
Competition	Knowledge	Status
Completion	Leading	Structure
Contribution	Mastery	Supervision
Control	Mobility	Surroundings
Cooperation	Moral fulfillment	Teamwork
Creativity	Organization	Time freedom
Decision making	Physical activity	Variety
Development	Power	

If you were thinking about a career in this field, or any other field you're exploring, at least some of the associated values should match those you extracted from your list of working conditions. Take a second look at any values that don't match up. How important are they to you? What will happen if they are not satisfied on the job? Can you incorporate those personal values elsewhere? Your answers need to be brutally honest. As you continue your exploration, be sure to add to your list any additional values that occur to you.

Step 3   Calculating Your Economic Needs

Each of us grew up in an environment that provided for certain basic needs, such as food and shelter, and, to varying degrees, other needs that we now consider basic, such as cable television, E-mail, or an automobile. Needs such as privacy, space, and quiet, which at first glance may not appear to be monetary needs, may add to housing expenses and so should be considered as you examine your economic needs. For example, if you place a high value on a large, open living space for yourself, it would be difficult to satisfy that need without an associated high housing cost, especially in a densely populated city environment.

As you prepare to move into the world of work and become responsible for meeting your own basic needs, it is important to consider the salary you will need to be able to afford a satisfying standard of living. The three-step process outlined here will help you plan a budget, which in turn will allow you to evaluate the various career choices and geographic locations you are considering. The steps include (1) developing a realistic budget, (2) examining starting salaries, and (3) using a cost-of-living index.

Developing a Realistic Budget. Each of us has certain expectations for the kind of lifestyle we want to maintain. To begin the process of defining your economic needs, it will be helpful to determine what you expect to spend on routine monthly expenses. These expenses include housing, food, transportation, entertainment, utilities, loan repayments, and revolving charge accounts. A worksheet that details many of these expenses is shown in Exhibit 1.4. You may not currently spend anything for certain items, but you probably will have to once you begin supporting yourself. As you develop this budget, be generous in your estimates, but keep in mind any items that could be reduced or eliminated. If you are not sure about the cost of a certain item, talk with family or friends who would be able to give you a realistic estimate.

If this is new or difficult for you, start to keep a log of expenses right now. You may be surprised at how much you actually spend each month for food or stamps or magazines. Household expenses and personal grooming items can often loom very large in a budget, as can auto repairs or home maintenance.

Income taxes must also be taken into consideration when examining salary requirements. State and local taxes vary, so it is difficult to calculate exactly the effect of taxes on the amount of income you need to generate. To roughly estimate the gross income necessary to generate your minimum annual salary requirement, multiply the minimum salary you have calculated (see Exhibit 1.4) by a factor of 1.35. The resulting figure will be an approximation of what your gross income would need to be, given your estimated expenses.

Examining Starting Salaries. Starting salaries for each of the career tracks are provided throughout this book. These salary figures can be used in con-

Exhibit 1.4
ESTIMATED MONTHLY EXPENSES WORKSHEET

		Could Reduce Spending? (Yes/No)
Cable	$ _____	_____
Child care	_____	_____
Clothing	_____	_____
Educational loan repayment	_____	_____
Entertainment	_____	_____
Food		
At home	_____	_____
Meals out	_____	_____
Gifts	_____	_____
Housing		
Rent/mortgage	_____	_____
Insurance	_____	_____
Property taxes	_____	_____
Medical insurance	_____	_____
Reading materials	_____	_____
Newspapers	_____	_____
Magazines	_____	_____
Books	_____	_____
Revolving loans/charges	_____	_____
Savings	_____	_____
Telephone	_____	_____
Transportation		
Auto payment	_____	_____
Insurance	_____	_____
Parking	_____	_____
Gasoline	_____	_____
or		
Cab/train/bus fare	_____	_____
Utilities		
Electric	_____	_____
Gas	_____	_____
Water/sewer	_____	_____

	Could Reduce Spending? (Yes/No)
Vacations	
Miscellaneous expense 1	_____ _____
Expense: _____	
Miscellaneous expense 2	_____ _____
Expense: _____	
Miscellaneous expense 3	_____ _____
Expense: _____	
TOTAL MONTHLY EXPENSES:	_____ _____
YEARLY EXPENSES	
(Monthly expenses $\times$ 12):	_____ _____
INCREASE TO INCLUDE TAXES	
(Yearly expenses $\times$ 1.35):	_____ _____ =
MINIMUM ANNUAL SALARY	
REQUIREMENT:	_____

junction with the cost-of-living index (discussed in the next section) to determine whether you would be able to meet your basic economic needs in a given geographic location.

Using a Cost-of-Living Index. If you are thinking about trying to get a job in a geographic region other than the one where you now live, understanding differences in the cost of living will help you come to a more informed decision about making a move. By using a cost-of-living index, you can compare salaries offered and the cost of living in different locations with what you know about the salaries offered and the cost of living in your present location.

Many variables are used to calculate the cost-of-living index. Often included are housing, groceries, utilities, transportation, health care, clothing, and entertainment expenses. Right now you do not need to worry about the details associated with calculating a given index. The main purpose of this exercise is to help you understand that pay ranges for entry-level positions may not vary greatly, but the cost of living in different locations *can* vary tremendously.

Let's suppose you are considering a future as an occupational career counselor. According to information available from the CNN/*Money Magazine* website, in February 2002, an occupational career counselor working in the United States would earn a median base salary of $27,515. However, your earnings would also depend on several other factors, including what part of the country you lived in.

Thus, the median base salary would be

- $26,001 in Springfield, Missouri
- $28,481 in Denver, Colorado
- $28,923 in Minneapolis, Minnesota
- $31,906 in New York, New York
- $32,238 in San Francisco, California

At first glance, one might suppose that the most financially rewarding place to seek employment would be in New York or San Francisco. However, you might be surprised to see how these salary figures really look once you dig a little deeper into the actual cost of living in these cities.

For example, if you were living in Springfield and considering a move to Denver, Colorado, you would perhaps increase your salary by several thousand dollars. You would also presumably want to replicate or even improve your financial well-being. It turns out, however, that to live as well as in Denver as you do in Springfield on $26,001, you would need to make $30,556. The statistics show that your costs would rise across the board:

- Groceries are 18.07 percent more expensive in Denver.
- Housing is 40.35 percent more expensive.
- Utilities are 3.2 percent higher.
- Transportation is 15.03 percent higher.
- Health care is 30.86 percent higher.
- Miscellaneous goods are 1.75 percent higher.

Nevertheless, the difference between Springfield and Denver is not overwhelmingly daunting, and if lifestyle or other personal reasons were to make that an attractive move for you, you might feel rather encouraged by these numbers.

Let's see what would happen if the same occupational career counselor was exploring career possibilities in San Francisco and New York. In San Francisco, you would need to earn $58,933 to be able to afford the same things that you can get in Springfield for $26,001.

- Groceries are 33.69 percent higher.
- Housing is an astonishing 386.28 percent higher!
- Utilities go up by 77.94 percent.
- Transportation is higher by 43.81 percent.
- Health care is 73.66 percent more expensive.
- Miscellaneous goods and services would rise by 17.26 percent.

And not surprisingly, living in Manhattan would require an even larger income: $68,128.

- Groceries higher than Springfield by 54.65 percent.
- Housing goes up by 470.23 percent.
- Utilities are 119.20 percent more expensive.
- Transportation is 28.78 percent higher.
- Health care is 85.28 percent more.
- Miscellaneous goods and services go up 40.08 percent.

Nevertheless, one shouldn't become too discouraged by these figures. First of all, in the larger cities there are more opportunities for employment, as well as advancement and the option of linking up with other careers that your initial job may lead to. And you may have personal reasons that outweigh monetary concerns. On the other hand, if you were to begin your working life in one of the more expensive cities, you might be very pleasantly surprised to find what your salary can provide for should you decide to move out of the big city!

You can work through a similar exercise for any type of job you are considering and for many locations when current salary information is available. It will be worth your time to undertake this analysis if you are seriously considering a relocation. By doing so you will be able to make an informed choice.

Step 4 Exploring Your Longer-Term Goals

There is no question that when we first begin working, our goals are to use our skills and education in a job that will reward us with employment, income, and status relative to the preparation we brought with us to this position. If we are not being paid as much as we feel we should for our level of education or if job demands don't provide the intellectual stimulation we had hoped for, we experience unhappiness and as a result often seek other employment.

Most jobs we consider "good" are those that fulfill our basic "lower-level" needs of security, food, clothing, shelter, income, and productive work. But even when our basic needs are met and our jobs are secure and productive, we as individuals are constantly changing. As we change, the demands and expectations we place on our jobs may change. Fortunately, some jobs grow and change with us, and this explains why some people are happy throughout many years in a job.

But more often people are bigger than the jobs they fill. We have more goals and needs than any job could satisfy. These are "higher-level" needs of self-esteem, companionship, affection, and an increasing desire to feel we are employing ourselves in the most effective way possible. Not all of these higher-level needs can be met through employment, but for as long as we are employed, we increasingly demand that our jobs play their part in moving us along the path to fulfillment.

Another obvious but important fact is that we change as we mature. Although our jobs also have the potential for change, they may not change as frequently or as markedly as we do. There are increasingly fewer one-job, one-employer careers; we must think about a work future that may involve voluntary or forced moves from employer to employer. Because of that very real possibility, we need to take advantage of the opportunities in each position we hold. Acquiring the skills and competencies associated with each position will keep us viable and attractive as employees. This is particularly true in a job market that not only is technology/computer dependent, but also is populated with more and more small, self-transforming organizations rather than the large, seemingly stable organizations of the past.

It may be difficult in the early stages of the job search to determine whether the path you are considering can meet these longer-term goals. Reading about career paths and individual career histories in your field can be very helpful in this regard. Meeting and talking with individuals further along in their careers can be enlightening as well. Older workers can provide valuable guidance on "self-managing" your career, which will become an increasingly valuable skill in the future. Some of these ideas may seem remote as you read this now, but you should be able to appreciate the need to ensure that you are growing, developing valuable new skills, and researching other employers who might be interested in your particular skills package.

Let's suppose you are drawn to a career as a substance abuse counselor. Learning more about the career potential would involve speaking to a recent graduate in the field, as well as with his or her supervisor and with the director of a social services agency. In this way you'd gain a better understanding of how your responsibilities would change with time, as well as a sense of how these professionals cope with working in a very stressful field.

Step 5 Enumerating Your Skill Base

In terms of the job search, skills can be thought of as capabilities that can be developed in school, at work, or by volunteering and then used in specific job settings. Many studies have documented the kinds of skills that employers seek in entry-level applicants. For example, some of the most desired skills for individuals interested in the teaching profession are the ability to interact effectively with students one-on-one, to manage a classroom, to adapt to varying situations as necessary, and to get involved in school activities. Business employers have also identified important qualities, including enthusiasm for the employer's product or service, a businesslike mind, the ability to follow written or oral instructions, the ability to demonstrate self-control, the confidence to suggest new ideas, the ability to communicate with all members of a group, an awareness of cultural differences, and loyalty, to name just a few. You will find that many of these skills are also in the repertoire of qualities demanded in your college major.

To be successful in obtaining any given job, you must be able to demonstrate that you possess a certain mix of skills that will allow you to carry out the duties required by that job. This skill mix will vary a great deal from job to job; to determine the skills necessary for the jobs you are seeking, you can read job advertisements or more generic job descriptions, such as those found later in this book. If you want to be effective in the job search, you must directly show employers that you possess the skills needed to be successful in filling the position. These skills will initially be described on your résumé and then discussed again during the interview process.

Skills are either general or specific. To develop a list of skills relevant to employers, you must first identify the general skills you possess, then list specific skills you have to offer, and, finally, examine which of these skills employers are seeking.

Identifying Your General Skills. Because you possess or will possess a college degree, employers will assume that you can read and write, perform certain basic computations, think critically, and communicate effectively. Employers will want to see that you have acquired these skills, and they will want to know which additional general skills you possess.

One way to begin identifying skills is to write an experiential diary. An experiential diary lists all the tasks you were responsible for completing for each job you've held and then outlines the skills required to do those tasks. You may list several skills for any given task. This diary allows you to distinguish between the tasks you performed and the underlying skills required to complete those tasks. Here's an example:

Tasks	Skills
Answering telephone	Effective use of language, clear diction, ability to direct inquiries, ability to solve problems
Waiting on tables	Poise under conditions of time and pressure, speed, accuracy, good memory, simultaneous completion of tasks, sales skills

For each job or experience you have participated in, develop a worksheet based on the example shown here. On a résumé, you may want to describe these skills rather than simply listing tasks. Skills are easier for the employer to appreciate, especially when your experience is very different from the employment you are seeking. In addition to helping you identify general skills, this experiential diary will prepare you to speak more effectively in an interview about the qualifications you possess.

Identifying Your Specific Skills. It may be easier to identify your specific skills because you can definitely say whether you can speak other languages, program a computer, draft a map or diagram, or edit a document using appropriate symbols and terminology.

Using your experiential diary, identify the points in your history where you learned how to do something very specific, and decide whether you have a beginning, intermediate, or advanced knowledge of how to use that particular skill. Right now, be sure to list *every* specific skill you have, and don't consider whether you like using the skill. Write down a list of specific skills you have acquired and the level of competence you possess—beginning, intermediate, or advanced.

Relating Your Skills to Employers. You probably have thought about a couple of different jobs you might be interested in obtaining, and one way to begin relating the general and specific skills you possess to a potential employer's needs is to read actual advertisements for these types of positions (see Part Two for resources listing actual job openings).

Let's suppose you are interested in a position as a research assistant for a nonprofit organization that focuses on juvenile justice issues. The organization for which you want to work has been given a grant to examine the success rates of various rehabilitation efforts. The job announcement for this position could be something along these lines: "Research assistant responsible for maintaining case documents, serving as liaison with public defender's office, and working with senior research staff to prepare research reports. Previous experience in the area of juvenile issues desirable. College degree required."

Your next step would be to determine what is generally expected of a research assistant working in a social services setting. While it is hard to categorize exactly what is expected, it is safe to assume that research assistants are usually involved in maintaining records and databases, preparing reports, and helping to coordinate the output of senior researchers.

As you start to read job announcements, begin to build a working list of what skills you will need to enter a particular career path. Many listings of available positions will describe quite clearly what is required of a potential candidate. You will soon notice that there are two kinds of skills: general and specific.

The following is a sample list of skills that you would need to be successful as a research assistant.

JOB: RESEARCH ASSISTANT FOR NONPROFIT
JUVENILE JUSTICE ORGANIZATION

General Skills	Specific Skills
Interviewing	Obtaining informed consent
Record keeping	from research participants
Database management	Working with public defenders
Word processing	office to obtain court records
Meeting deadlines	Serving as liaison with
Note taking at meetings	residential treatment staff
Organizing conferences	Occasionally visiting prisons for
Writing summary reports	interview purposes

On a separate piece of paper, generate a list—as comprehensive as possible—of the skills needed for a job that particularly interests you. The list of skills that you come up with will be valuable for many other positions that you might apply for. Many of the specific skills, in fact, might also cross over to other positions. For example, the interviewing and record-keeping aspect of a research assistant's job are also part of the work of public assistance administration, as well as for positions in human resource management.

Now review the list of skills that are required for jobs you are considering, and check off those skills that *you know you possess*. You should refer to these specific skills on the résumé that you write for this type of job. See Chapter 2 for details on résumé writing.

Step 6   Recognizing Your Preferred Skills

In the previous section you developed a comprehensive list of skills that relate to particular career paths that are of interest to you. You can now relate these to skills that you prefer to use. We all use a wide range of skills (some researchers say individuals have a repertoire of about five hundred skills), but we may not particularly be interested in using all of them in our work. There may be some skills that come to us more naturally or that we use successfully time and time again and that we want to continue to use; these are best described as our preferred skills. For this exercise use the list of skills that you created for the previous section, and decide which of them you are *most interested in using* in future work and how often you would like to use them. You might be interested in using some skills only occasionally, while others you would like to use more regularly. You probably also have skills that you hope you can use constantly.

As you examine job announcements, look for matches between this list of preferred skills and the qualifications described in the advertisements. These skills should be highlighted on your résumé and discussed in job interviews.

Step 7   Assessing Skills Needing Further Development

Previously you compiled a list of general and specific skills required for given positions. You already possess some of these skills; those that remain to be developed are your underdeveloped skills.

If you are just beginning the job search, there may be gaps between the qualifications required for some of the jobs you're considering and skills you possess. The thought of having to admit to and talk about these underdeveloped skills, especially in a job interview, is a frightening one. One way to put a healthy perspective on this subject is to target and relate your exploration of underdeveloped skills to the types of positions you are seeking. Recognizing these shortcomings and planning to overcome them with either on-the-job training or additional formal education can be a positive way to address the concept of underdeveloped skills.

On your worksheet or in your journal, make a list of up to five general or specific skills required for the positions you're interested in that you *don't currently possess*. For each item list an idea you have for specific action you could take to acquire that skill. Do some brainstorming to come up with possible actions. If you have a hard time generating ideas, talk to people currently working in this type of position, professionals in your college career services office, trusted friends, family members, or members of related professional associations.

If, for example, you are interested in a job for which you don't have some specific required experience, you could locate training opportunities such as classes or workshops offered through a local college or university, community college, or club or association that would help you build the level of expertise you need for the job.

You will notice in this book that many excellent positions for your major demand computer skills. While basic word processing has been something you've done all through college, you may be surprised at the additional computer skills required by employers. Many positions for college graduates will ask for some familiarity with spreadsheet programming, and frequently some database-management software familiarity is a job demand as well. Desktop publishing software, graphics programs, and basic Web-page design also pop up frequently in job ads for college graduates. If your degree program hasn't introduced you to a wide variety of computer applications, what are your options? If you're still in college, take what computer courses you can before you graduate. If you've already graduated, look at evening programs, continuing education courses, or tutorial programs that may be available commercially. Developing a modest level of expertise will encourage you to be more confident in suggesting to potential employers that you can continue to add to your skill base on the job.

In Chapter 5 on interviewing, we will discuss in detail how to effectively address questions about underdeveloped skills. Generally speaking, though, employers want genuine answers to these types of questions. They want you to reveal "the real you," and they also want to see how you answer difficult questions. In taking the positive, targeted approach discussed above, you show the employer that you are willing to continue to learn and that you have a plan for strengthening your job qualifications.

Using Your Self-Assessment

Exploring entry-level career options can be an exciting experience if you have good resources available and will take the time to use them. Can you effectively complete the following tasks?

1. Understand your personality traits and relate them to career choices
2. Define your personal values
3. Determine your economic needs
4. Explore longer-term goals
5. Understand your skill base
6. Recognize your preferred skills
7. Express a willingness to improve on your underdeveloped skills

If so, then you can more meaningfully participate in the job search process by writing a more effective résumé, finding job titles that represent work you are interested in doing, locating job sites that will provide the opportunity for you to use your strengths and skills, networking in an informed way, participating in focused interviews, getting the most out of follow-up contacts, and evaluating job offers to find those that create a good match between you and the employer. The remaining chapters in Part One guide you through these next steps in the job search process. For many job seekers, this process can take anywhere from three months to a year to implement. The time you will need to put into your job search will depend on the type of job you want and the geographic location where you'd like to work. Think of your effort as a job in itself, requiring you to set aside time each week to complete the needed work. Carefully undertaken efforts may reduce the time you need for your job search.

The Résumé and Cover Letter

The task of writing a résumé may seem overwhelming if you are unfamiliar with this type of document, but there are some easily understood techniques that can and should be used. This section was written to help you understand the purpose of the résumé, the different types of résumé formats available, and how to write the sections of information traditionally found on a résumé. We will present examples and explanations that address questions frequently posed by people writing their first résumé or updating an old résumé.

Even within the formats and suggestions given, however, there are infinite variations. True, most résumés follow one of the outlines suggested, but you should feel free to adjust the résumé to suit your needs and make it expressive of your life and experience.

Why Write a Résumé?

The purpose of a résumé is to convince an employer that you should be interviewed. Whether you're mailing, faxing, or E-mailing this document, you'll want to present enough information to show that you can make an immediate and valuable contribution to an organization. A résumé is not an in-depth historical or legal document; later in the job search process you may be asked to document your entire work history on an application form and attest to its validity. The résumé should, instead, highlight relevant information pertaining directly to the organization that will receive the document or to the type of position you are seeking.

We will discuss four types of résumés in this chapter: chronological, functional, targeted, and digital. The reasons for using one type of résumé over another and the typical format for each are addressed in the following sections.

The Chronological Résumé

The chronological résumé is the most common of the various résumé formats and therefore the format that employers are most used to receiving. This type of résumé is easy to read and understand because it details the chronological progression of jobs you have held. (See Exhibit 2.1.) It begins with your most recent employment and works back in time. If you have a solid work history or have experience that provided growth and development in your duties and responsibilities, a chronological résumé will highlight these achievements. The typical elements of a chronological résumé include the heading, a career objective, educational background, employment experience, activities, and references.

The Heading
The heading consists of your name, address, telephone number, and other means of contact. This may include a fax number, E-mail address, and your home-page address. If you are using a shared E-mail account or a parent's business fax, be sure to let others who use these systems know that you may receive important professional correspondence via these systems. You wouldn't want to miss a vital E-mail or fax! Likewise, if your résumé directs readers to a personal home page on the Web, be certain it's a professional personal home page designed to be viewed and appreciated by a prospective employer. This may mean making substantial changes in the home page you currently mount on the Web.

We suggest that you spell out your full name in your résumé heading and type it in all capital letters in bold type. After all, you are the focus of the résumé! If you have a current as well as a permanent address and you include both in the heading, be sure to indicate until what date your current address will be valid. The two-letter state abbreviation should be the only abbreviation that appears in your heading. Don't forget to include the zip code with your address and the area code with your telephone number.

The Objective
As you formulate the wording for this part of your résumé, keep the following points in mind.

Exhibit 2.1
CHRONOLOGICAL RÉSUMÉ

DOMINIQUE WILSON

247 Central Avenue
Plymouth, ME 20345
(until May 2002)

5722 Parker Street
Chicago, IL 60633
(773) 555-2112

OBJECTIVE
Entry-level interviewer or research position. Special interest in computer applications to the research process.

EDUCATION
Bachelor of Arts in Sociology
Rollins College, Portland, ME 2002
Minor: Computer Systems Technology

HONORS/AWARDS
Dean's List, 2001, 2002
Residential Life Award for dorm leadership, 2000
Outstanding Sociology Research Paper Award, 2001

EXPERIENCE
Intern, Portland Selectman's Office, Portland, ME, Summer 2001
A full-time summer internship collecting data on all established cemeteries within the city limits. Worked closely with Planning Board, Selectmen, and Town Administrator to draw up maps, inventories, and registers.

Media Support, Gordon Research Conferences, Rockport, ME, Summer 1999 and 2000
Two summers, with increases in pay and responsibility, providing media support for a weekly international conference of scientists. Full responsibility for climate control of multiple venues and inventory and maintenance of costly equipment.

Pastry Chef, Cafe Brioche, South Portland, ME, School year 2000
Evening baker for the city's most notable European style bakery. Extensive training and high standards of personal responsibility and motivation.

continued

COMMUNITY SERVICE
Volunteer, Medical Records Department, Maine Medical Center, Portland, ME.
Donated over 100 hours assisting in the cataloging, data entry, and systems
design for a new medical records department. Position required confidentiality
and discretion.

REFERENCES
Personal and professional references available
upon request.

The Objective Focuses the Résumé. Without a doubt this is the most challenging part of the résumé for most writers. Even for individuals who have
decided on a career path, it can be difficult to encapsulate all they want to
say in one or two brief sentences. For job seekers who are unfocused or
unclear about their intentions, trying to write this section can inhibit the
entire résumé writing process.

Recruiters tell us time and time again that the objective creates a frame
of reference for them. It helps them see how you express your goals and career
focus. In addition, the statement may indicate in what ways you can immediately benefit an organization. Given the importance of the objective, every
point covered in the résumé should relate to it. If information doesn't relate,
it should be omitted. You'll file a number of résumé variations in your computer. There's no excuse for not being able to tailor a résumé to individual
employers or specific positions.

Choose an Appropriate Length. Because of the brevity necessary for a
résumé, you should keep the objective as short as possible. Although objectives of only four or five words often don't show much direction, objectives
that take three full lines could be viewed as too wordy and might possibly
be ignored.

Consider Which Type of Objective Statement You Will Use. There are
many ways to state an objective, but generally there are four forms this statement can take: (1) a very general statement; (2) a statement focused on a
specific position; (3) a statement focused on a specific industry; or (4) a summary of your qualifications. In our contacts with employers, we often hear
that many résumés don't exhibit any direction or career goals, so we suggest
avoiding general statements when possible.

1. General Objective Statement. General objective statements look like the following:

- An entry-level educational programming coordinator position
- An entry-level marketing position

This type of objective would be useful if you know what type of job you want but you're not sure which industries interest you.

2. Position-Focused Objective. Following are examples of objectives focusing on a specific position:

- To obtain the position of conference coordinator at State College
- To obtain a position as assistant editor at *Time* magazine

When a student applies for an advertised job opening, this type of focus can be very effective. The employer knows that the applicant has taken the time to tailor the résumé specifically for this position.

3. Industry-Focused Objective. Focusing on a particular industry in an objective could be stated as follows:

- To begin a career as an applications engineer in the biomedical device industry

4. Summary of Qualifications Statement. The summary of qualifications can be used instead of an objective or in conjunction with an objective. The purpose of this type of statement is to highlight relevant qualifications gained through a variety of experiences. This type of statement is often used by individuals with extensive and diversified work experience. An example of a qualifications statement follows:

My degree in sociology and three years of volunteer experience on a suicide prevention hotline have given me a strong foundation for a career in social services administration, with a particular emphasis on youth intervention programs.

Support Your Objective. A résumé that contains any one of these types of objective statements should then go on to demonstrate why you are qualified to get the position. Listing academic degrees can be one way to indicate qualifications. Another demonstration would be in the way previous experiences, both volunteer and paid, are described. Without this kind of documentation in the body of the résumé, the objective looks unsupported. Think of the résumé as telling a connected story about you. All the elements should work together to form a coherent picture that ideally should relate to your statement of objective.

Education

This section of your résumé should indicate the exact name of the degree you will receive or have received, spelled out completely with no abbreviations. The degree is generally listed after the objective, followed by the institution name and location, and then the month and year of graduation. This section could also include your academic minor, grade point average (GPA), and appearance on the Dean's List or President's List.

If you have enough space, you might want to include a section listing courses related to the field in which you are seeking work. The best use of a "related courses" section would be to list some course work that is not traditionally associated with the major. Perhaps you took several computer courses outside your degree that will be helpful and related to the job prospects you are entertaining. Several education section examples are shown here:

- Bachelor of Arts Degree in Sociology
  Black Hills College, Minot, North Dakota, May 2002
  Minor: Native American Studies
- Bachelor of Arts in Interdisciplinary Studies, a
  self-designed program focusing on Sociology and
  Anthropology
  University of Southern Maine, Portland, ME, December, 2002
- Bachelor of Arts Degree in Sociology
  University of Iowa, Iowa City, Iowa 2002

An example of a format for a related courses section follows:

Psychology of Aging	Human Resource Management
Methods in Social Research	Cross-cultural Communications
Counseling	Technical Writing

Experience

The experience section of your résumé should be the most substantial part and should take up most of the space on the page. Employers want to see what kind of work history you have. They will look at your range of experiences, longevity in jobs, and specific tasks you are able to complete. This section may also be called "work experience," "related experience," "employment history," or "employment." No matter what you call this section, some important points to remember are the following:

1. **Describe your duties** as they relate to the position you are seeking.
2. **Emphasize major responsibilities** and indicate increases in responsibility. Include all relevant employment experiences: summer, part-time, internships, cooperative education, or self-employment.
3. **Emphasize skills**, especially those that transfer from one situation to another. The fact that you coordinated a student organization, chaired meetings, supervised others, and managed a budget leads one to suspect that you could coordinate other things as well.
4. **Use descriptive job titles** that provide information about what you did. A "Student Intern" should be more specifically stated as, for example, "Civil Engineering Intern." "Volunteer" is also too general; a title such as "Peer Writing Tutor" would be more appropriate.
5. **Create word pictures** by using active verbs to start sentences. Describe *results* you have produced in the work you have done.

A limp description would say something such as the following: "My duties included helping with production, proofreading, and editing. I used a design and page layout program." An action statement would be stated as follows: "Coordinated and assisted in the creative marketing of brochures and seminar promotions, becoming proficient in Quark."

Remember, an accomplishment is simply a result, a final measurable product that people can relate to. A duty is not a result; it is an obligation—every job holder has duties. For an effective résumé, list as many results as you can. To make the most of the limited space you have and to give your description impact, carefully select appropriate and accurate descriptors from the list of action words in Exhibit 2.2.

Here are some traits that employers tell us they like to see:

- Teamwork
- Energy and motivation
- Learning and using new skills
- Versatility

Exhibit 2.2
RÉSUMÉ ACTION VERBS

Achieved	Eliminated	Monitored
Acted	Ensured	Negotiated
Administered	Established	Observed
Advised	Estimated	Obtained
Analyzed	Evaluated	Operated
Assessed	Examined	Organized
Assisted	Explained	Participated
Attained	Facilitated	Performed
Balanced	Finalized	Planned
Budgeted	Generated	Predicted
Calculated	Handled	Prepared
Collected	Headed	Presented
Communicated	Helped	Processed
Compiled	Identified	Produced
Completed	Illustrated	Projected
Composed	Implemented	Proposed
Conceptualized	Improved	Provided
Condensed	Increased	Qualified
Conducted	Influenced	Quantified
Consolidated	Informed	Questioned
Constructed	Initiated	Realized
Controlled	Innovated	Received
Converted	Instituted	Recommended
Coordinated	Instructed	Recorded
Corrected	Integrated	Reduced
Created	Interpreted	Reinforced
Decreased	Introduced	Reported
Defined	Learned	Represented
Demonstrated	Lectured	Researched
Designed	Led	Resolved
Determined	Maintained	Reviewed
Developed	Managed	Scheduled
Directed	Mapped	Selected
Documented	Marketed	Served
Drafted	Met	Showed
Edited	Modified	Simplified

Sketched	Studied	Tested
Sold	Submitted	Transacted
Solved	Summarized	Updated
Staffed	Systematized	Verified
Streamlined	Tabulated	

- Critical thinking
- Understanding how profits are created
- Organizational acumen
- Communicating directly and clearly, in both writing and speaking
- Risk taking
- Willingness to admit mistakes
- High personal standards

Solutions to Frequently Encountered Problems

Repetitive Employment with the Same Employer
EMPLOYMENT: The Foot Locker, Portland, Oregon. Summer 2001, 2002, 2003. Initially employed in high school as salesclerk. Due to successful performance, asked to return next two summers at higher pay with added responsibility. Ranked as the #2 salesperson the first summer and #1 the next two summers. Assisted in arranging eye-catching retail displays; served as manager of other summer workers during owner's absence.

A Large Number of Jobs
EMPLOYMENT: Recent Hospitality Industry Experience: Affiliated with four upscale hotel/restaurant complexes (September 2001–February 2004), where I worked part- and full-time as a waiter, bartender, disc jockey, and bookkeeper to produce income for college.

Several Positions with the Same Employer
EMPLOYMENT: Coca-Cola Bottling Co., Burlington, Vermont, 2001–2004. In four years, I received three promotions, each with increased pay and responsibility.

Summer Sales Coordinator: Promoted to hire, train, and direct efforts of add-on staff of fifteen college-age route salespeople hired to meet summer peak demand for product.

Sales Administrator: Promoted to run home office sales desk, managing accounts and associated delivery schedules for professional sales force of ten people. Intensive phone work, daily interaction with all personnel, and strong knowledge of product line required.

Route Salesperson: Summer employment to travel and tourism industry sites that use Coke products. Met specific schedule demands, used good communication skills with wide variety of customers, and demonstrated strong selling skills. Named salesperson of the month for July and August of that year.

Questions Résumé Writers Often Ask

How Far Back Should I Go in Terms of Listing Past Jobs?
Usually, listing three or four jobs should suffice. If you did something back in high school that has a bearing on your future aspirations for employment, by all means list the job. As you progress through your college career, high school jobs will be replaced on the résumé by college employment.

Should I Differentiate Between Paid and Nonpaid Employment?
Most employers are not initially concerned about how much you were paid. They are anxious to know how much responsibility you held in your past employment. There is no need to specify that your work was as a volunteer if you had significant responsibilities.

How Should I Represent My Accomplishments or Work-Related Responsibilities?
Succinctly, but fully. In other words, give the employer enough information to arouse curiosity but not so much detail that you leave nothing to the imagination. Besides, some jobs merit more lengthy explanations than others. Be sure to convey any information that can give an employer a better understanding of the depth of your involvement at work. Did you supervise others? How many? Did your efforts result in a more efficient operation? How much did you increase efficiency? Did you handle a budget? How much? Were you promoted in a short time? Did you work two jobs at once or fifteen hours per week after high school? Where appropriate, quantify.

Should the Work Section Always Follow the Education Section on the Résumé?

Always lead with your strengths. If your education closely relates to the employment you now seek, put this section after the objective. If your education does not closely relate but you have a surplus of good work experiences, consider reversing the order of your sections to lead with employment, followed by education.

How Should I Present My Activities, Honors, Awards, Professional Societies, and Affiliations?

This section of the résumé can add valuable information for an employer to consider if used correctly. The rule of thumb for information in this section is to include only those activities that are in some way relevant to the objective stated on your résumé. If you can draw a valid connection between your activities and your objective, include them; if not, leave them out.

Granted, this is hard to do. Playing center on the championship basketball team or serving as coordinator of the biggest homecoming parade ever held are roles that have meaning for you and represent personal accomplishments you'd like to share. But the résumé is a brief document, and the information you provide on it should help the employer make a decision about your job eligibility. Including personal details can be confusing and could hurt your candidacy. Limiting your activity list to a few significant experiences can be very effective.

If you are applying for a position as a safety officer, your certificate in Red Cross lifesaving skills or CPR would be related and valuable. You would want to include it. If, however, you are applying for a job as a junior account executive in an advertising agency, that information would be unrelated and superfluous. Leave it out.

Professional affiliations and honors should all be listed; especially important are those related to your job objective. Social clubs and activities need not be a part of your résumé unless you hold a significant office or you are looking for a position related to your membership. Be aware that most prospective employers' principal concerns are related to your employability, not your social life. If you have any, publications can be included as an addendum to your résumé.

The focus of the résumé is your experience and education. It is not necessary to describe your involvement in activities. However, if your résumé needs to be lengthened, this section provides the freedom either to expand on or mention only briefly the contributions you have made. If you have made significant contributions (e.g., an officer of an organization or a particularly long tenure with a group), you may choose to describe them in more detail. It is not always necessary to include the dates of your memberships with your activities the way you would include job dates.

There are various ways in which to present additional information. You may give this section a number of different titles. Assess what you want to list, and then use an appropriate title. Do not use "extracurricular activities." This terminology is scholastic, not professional, and therefore not appropriate. The following are two examples:

- ACTIVITIES: Society for Technical Communication, Student Senate, Student Admissions Representative, Senior Class Officer
- ACTIVITIES:
  - Society for Technical Communication Member
  - Student Senator
  - Student Admissions Representative
  - Senior Class Officer

The position you are looking for will determine what you should or should not include. Always look for a correlation between the activity and the prospective job.

How Should I Handle References?

The use of references is considered a part of the interview process, and they should never be listed on a résumé. You would always provide references to a potential employer if requested to, so it is not even necessary to include this section on the résumé if space does not permit. If space is available, it is acceptable to include one of the following statements:

- REFERENCES: Furnished upon request.
- REFERENCES: Available upon request.

Individuals used as references must be protected from unnecessary contacts. By including names on your résumé, you leave your references unprotected. Overuse and abuse of your references will lead to less-than-supportive comments. Protect your references by giving out their names only when you are being considered seriously as a candidate for a given position.

The Functional Résumé

The functional résumé departs from a chronological résumé in that it organizes information by specific accomplishments in various settings: previous jobs, volunteer work, associations, and so forth. This type of résumé permits you to stress the substance of your experiences rather than the position titles you have held. (See Exhibit 2.3.) You should consider using a functional résumé if you have held a series of similar jobs that relied on the same skills or abilities.

The Objective
A functional résumé begins with an objective that can be used to focus the contents of the résumé.

Specific Accomplishments
Specific accomplishments are listed on this type of résumé. Examples of the types of headings used to describe these capabilities might include research, computer skills, teaching, communication, production, management, marketing, or writing. The headings you choose will directly relate to your experience and the tasks that you carried out. Each accomplishment section contains statements related to your experience in that category, regardless of when or where it occurred. Organize the accomplishments and the related tasks you describe in their order of importance as related to the position you seek.

Experience or Employment History
Your actual work experience is condensed and placed after the specific accomplishments section. It simply lists dates of employment, position titles, and employer names.

Education
The education section of a functional résumé is identical to that of the chronological résumé, but it does not carry the same visual importance because it is placed near the bottom of the page.

References
Because actual reference names are never listed on a résumé, a statement of reference availability is optional.

Exhibit 2.3
FUNCTIONAL RÉSUMÉ

MARY ELLEN HUBER

26 Walnut Street	Smith Creek
Madison, WI	Brattleboro, VT 05763
(217) 555-2336	(802) 555-4356
(until May 2002)	

OBJECTIVE

An entry-level position in a dynamic human resource department. My special interest is in benefits counseling and administration.

CAPABILITIES

- Strong communication and interpersonal skills
- Proven administrative ability, with attention to detail
- High energy, task oriented, decision maker

SELECTED ACCOMPLISHMENTS

Counseling—Numerous counseling experiences that have built upon formal college counseling courses: peer leader for alcohol and drug awareness, associate dorm resident head providing counseling and support, volunteer coordinator for student community service group, and two years as a student admissions representative.

Administration—Four years work-study experience in the Dean of Students office: booking appointments, dealing with sensitive issues, heavy telephone use, establishing and maintaining files, records, and correspondence for easy retrieval, word processing, and meeting and welcoming many visitors and dignitaries.

Multitasking Skills—My summer and winter jobs during my college years were for a very busy catering firm, where I learned to meet with clients, prepare sophisticated food under rigorous quality and time standards, develop cost estimates, decorate, set up, and break down large events—sometimes performing all functions in one day!

AWARDS

Dean's List (six semesters)
Employee of the Month (six times over three years)
American Marketing Association Award for Leadership, 2001

EMPLOYMENT HISTORY
Falling Birch Catering, Ludlow, VT, 1997–2001
Office of the Dean of Students, University of Wisconsin, Madison, WI,
   1997–2002

EDUCATION
Bachelor of Arts in Sociology
University of Wisconsin, Madison, WI, 2002

REFERENCES
Provided upon request.

The Targeted Résumé

The targeted résumé focuses on specific work-related capabilities you can bring to a given position within an organization. (See Exhibit 2.4.) It should be sent to an individual within the organization who makes hiring decisions about the position you are seeking.

The Objective
The objective on this type of résumé should be targeted to a specific career or position. It should be supported by the capabilities, accomplishments, and achievements documented in the résumé.

Capabilities
Capabilities should be statements that illustrate tasks you believe you are capable of based on your accomplishments, achievements, and work history. Each should relate to your targeted career or position. You can stress your qualifications rather than your employment history. This approach may require research to obtain an understanding of the nature of the work involved and the capabilities necessary to carry out that work.

Accomplishments/Achievements
This section relates the various activities you have been involved in to the job market. These experiences may include previous jobs, extracurricular activities at school, internships, and part-time summer work.

Experience
Your work history should be listed in abbreviated form and may include position title, employer name, and employment dates.

Exhibit 2.4
TARGETED RÉSUMÉ

MARK GODWIN

Charles Smith House, 302
Grinnell College
Grinnell, IA 52342
(319) 555-2901
(until May 2002)

518 Dorset Avenue
Minneapolis, MN 55401
(612) 555-2443

JOB TARGET
Job Placement Specialist position with human service/social welfare agency.

CAPABILITIES
- Excellent counseling and communication skills
- Knowledge of the nonprofessional job market
- Strong computer skills
- Solid administrative experience

ACHIEVEMENTS
- Member of the original development team for my college office of volunteer services, providing outreach to the community through student labor
- Coauthored a booklet on area nonprofit organizations and their employment needs

WORK HISTORY
2001–Present   Student Administrator, Office of Community Service, Grinnell College, Grinnell, IA
- Maintain database of clients and match student talent to area volunteer needs

1997–Present   Student Worker, Career Development Office, Grinnell College, Grinnell, IA
- Peer career counselor
- Staff résumé clinics
- Host employers for onsite recruiting

1999–2000 (summers)   Staff, Harkin Bike Shop, Minneapolis, MN
- Increased responsibilities and remuneration each summer—now supervise all part-time staff
- Sell and service a variety of cycling products
- Teach basic bike rebuilding and repair

EDUCATION

Bachelor of Arts in Sociology with a minor in Psychology, 2002

Grinnell College, Grinnell, IA

Regents College, London, England, Spring 1999 Exchange Program

---

Education

Because this type of résumé is directed toward a specific job target and an individual's related experience, the education section is not prominently located at the top of the résumé as is done on the chronological résumé.

Digital Résumés

Today's employers have to manage an enormous number of résumés. One of the most frequent complaints the writers of this series hear from students is the failure of employers to even acknowledge the receipt of a résumé and cover letter. Frequently, the reason for this poor response or nonresponse is the volume of applications received for every job. In an attempt to better manage the considerable labor investment involved in processing large numbers of résumés, many employers are requiring digital submission of résumés (see Exhibit 2.5). There are two types of digital résumés: those that can be E-mailed or posted to a website, called *electronic résumés*, and those that can be "read" by a computer, commonly called *scannable résumés*. Though the format may be a bit different from the traditional "paper" résumé, the goal of both types of digital résumés is the same—to get you an interview! These résumés must be designed to be "technologically friendly." What that basically means to you is that they should be free of graphics and fancy formatting.

Electronic Résumés

Sometimes referred to as plain-text résumés, electronic résumés are designed to be E-mailed to an employer or posted to one of many commercial Internet databases such as CareerMosaic.com, America's Job Bank (ajb.dni.us), or Monster.com.

Some technical considerations:

- Electronic résumés must be written in American Standard Code for Information Interchange (ASCII), which is simply a plain-text format. These characters are universally recognized so that every computer can accurately read and understand them. To create an ASCII file of your

Exhibit 2.5
DIGITAL RÉSUMÉ

JOHN J. DOE — Put your name at the
224 University Place — top on its own line.
Downstate, IL 60000
Phone: 555/555-1234 — Put your phone number
Cell: 555/123-4567 — on its own line.
Website: mwu.edu/j-doe — Use a standard-width
E-mail: j-doe@mwu.edu — typeface.

KEYWORD SUMMARY
Ph.D. Sociology (Social Stratification) 2002, Dean's — Keywords make your
   List, Lecturer, Publications, Teaching Assistant — résumé easier to find in
Microsoft Office Suite — a database.
Spanish

EDUCATION — Capital letters
Ph.D., Sociology (Social Stratification), 2002 — emphasize headings.
University of Texas, Austin, TX
Bachelor of Arts Degree in Sociology, 1996
University of North Carolina, Chapel Hill, NC — No line should exceed
   sixty-five characters.

SCHOLARSHIPS & HONORS
Listed in Who's Who in American Schools, 2001 — End each line by
Dean's List, University of North Carolina, 1994–1996 — hitting the enter key.

TEACHING
Lecturer, Tulane University, 2000–Present
General Sociology: Social Stratification; Race, Class,
   and Gender
Teaching Assistant, University of Texas, 1999–2001
General Sociology

PROFESSIONAL ORGANIZATIONS
American Sociological Association
Sociological Practice Association

PUBLICATIONS
* Doe, J., The Changing role of religion in the lives of migrant farm workers.
   Journal for the Study of Religion, 2001.
* Anderson, J. P., and Doe, J., Social cognition and social relations of adolescent
   migrant workers. International Journal of Behavioral Development, 2000.

```
COMMITTEES
Graduate School Council, Cornell University, 2000–2002.

REFERENCES
Furnished upon request.
```

current résumé, open your document, then save it as a text or ASCII file. This will eliminate all formatting. Edit as needed using your computer's text editor application.

- Use a standard-width typeface. Courier is a good choice because it is the font associated with ASCII in most systems.
- Use a font size of 11 to 14 points. A 12-point font is considered standard.
- Your margin should be left-justified.
- Do not exceed sixty-five characters per line because the word-wrap function doesn't operate in ASCII.
- Do not use boldface, italics, underlining, bullets, or various font sizes. Instead, use asterisks, plus signs, or all capital letters when you want to emphasize something.
- Avoid graphics and shading.
- Use as many "keywords" as you possibly can. These are words or phrases usually relating to skills or experience that either are specifically used in the job announcement or are popular buzzwords in the industry.
- Minimize abbreviations.
- Your name should be the first line of text.
- Conduct a "test run" by E-mailing your résumé to yourself and a friend before you send it to the employer. See how it transmits, and make any changes you need to. Continue to test it until it's exactly how you want it to look.
- Unless an employer specifically requests that you send the résumé in the form of an attachment, don't. Employers can encounter problems opening a document as an attachment, and there are always viruses to consider.
- Don't forget your cover letter. Send it along with your résumé as a single message.

Scannable Résumés

Some companies are relying on technology to narrow the candidate pool for available job openings. Electronic Applicant Tracking uses imaging to scan, sort, and store résumé elements in a database. Then, through OCR (Optical Character Recognition) software, the computer scans the résumés for keywords and phrases. To have the best chance at getting an interview, you want to increase the number of "hits"—matches of your skills, abilities, experience, and education to those the computer is scanning for—your résumé will get. You can see how critical using the right keywords is for this type of résumé.

Technical considerations include:

- Again, do not use boldface (newer systems may read this OK, but many older ones won't), italics, underlining, bullets, shading, graphics, or multiple font sizes. Instead, for emphasis, use asterisks, plus signs, or all capital letters. Minimize abbreviations.
- Use a popular typeface such as Courier, Helvetica, Ariel, or Palatino. Avoid decorative fonts.
- Font size should be between 11 and 14 points.
- Do not compress the spacing between letters.
- Use horizontal and vertical lines sparingly; the computer may misread them as the letters L or I.
- Left-justify the text.
- Do not use parentheses or brackets around telephone numbers, and be sure your phone number is on its own line of text.
- Your name should be the first line of text and on its own line. If your résumé is longer than one page, be sure to put your name on the top of all pages.
- Use a traditional résumé structure. The chronological format may work best.
- Use nouns that are skill-focused, such as management, writer, and programming. This is different from traditional paper résumés, which use action-oriented verbs.
- Laser printers produce the finest copies. Avoid dot-matrix printers.
- Use standard, light-colored paper with text on one side only. Since the higher the contrast, the better, your best choice is black ink on white paper.
- Always send original copies. If you must fax, set the fax on fine mode, not standard.
- Do not staple or fold your résumé. This can confuse the computer.
- Before you send your scannable résumé, be certain the employer uses this technology. If you can't determine this, you may want to send two versions (scannable and traditional) to be sure your résumé gets considered.

Résumé Production and Other Tips

An ink-jet printer is the preferred option for printing your résumé. Begin by printing just a few copies. You may find a small error or you may simply want to make some changes, and it is less frustrating and less expensive if you print in small batches.

Résumé paper color should be carefully chosen. You should consider the types of employers who will receive your résumé and the types of positions for which you are applying. Use white or ivory paper for traditional or conservative employers or for higher-level positions.

Black ink on sharp, white paper can be harsh on the reader's eyes. Think about an ivory or cream paper that will provide less contrast and be easier to read. Pink, green, and blue tints should generally be avoided.

Many résumé writers buy packages of matching envelopes and cover sheet stationery that, although not absolutely necessary, help convey a professional impression.

If you'll be producing many cover letters at home, be sure you have high-quality printing equipment. Learn standard envelope formats for business, and retain a copy of every cover letter you send out. You can use the copies to take notes of any telephone conversations that may occur.

If attending a job fair, either carry a briefcase or place your résumé in a nicely covered legal-size pad holder.

The Cover Letter

The cover letter provides you with the opportunity to tailor your résumé by telling the prospective employer how you can be a benefit to the organization. It allows you to highlight aspects of your background that are not already discussed in your résumé and that might be especially relevant to the organization you are contacting or to the position you are seeking. Every résumé should have a cover letter enclosed when you send it out. Unlike the résumé, which may be mass-produced, a cover letter is most effective when it is individually prepared and focused on the particular requirements of the organization in question.

A good cover letter should supplement the résumé and motivate the reader to review the résumé. The format shown in Exhibit 2.6 is only a suggestion to help you decide what information to include in writing a cover letter.

Begin the cover letter with your street address six lines down from the top. Leave three to five lines between the date and the name of the person to whom you are addressing the cover letter. Make sure you leave one blank line between the salutation and the body of the letter and between paragraphs. After typing "Sincerely," leave four blank lines and type your name. This should leave plenty of room for your signature. A sample cover letter is shown in Exhibit 2.7.

The following guidelines will help you write good cover letters:

1. Be sure to type your letter neatly; ensure there are no misspellings.
2. Avoid unusual typefaces, such as script.
3. Address the letter to an individual, using the person's name and title. To obtain this information, call the company. If answering a blind newspaper advertisement, address the letter "To Whom It May Concern" or omit the salutation.
4. Be sure your cover letter directly indicates the position you are applying for and tells why you are qualified to fill it.
5. Send the original letter, not a photocopy, with your résumé. Keep a copy for your records.
6. Make your cover letter no more than one page.
7. Include a phone number where you can be reached.
8. Avoid trite language and have someone read the letter over to react to its tone, content, and mechanics.
9. For your own information, record the date you send out each letter and résumé.

Exhibit 2.6
COVER LETTER FORMAT

Your Street Address
Your Town, State, Zip
Phone Number
Fax Number
Date   E-mail

Name
Title
Organization
Address

Dear _____:

First Paragraph. In this paragraph state the reason for the letter, name the specific position or type of work you are applying for, and indicate from which resource (career services office, website, newspaper, contact, employment service) you learned of this opening. The first paragraph can also be used to inquire about future openings.

Second Paragraph. Indicate why you are interested in this position, the company, or its products or services, and what you can do for the employer. If you are a recent graduate, explain how your academic background makes you a qualified candidate. Try not to repeat the same information found in the résumé.

Third Paragraph. Refer the reader to the enclosed résumé for more detailed information.

Fourth Paragraph. In this paragraph say what you will do to follow up on your letter. For example, state that you will call by a certain date to set up an interview or to find out if the company will be recruiting in your area. Finish by indicating your willingness to answer any questions they may have. Be sure you have provided your phone number.

Sincerely,

Type your name
Enclosure

Exhibit 2.7
SAMPLE COVER LETTER

28 Lake Street
Minneapolis, MN 55408
612-555-0020

May 5, 2002

Mr. Jeff Pettit
Director of Personnel
Community Action Base
852 Front Street, Suite 15
St. Paul, MN 55103

Dear Mr. Pettit:

This month I will graduate from the University of Minnesota with a bachelor's degree in sociology. I've been interested in your organization for several years and was very intrigued when I saw a posting for a job opening on the community services jobs website. I'm eager to learn more about the research assistant position and am writing to explore the opportunity for employment with Community Action Base.

The advertisement indicated that you were looking for someone with the skills for and interest in working accurately with numbers and details. I believe my résumé outlines a work and education history that you will find most interesting and relevant. Beginning with office duties for a local Internet provider, I added to my experience during college by working in the financial aid office as a data analyst. I gained some strong interpersonal skills and became more skillful at dealing with people in stressful situations. My sociology major and courses in psychology and counseling proved helpful. My work style is task oriented, productive, and flexible around shifting priorities.

As you will see by the enclosed résumé, I have had exposure to considerable technology, both through my studies and in my work with the online service provider. I am thoroughly familiar with the computers, database management, and online research systems that you mention in your ad. In addition, I have good spreadsheet experience and my word processing skills are excellent.

I would like to meet with you to discuss how my education and experience would be consistent with your needs. I will contact your office next week to discuss the possibility of an interview. In the meantime, if you have any questions or require additional information, please contact me at my home number listed above.

Sincerely,

Matthew Shaw
Enclosure

Researching Careers

As a sociology major, you've learned *about* sociology, but you have yet to learn how to really *do* sociology. True, sociology is not like accounting or computer programming, where you often learn by doing. On the other hand, it can be a more exciting challenge to find your own individual career path. The first step is launching an investigation into what jobs are out there for sociology majors. The next step is starting to answer the question: What do I become?

What Do They Call the Job You Want?

There is every reason to be unaware. One reason for confusion is perhaps a mistaken assumption that a college education provides job training. In most cases it does not. Of course, applied fields such as engineering, management, or education provide specific skills for the workplace as well as an education, whereas most liberal arts degrees simply provide an education. Regardless, your overall college education exposes you to numerous fields of study and teaches you quantitative reasoning, critical thinking, writing, and speaking, all of which can be successfully applied to a number of different job fields. But it still remains up to you to choose a job field and to learn how to articulate the benefits of your education in a way the employer will appreciate.

As indicated in Chapter 1 on self-assessment, your first task is to understand and value what parts of that education you enjoyed and were good at and would continue to enjoy in your life's work. Did your writing courses encourage you in your ability to express yourself in writing? Did you enjoy the research process, and did you find that your work was well received? Did you enjoy any of your required quantitative subjects such as algebra or calculus?

The answers to questions such as these provide clues to skills and interests you bring to the employment market over and above the credential of your degree. In fact, it is not an overstatement to suggest that most employers who demand a college degree immediately look beyond that degree to you as a person and your own individual expression of what you like to do and think you can do for them, regardless of your major.

Collecting Job Titles

The world of employment is a big place, and even seasoned veterans of the job hunt can be surprised about what jobs are to be found in what organizations. You need to become a bit of an explorer and adventurer and be willing to try a variety of techniques to begin a list of possible occupations that might use your talents and education. Once you have a list of possibilities that you are interested in and qualified for, you can move on to find out what kinds of organizations have these job titles.

Only you will be able to define for yourself what work you want and where you *want* to work! As a social researcher or personnel manager (or any of the dozens of other careers you might select) you may be drawn to working in large corporations, on college campuses, in state government, or in small community organizations. Each environment presents a different "culture" with associated norms in the pace of work, the kind of information you'll be using in your job, and the background and training of those you'll be working alongside. Your job title might be the same in each situation, but not all locations may present the same "fit" for you.

It's also important to keep your options open as much as possible. Your interest in social relationships might lead you to graduate school, but you could also find compatible careers in human resources, teaching, training, public relations, counseling, and sales. Each job title in this list can be found in a variety of settings.

Take training, for example. Trainers write policy and procedural manuals and actively teach to assist all levels of employees in mastering various tasks and work-related systems. Trainers exist in all large corporations, banks, consumer goods manufacturers, medical diagnostic equipment firms, sales organizations, and any organization that has processes or materials that need to be presented to and learned by the staff.

In reading job descriptions or want ads for any of these positions, you would find your four-year degree a "must." However, the academic major might be less important than your own individual skills in critical thinking, analysis, report writing, public presentations, and interpersonal communication. Even more important than thinking or knowing you have certain skills are your ability to express those skills concretely and the examples you use to illustrate them to an employer.

The best beginning to a job search is to create a list of job titles you might want to pursue, learn more about the nature of the jobs behind those titles, and then discover what kinds of employers hire for those positions. In the following section we'll teach you how to build a job title directory to use in your job search.

Developing a Job Title Directory That Works for You

A job title directory is simply a complete list of all the job titles you are interested in, are intrigued by, or think you are qualified for. After combining the understanding gained through self-assessment with your own individual interests and the skills and talents you've acquired with your degree, you'll soon start to read and recognize a number of occupational titles that seem right for you. There are several resources you can use to develop your list, including computer searches, books, and want ads.

Computerized Interest Inventories. One way to begin your search is to identify a number of jobs that call for your degree and the particular skills and interests you identified as part of the self-assessment process. There are excellent interactive career-guidance programs on the market to help you produce such selected lists of possible job titles. Most of these are available at high schools and colleges and at some larger town and city libraries. Two of the industry leaders are CHOICES and DISCOVER. Both allow you to enter interests, values, educational background, and other information to produce lists of possible occupations and industries. Each of the resources listed here will produce different job title lists. Some job titles will appear again and again, while others will be unique to a particular source. Investigate all of them!

Reference Sources. Books on the market that may be available through your local library or career counseling office also suggest various occupations related to specific majors. The following are only a few of the many good books on the market: *The College Board Guide to 150 Popular College Majors, College Majors and Careers: A Resource Guide for Effective Life Planning* both by Paul Phifer, and *Kaplan's What to Study: 101 Fields in a Flash.* All of these books list possible job titles within the academic major.

Sociology majors will find about fifty job titles for which they are generally qualified. You'll be familiar with some of these, such as social services counselor. Other positions, such as penologist or social ecologist, will be new to you.

Another good source is the *Occupational Thesaurus.* Here, job titles are given under general category headings. If you discovered "counselor" as a job title in the book *What Can I Do With a Major in . . . ?*, you can then go to the *Occupational Thesaurus*, which lists scores of jobs under that title. Under "Medical Services," for instance, there is a list of more than thirty associated job titles, including grievances counselor, community relations officer, alcoholism and drug addiction researcher, and non-diagnostic interviewer. By cross-checking suggested occupations in several different sources you will be able to expand the possibilities for your job search.

Each job title deserves your consideration. Like removing the layers of an onion, the search for job titles can go on and on! As you spend time doing this activity, you are actually learning more about the value of your degree. What's important in your search at this point is not to become critical or selective but rather to develop as long a list of possibilities as you can. Every source used will help you add new and potentially exciting jobs to your growing list.

Classified Ads. It has been well publicized that the classified ad section of the newspaper represents only about 10 to 15 percent of the current job market. Nevertheless, the weekly classified ads can be a great help to you in your search. Although they may not be the best place to look for a job, they can teach you a lot about the job market. Classified ads provide a good education in job descriptions, duties, responsibilities, and qualifications. In addition, they provide insight into which industries are actively recruiting and some indication of the area's employment market. This is particularly helpful when seeking a position in a specific geographic area and/or a specific field. For your purposes, classified ads are a good source for job titles to add to your list.

Read the Sunday classified ads in a major market newspaper for several weeks in a row. Cut and paste all the ads that interest you and seem to call for something close to your education, skills, experience, and interests. Remember that classified ads are written for what an organization *hopes* to find, you don't have to meet absolutely every criterion. However, if certain requirements are stated as absolute minimums and you cannot meet them, it's best not to waste your time and that of the employer.

The weekly classified want ads exercise is important because these jobs are out in the marketplace. They truly exist, and people with your qualifications are being sought to apply. What's more, many of these advertisements describe the duties and responsibilities of the job advertised and give you a beginning sense of the challenges and opportunities such a position presents. Some will indicate salary, and that will be helpful as well. This information will better define the jobs for you and provide some good material for possible interviews in that field.

Exploring Job Descriptions

Once you've arrived at a solid list of possible job titles that interest you and for which you believe you are somewhat qualified, it's a good idea to do some research on each of these jobs. The preeminent source for such job information is the *Dictionary of Occupational Titles*, or *DOT* (wave.net/upg/immigration/dot_index.html). This directory lists every conceivable job and provides excellent up-to-date information on duties and responsibilities, interactions with associates, and day-to-day assignments and tasks. These descriptions provide a thorough job analysis, but they do not consider the possible employers or the environments in which a job may be performed. So, although a position as public relations officer may be well defined in terms of duties and responsibilities, it does not explain the differences in doing public relations work in a college or a hospital or a factory or a bank. You will need to look somewhere else for work settings.

Learning More About Possible Work Settings

After reading some job descriptions, you may choose to edit and revise your list of job titles once again, discarding those you feel are not suitable and keeping those that continue to hold your interest. Or you may wish to keep your list intact and see where these jobs may be located. For example, if you are interested in public relations and you appear to have those skills and the requisite education, you'll want to know what organizations do public relations. How can you find that out? How much income does someone in public relations make a year and what is the employment potential for the field of public relations?

To answer these and many other questions about your list of job titles, we recommend you try any of the following resources: *Careers Encyclopedia*, the professional societies and resources found throughout this book, *College to Career: The Guide to Job Opportunities*, and the *Occupational Outlook Handbook* (http://stats.bls.gov/ocohome.htm). Each of these resources, in a different way, will help to put the job titles you have selected into an employer context. Perhaps the most extensive discussion is found in the *Occupational Outlook Handbook*, which gives a thorough presentation of the nature of the work, the working conditions, employment statistics, training, other qualifications, and advancement possibilities as well as job outlook and earnings. Related occupations are also detailed, and a select bibliography is provided to help you find additional information.

Continuing with our public relations example, your search through these reference materials would teach you that the public relations jobs you find attractive are available in larger hospitals, financial institutions, most corporations (both consumer goods and industrial goods), media organizations, and colleges and universities.

Networking to Get the Complete Story

You now have not only a list of job titles but also, for each of these job titles, a description of the work involved and a general list of possible employment settings in which to work. You'll want to do some reading and keep talking to friends, colleagues, teachers, and others about the possibilities. Don't neglect to ask if the career office at your college maintains some kind of alumni network. Often such alumni networks will connect you with another graduate from the college who is working in the job title or industry you are seeking information about. These career networkers offer what assistance they can. For some it is a full day "shadowing" the alumnus as he or she goes about the job. Others offer partial-day visits, tours, informational interviews, résumé reviews, job postings, or, if distance prevents a visit, telephone interviews. As fellow graduates, they'll be frank and informative about their own jobs and prospects in their field.

Take them up on their offer and continue to learn all you can about your own personal list of job titles, descriptions, and employment settings. You'll probably continue to edit and refine this list as you learn more about the realities of the job, the possible salary, advancement opportunities, and supply and demand statistics.

In the next section we'll describe how to find the specific organizations that represent these industries and employers so that you can begin to make contact.

Where Are These Jobs, Anyway?

Having a list of job titles that you've designed around your own career interests and skills is an excellent beginning. It means you've really thought about who you are and what you are presenting to the employment market. It has caused you to think seriously about the most appealing environments to work in, and you have identified some employer types that represent these environments.

The research and the thinking that you've done thus far will be used again and again. They will be helpful in writing your résumé and cover letters, in talking about yourself on the telephone to prospective employers, and in answering interview questions.

Now is a good time to begin to narrow the field of job titles and employment sites down to some specific employers to initiate the employment contact.

Finding Out Which Employers Hire People Like You

This section will provide tips, techniques, and specific resources for developing an actual list of specific employers that can be used to make contacts. It is only an outline that you must be prepared to tailor to your own particular needs and according to what you bring to the job search. Once again, it is important to communicate with others along the way exactly what you're looking for and what your goals are for the research you're doing. Librarians, employers, career counselors, friends, friends of friends, business contacts, and bookstore staff will all have helpful information on geographically specific and new resources to aid you in locating employers who'll hire you.

Identifying Information Resources

Your interview wardrobe and your new résumé might have put a dent in your wallet, but the resources you'll need to pursue your job search are available for free (although you may choose to copy materials on a machine instead of taking notes by hand). The categories of information detailed here are not hard to find and are yours for the browsing.

Numerous resources described in this section will help you identify actual employers. Use all of them or any others that you identify as available in your geographic area. As you become experienced in this process, you'll quickly figure out which information sources are helpful and which are not. If you live in a rural area, a well-planned day trip to a major city that includes a college career office, a large college or city library, state and federal employment centers, a chamber of commerce office, and a well-stocked bookstore can produce valuable results.

There are many excellent resources available to help you identify actual job sites. They are categorized into employer directories (usually indexed by product lines and geographic location), geographically based directories (designed to highlight particular cities, regions, or states), career-specific directories (e.g., *Sports MarketPlace*, which lists tens of thousands of firms involved with sports), periodicals and newspapers, targeted job posting publications, and videos. This is by no means meant to be a complete treatment of resources but rather a starting point for identifying useful resources.

Working from the more general references to highly specific resources, we provide a basic list to help you begin your search. Many of these you'll find easily available. In some cases reference librarians and others will suggest even better materials for your particular situation. Start to create your own customized bibliography of job search references. Use copying services to save time and to allow you to carry away information about organizations' missions, locations, company officers, phone numbers, and addresses.

Geographically Based Directories. The Job Bank series published by Bob Adams, Inc. (aip.com) contains detailed entries on each area's major employers, including business activity, address, phone number, and hiring contact name. Many listings specify educational backgrounds being sought in potential employees. Each volume contains a solid discussion of each city's or state's major employment sectors. Organizations are also indexed by industry. Job Bank volumes are available for the following places: Atlanta, Boston, Chicago, Dallas–Ft. Worth, Denver, Detroit, Florida, Houston, Los Angeles, Minneapolis, New York, Ohio, Philadelphia, San Francisco, Seattle, St. Louis, Washington, D.C., and other cities throughout the Northwest.

National Job Bank (careercity.com) lists employers in every state, along with contact names and commonly hired job categories. Included are many small companies often overlooked by other directories. Companies are also indexed by industry. This publication provides information on educational backgrounds sought and lists company benefits.

Periodicals and Newspapers. Several sources are available to help you locate which journals or magazines carry job advertisements in your field. Other resources help you identify opportunities in other parts of the country.

- *Where the Jobs Are: A Comprehensive Directory of 1200 Journals Listing Career Opportunities*
  Links specific occupational titles to corresponding periodicals that carry job listings for your field.
- *Corptech Fast 5000 Company Locator*
  Profiles high technology companies throughout the country. The locator is indexed by company name and city.
- *National Business Employment Weekly* (nbew.com)
  Compiles want ads from four regional editors of the *Wall Street Journal* (http://interactive.wsj.com). Most are business and management positions.
- *National Ad Search* (nationaladsearch.com)
  Reprints ads from seventy-five metropolitan newspapers across the country. Although the focus is on management positions, technical and professional postings are also included. *Caution:* Watch deadline dates carefully on listings, because they may have already passed by the time the ad is printed.
- *The Federal Jobs Digest* (jobsfed.com) and *Federal Career Opportunities*
  Lists government positions.
- *World Chamber of Commerce Directory* (chamberofcommerce.org)
  Lists addresses for chambers worldwide, state boards of tourism, convention and visitors' bureaus, and economic development organizations. This information not only helps locate employers but provides information on employers planning to relocate into a specific geographic area and trade shows that will take place near you where you can meet potential employers.

This list is certainly not exhaustive; use it to begin your job search work.

Targeted Job Posting Publications. Although the resources that follow are national in scope, they are either targeted to one medium of contact (telephone), focused on specific types of jobs, or less comprehensive than the sources previously listed.

- *Job Hotlines USA* (careers.org/topic/01_002.html)
  Pinpoints more than 1,000 hard-to-find telephone numbers

for companies and government agencies that use prerecorded
job messages and listings. Very few of the telephone numbers listed
are toll-free, and sometimes recordings are long, so—callers, beware!

- *The Job Hunter* (jobhunter.com)
  A national biweekly newspaper listing business, arts, media,
  government, human services, health, community-related, and student
  services job openings.
- *Current Jobs for Graduates* (graduatejobs.com)
  A national employment listing for liberal arts professions, including
  editorial positions, management opportunities, museum work,
  teaching, and nonprofit work.
- *Environmental Opportunities* (ecojobs.com)
  Serves environmental job interests nationwide by listing
  administrative, marketing, and human resources positions along with
  education-related jobs and positions directly related to a degree in an
  environmental field.
- *Y National Vacancy List* (ymcahrm.ns.ca/employed/jobleads.html)
  Shows YMCA professional vacancies, including development,
  administration, programming, membership, and recreation postings.
- *ARTSearch*
  A national employment service bulletin for the arts, including
  administration, managerial, marketing, and financial management
  jobs.
- *Community Jobs*
  An employment newspaper for the nonprofit sector that provides a
  variety of listings, including project manager, canvas director,
  government relations specialist, community organizer, and program
  instructor.
- *College Placement Council Annual: A Guide to Employment
  Opportunities for College Graduates*
  An annual guide containing solid job-hunting information and, more
  important, displaying ads from large corporations actively seeking
  recent college graduates in all majors. Company profiles provide brief
  descriptions and available employment opportunities. Contact names
  and addresses are given. Profiles are indexed by organization name,
  geographic location, and occupation.
- *National Association of Colleges and Employers* (naceweb.org)
  Job Choices series includes four books: *Planning Job Choices, Job
  Choices: Diversity Edition, Job Choices in Business,* and *Job Choices in*

Science, Engineering, and Technology. The website provides a listing of other books that can be helpful to a wide variety of job seekers.

Videos. You may be one of the many job seekers who likes to get information via a medium other than paper. Many career libraries, public libraries, and career centers in libraries carry an assortment of videos that will help you learn new techniques and get information helpful in the job search.

Locating Information Resources

Throughout these introductory chapters, we have continually referred you to various websites for information on everything from job listings to career information. Using the Web gives you a mobility at your computer that you don't enjoy if you rely solely on books or newspapers or printed journals. Moreover, material on the Web, if the site is maintained, can be up-to-date, which may be crucial if you are looking at a cutting-edge career in which technology changes almost daily. Federal government sites offer the option in some cases of downloading application materials, and many will accept your résumé online.

You'll eventually identify the information resources that work best for you, but make certain you've covered the full range of resources before you begin to rely on a smaller list. Here's a short list of informational sites that many job seekers find helpful:

- Public and college libraries
- College career centers
- Bookstores
- Internet
- Local and state government personnel offices

Each one of these sites offers a collection of resources that will help you get the information you need.

As you meet and talk with service professionals at all these sites, be sure to let them know what you're doing. Inform them of your job search, what you've already accomplished, and what you're looking for. The more people who know you're job seeking, the greater the possibility that someone will have information or know someone who can help you along your way.

Public and College Libraries. Large city libraries, college and university libraries, and even well-supported town library collections contain a variety of resources to help you conduct a job search. It is not uncommon for libraries to have separate "vocational choices" sections with books, tapes, computer terminals, and associated materials relating to job search and selection. Some are now even making résumé-creation software available for use by patrons.

Some of the publications we name throughout this book are expensive reference items that are rarely purchased by individuals. In addition, libraries carry a wide range of newspapers and telephone yellow pages as well as the usual array of books. If resources are not immediately available, many libraries have loan arrangements with other facilities and can make information available to you relatively quickly.

Take advantage not only of the reference collections but also of the skilled and informed staff. Let them know exactly what you are looking for, and they'll have their own suggestions. You'll be visiting the library frequently, and the reference staff will soon come to know who you are and what you're working on. They'll be part of your job search network!

College Career Centers. Career libraries, which are found in career centers at colleges and universities and sometimes within large public libraries, contain a unique blend of the job search resources housed in other settings. In addition, career libraries often purchase a number of job listing publications, each of which targets a specific industry or type of job. You may find job listings specifically for entry-level positions for your major. Ask about job posting newsletters or newspapers focused on careers in the area that most interests you. Each center will be unique, but you are certain to discover some good sources of jobs.

Most college career libraries now hold growing collections of video material on specific industries and on aspects of your job search process, including dress and appearance, how to manage the luncheon or dinner interview, how to be effective at a job fair, and many other titles. Some larger corporations produce handsome video materials detailing the variety of career paths and opportunities available in their organizations.

Some career libraries also house computer-based career planning and information systems. These interactive computer programs help you to clarify your values and interests and will combine them with your education to provide possible job titles and industry locations. Some even contain extensive lists of graduate school programs.

One specific kind of service a career library will be able to direct you to is computerized job search services. These services, of which there are many, are run by private companies, individual colleges, or consortiums of colleges. They attempt to match qualified job candidates with potential employers. The candidate submits a résumé (or an application) to the service. This information (which can be categorized into hundreds of separate fields of data) is entered into a computer database. Your information is then compared with the information from employers about what they desire in a prospective employee. If there is a match between what they want and what you have indicated you can offer, the job search service or the employer will contact you directly to continue the process.

Computerized job search services can complement an otherwise complete job search program. They are *not*, however, a substitute for the kinds of activities described in this book. They are essentially passive operations that are random in nature. If you have not listed skills, abilities, traits, experiences, or education *exactly* as an employer has listed its needs, there is simply no match.

Consult with the staff members at the career libraries you use. These professionals have been specifically trained to meet the unique needs you present. Often you can just drop in and receive help with general questions, or you may want to set up an appointment to speak one-on-one with a career counselor to gain special assistance.

Every career library is different in size and content, but each can provide valuable information for the job search. Some may even provide limited counseling. If you have not visited the career library at your college or alma mater, call and ask if these collections are still available for your use. Be sure to ask about other services that you can use as well.

If you are not near your own college as you work on your job search, call the career office and inquire about reciprocal agreements with other colleges that are closer to where you live. Very often, your own alma mater can arrange for you to use a limited menu of services at another school. This typically would include access to a career library and job posting information and might include limited counseling.

Bookstores. Any well-stocked bookstore will carry some job search books that are worth buying. Some major stores will even have an extensive section devoted to materials, including excellent videos, related to the job search process. You will also find copies of local newspapers and business magazines. The one advantage that is provided by resources purchased at a bookstore is that you can read and work with the information in the comfort of your own home and do not have to conform to the hours of operation of a library, which can present real difficulties if you are working full-time as you seek employment. A few minutes spent browsing in a bookstore might be a beneficial break from your job search activities and turn up valuable resources.

Internet. The World Wide Web has made the search and retrieval of information faster, and in many cases, more efficient. Using search engines such as Netscape, Yahoo!, Google, AltaVista, or MSN, it is possible to find great quantities of information about careers in general, specific employers, and job openings. The Internet should be an important part of any job search strategy.

Use of keywords and/or topics in your specific discipline to search the Web will open numerous opportunities for insight and further exploration. It is important to not only look at "career" websites such as Monster.com, BrassRing.com, or CareerBuilder.com, but to also read the websites of particular employers. Go beyond reading only their career or employment page. Make sure that you read their pages for customers or clients. Learn how they are promoting themselves to the people who buy or use their services. Pay particular attention to the "news" pages on an employer website. There is a great deal to be learned about an organization by reading its "news" page!

Learning which Internet sites are most accurate and fruitful for your job search will take time, persistence, and caution. There's no doubt about it, the Web is a job hunter's best friend. But it can also be an overwhelmingly abundant source of information—so much information that it becomes difficult to identify what's important and what is not. A simple search under a keyword or phrase can bring up sites that will be very meaningful for you and sites whose information is trivial and irrelevant to your job search. You need a strategy to master the Web, just as we advise a strategy to master the job search. Here are some suggestions:

1. Thoroughly utilize the websites identified throughout this guide. They've been chosen with you in mind, and many of them will be very helpful to you.
2. Begin to build your own portfolio of websites on your computer. Use the "bookmarking" function on your Web browser to build a series of bookmark folders for individual categories of good websites. You may have a folder for "entry-level job ad" sites and another folder for "professional associations," and so on. Start your folders with the sites in this book that seem most helpful to you.

3. Visit your college career center (or ask for reciprocity consideration at a local college) and your nearby local and/or state and university libraries. All of these places have staff who are skilled researchers and can help you locate and identify more sites that are more closely targeted to your growing sense of job direction.

4. Use the E-mail function or Webmaster address that you'll find on many sites. Some sites encourage questions via E-mail. We have found that the response time to E-mail questions for website mailboxes can vary considerably, but more often than not, replies are quite prompt. Sometimes a website will list the E-mail of the "Webmaster" or "Webguru," and we have contacted those individuals with good success as well. So, if you have a question about a website, use these options to get satisfaction.

Local and State Government Personnel Offices. You'll learn that it's most efficient to establish a routine for checking job postings. Searching for a job is a full-time job (or should be!), and you don't want to waste time or feel that you're going around in circles. So, establish a routine by which each week, on the most appropriate day, you check out that day's resources. For example, if you live in a midsize city with a daily paper, you'll probably give the want ads a once-over every morning so that you can act immediately on any good job opening.

The same strategy applies to your local and state government personnel offices. Find out when and how they post jobs, and put those offices on your weekly checklist, so that you don't miss any reasonable openings. Your local municipality's personnel office may simply use a bulletin board in the town hall or a clipboard on a counter in the office. Make these stops part of your weekly routine, and you'll find that people begin to recognize you and become aware of your job search, which could prove to be very helpful. Most local governmental units are required to post jobs in public places for a stated period before the hiring process begins. It should be easy to find out where and how they do this. Keep a close eye on those sites.

State personnel offices are larger, less casual operations, but the principles are the same. State jobs are advertised, and the office can tell you what advertising mechanisms they use—which newspapers, what websites, and when jobs are posted. The personnel offices themselves are worth a visit, if you are close enough. In addition to all the current job postings, many state personnel offices have "spec sheets," which are detailed job specifications of all the positions they are apt to advertise. You could pick up a spec sheet for every job related to your major and keep them in a file for later reference when such a job is advertised.

Many state personnel offices also publish a weekly or biweekly "open recruitment" listing of career opportunities that have not yet been filled. These listings are categorized by job title as well as by branch of government, and often by whether a test is needed to qualify for the position or not. An increasing number of state personnel or human resources offices are online and offer many services on the Web. A fine general website that can help you locate your state personnel office is piperinfo.com/state/index.cfm. While each state's site is different, you can count on access to the state human resources office and sometimes even the human resources offices of many of the state's larger cities. For example, the State of Connecticut lists an additional twenty-seven city sites that each have human resources departmental listings. So, you could search the State of Connecticut Human Resource Office and then jump to the City of Stamford and review city jobs on its site.

Career/Job Fairs. Career and/or job fairs are common occurrences on most college campuses. The career services office usually sponsors one or more of these each year. Specific student organizations and academic departments on campus may sponsor them as well. In addition, commercial organizations will sponsor these events in major cities. Watch the employment section of local newspapers and/or the general career Internet sites for announcements of these events near you.

It is important to begin to attend these as early in your college career as possible. By introducing yourself to recruiters and learning what they look for and value in their top candidates, you can better plan your personal career development throughout your college years. However, if you are getting ready to graduate and will now begin attending these events for the purpose of finding an entry-level position, it is advisable that you use them to not only promote yourself but to learn more about the hiring organizations that recruit from your institution.

In addition to coming prepared to tell the recruiter about yourself and why you are interested in the organization, do some preliminary research on the companies that will be participating in the career or job fair and be prepared to ask the recruiter questions about the ideal candidates whom they seek, the type of opportunities that they offer to entry-level professionals, and their hiring process. In other words, use the career or job fair to increase your knowledge of the organizations in which you think you may have an interest, but do not monopolize the recruiter's time. There are others who will want to talk to the representative as well.

Information Sessions. Many recruiters come to campus and sponsor information sessions either in the school or department or in the student center. Look for these events to be advertised in your school paper and on bulletin boards around campus. Often the recruiters will be interested in specific types of majors. However, if you have researched the company in the library and on the Internet, and feel that you have unique qualifications that match its needs, you should attend.

When attending an information session, bring a résumé that is specifically tailored to the organization sponsoring the session. Dress professionally, whenever possible, but do not let a lab or athletic practice keep you from attending a session sponsored by an organization in which you have a strong interest. Arrive on time and do not attempt to talk to the presenters before the program begins. Listen to the presentation and take notes. After the presentation, ask questions from the audience that will be of general interest to the entire group, not specifically to you. For example, an appropriate question might be "What are the promotional opportunities within your organization?" An inappropriate question might be "I know you are here in the Business School tonight, but do you ever hire my major?"

When the question-and-answer period concludes, go up to the presenter(s) and introduce yourself. Explain briefly why you are interested in the organization and how you believe that your skills and experiences fit, and ask a question that is specific to you. Do not monopolize the presenter's time. Follow up with a letter and résumé after this event and thank the presenter for taking time to answer your questions.

Networking

Networking is the process of deliberately establishing relationships to get career-related information or to alert potential employers that you are available for work. Networking is critically important to today's job seeker for two reasons: it will help you get the information you need, and it can help you find out about *all* of the available jobs.

Getting the Information You Need

Networkers will review your résumé and give you feedback on its effectiveness. They will talk about the job you are looking for and give you a candid appraisal of how they see your strengths and weaknesses. If they have a good sense of the industry or the employment sector for that job, you'll get their feelings on future trends in the industry as well. Some networkers will be very forthcoming about salaries, job-hunting techniques, and suggestions for your job search strategy. Many have been known to place calls right from the interview desk to friends and associates who might be interested in you. Each networker will make his or her own contribution, and each will be valuable.

Because organizations must evolve to adapt to current global market needs, the information provided by decision makers within various organizations will be critical to your success as a new job market entrant. For example, you might learn about the concept of virtual organizations from a networker. Virtual organizations coordinate economic activity to deliver value to customers by using resources outside the traditional boundaries of the organization. This concept is being discussed and implemented by chief executive officers of many organizations, including Ford Motor, Dell, and IBM. Networking can help you find out about this and other trends currently affecting the industries under your consideration.

Finding Out About All of the Available Jobs

Not every job that is available at this very moment is advertised for potential applicants to see. This is called the *hidden job market*. Only 15 to 20 percent of all jobs are formally advertised, which means that 80 to 85 percent of available jobs do not appear in published channels. Networking will help you become more knowledgeable about all the employment opportunities available during your job search period.

Although someone you might talk to today doesn't know of any openings within his or her organization, tomorrow or next week or next month an opening may occur. If you've taken the time to show an interest in and knowledge of their organization, if you've shown the company representative how you can help achieve organizational goals and that you can fit into the organization, you'll be one of the first candidates considered for the position.

Networking: A Proactive Approach

Networking is a proactive rather than a reactive approach. You, as a job seeker, are expected to initiate a certain level of activity on your own behalf; you cannot afford to simply respond to jobs listed in the newspaper. Being proactive means building a network of contacts that includes informed and interested decision makers who will provide you with up-to-date knowledge of the current job market and increase your chances of finding out about employment opportunities appropriate for your interests, experience, and level of education.

An old axiom of networking says, "You are only two phone calls away from the information you need." In other words, by talking to enough people, you will quickly come across someone who can offer you help. Start with your professors. Each of them probably has a wide circle of contacts. In their work and travel they might have met someone who can help you or direct you to someone who can.

Control and the Networking Process

In deliberately establishing relationships, the process of networking begins with you in control—*you* are contacting specific individuals. As your network expands and you establish a set of professional relationships, your search for information or jobs will begin to move outside of your total control. A part of the networking process involves others assisting you by gathering information for you or recommending you as a possible job candidate. As additional people become a part of your networking system, you will have less knowledge about activities undertaken on your behalf; you will undoubtedly be contacted by individuals whom you did not initially approach. If you want to function effectively in surprise situations, you must be prepared at all times to talk with strangers about the informational or employment needs that motivated you to become involved in the networking process.

Preparing to Network

In deliberately establishing relationships, maximize your efforts by organizing your approach. Five specific areas in which you can organize your efforts include reviewing your self-assessment, reviewing your research on job sites and organizations, deciding who it is you want to talk to, keeping track of all your efforts, and creating your self-promotion tools.

Review Your Self-Assessment

Your self-assessment is as important a tool in preparing to network as it has been in other aspects of your job search. You have carefully evaluated your personal traits, personal values, economic needs, longer-term goals, skill base, preferred skills, and underdeveloped skills. During the networking process you will be called upon to communicate what you know about yourself and relate it to the information or job you seek. Be sure to review the exercises that you completed in the self-assessment section of this book in preparation for networking. We've explained that you need to assess what skills you have acquired from your major that are of general value to an employer and to be ready to express those in ways employers can appreciate as useful in their own organizations.

Review Research on Job Sites and Organizations

In addition, individuals assisting you will expect that you'll have at least some background information on the occupation or industry of interest to you.

Refer to the appropriate sections of this book and other relevant publications to acquire the background information necessary for effective networking. They'll explain how to identify not only the job titles that might be of interest to you but also what kinds of organizations employ people to do that job. You will develop some sense of working conditions and expectations about duties and responsibilities—all of which will be of help in your networking interviews.

Decide Who It Is You Want to Talk To

Networking cannot begin until you decide who it is that you want to talk to and, in general, what type of information you hope to gain from your contacts. Once you know this, it's time to begin developing a list of contacts. Five useful sources for locating contacts are described here.

College Alumni Network. Most colleges and universities have created a formal network of alumni and friends of the institution who are particularly interested in helping currently enrolled students and graduates of their alma mater gain employment-related information.

One of the more interesting aspects of networking is discovering the many roads taken by former sociology majors. You will probably be surprised at the diverse settings, in both the private and public sectors, where sociology graduates work. The most difficult task might be in narrowing down your list of who you would find is interesting to talk to. Don't limit yourself to alumni in your regional area, as networking by telephone or even by E-mail can still be very productive.

It is usually a simple process to make use of an alumni network. Visit your college's website and locate the alumni office and/or your career center. Either or both sites will have information about your school's alumni network. You'll be provided with information on shadowing experiences, geographic information, or those alumni offering job referrals. If you don't find what you're looking for, don't hesitate to phone or E-mail your career center and ask what they can do to help you connect with an alum.

Alumni networkers may provide some combination of the following services: day-long shadowing experiences, telephone interviews, in-person interviews, information on relocating to given geographic areas, internship information, suggestions on graduate school study, and job vacancy notices.

If you have the opportunity to spend a day with an alum who works in human services, you'll have a clearer view of the possibilities for your degree. Seeing what the job entails on a day-to-day basis will clarify your decision-making process, helping you to determine if indeed this is the right field for you.

This member of your network will also be able to share with you his or her own views on the roles that a sociology major can play in a human services setting.

Present and Former Supervisors. If you believe you are on good terms with present or former job supervisors, they may be an excellent resource for providing information or directing you to appropriate resources that would have information related to your current interests and needs. Additionally, these supervisors probably belong to professional organizations that they might be willing to utilize to get information for you.

Let's suppose you are seeking a job in human resource management. As a student, you've worked part-time and summers for a local real estate office. Though it might seem at first that your employer will not have the connections to local manufacturers that you need, don't get discouraged! In fact, it is more likely that your supervisor belongs to the local Chamber of Commerce, a venue through which he or she has formed ties with other Chamber of Commerce members. Working through organizations such as Chamber of Commerce can allow you to identify potential employers as well as obtain the names and numbers of people who can help you in the networking phase of the job search.

Employers in Your Area. Although you may be interested in working in a geographic location different from the one where you currently reside, don't overlook the value of the knowledge and contacts those around you are able to provide. Use the local telephone directory and newspaper to identify the types of organizations you are thinking of working for or professionals who have the kinds of jobs you are interested in. Recently, a call made to a local hospital's financial administrator for information on working in health-care financial administration yielded more pertinent information on training seminars, regional professional organizations, and potential employment sites than a national organization was willing to provide.

Employers in Geographic Areas Where You Hope to Work. If you are thinking about relocating, identifying prospective employers or informational contacts in the new location will be critical to your success. Here are some tips for online searching. First, use a "metasearch" engine to get the most out of your search. Metasearch engines combine several engines into one powerful tool. We frequently use dogpile.com and metasearch.com for this purpose. Try using the city and state as your keywords in a search. *New Haven, Connecticut* will bring you to the city's website with links to the chamber of commerce, member businesses, and other valuable resources. By using looksmart.com you can locate newspapers in any area, and they, too, can provide valuable insight before you relocate. Of course, both dogpile and metasearch can lead you to yellow and white page directories in areas you are considering.

Professional Associations and Organizations. Professional associations and organizations can provide valuable information in several areas: career paths that you might not have considered, qualifications relating to those career choices, publications that list current job openings, and workshops or seminars that will enhance your professional knowledge and skills. They can also be excellent sources for background information on given industries: their health, current problems, and future challenges.

There are several excellent resources available to help you locate professional associations and organizations that would have information to meet your needs. Two especially useful publications are the *Encyclopedia of Associations* and *National Trade and Professional Associations of the United States.*

Keep Track of All Your Efforts

It can be difficult, almost impossible, to remember all the details related to each contact you make during the networking process, so you will want to develop a record-keeping system that works for you. Formalize this process by using your computer to keep a record of the people and organizations you want to contact. You can simply record the contact's name, address, and telephone number, and what information you hope to gain. Each entry might look something like this:

Contact Name	Address	Phone #	Purpose
Mr. Lee Perkins	13 Muromachi	73-8906	Local market
Osaka Branch	Osaka-shi		information

You could record this as a simple Word document and you could still use the "Find" function if you were trying to locate some data and could only recall the firm's name or the contact's name. If you're comfortable with database management and you have some database software on your computer, then you can put information at your fingertips even if you have only the zip code! The point here is not technological sophistication but good record keeping.

Once you have created this initial list, it will be helpful to keep more detailed information as you begin to actually make the contacts. Using the Network Contact Record form in Exhibit 4.1 will help you keep good information on all your network contacts. They'll appreciate your recall of details of your meetings and conversations, and the information will help you to focus your networking efforts.

Create Your Self-Promotion Tools

There are two types of promotional tools that are used in the networking process. The first is a résumé and cover letter, and the second is a one-minute "infomercial," which may be given over the telephone or in person.

Techniques for writing an effective résumé and cover letter are discussed in Chapter 2. Once you have reviewed that material and prepared these important documents, you will have created one of your self-promotion tools.

The one-minute infomercial will demand that you begin tying your interests, abilities, and skills to the people or organizations you want to network with. Think about your goal for making the contact to help you understand what you should say about yourself. You should be able to express yourself easily and convincingly. If, for example, you are contacting an alumnus of your institution to obtain the names of possible employment sites in a distant city, be prepared to discuss why you are interested in moving to that location, the types of jobs you are interested in, and the skills and abilities you possess that will make you a qualified candidate.

To create a meaningful one-minute infomercial, write it out, practice it as if it will be a spoken presentation, rewrite it, and practice it again if necessary until expressing yourself comes easily and is convincing.

Here's a simplified example of an infomercial for use over the telephone:

Hello, Mr. Jenkins? This is Peter Stone. Thanks for taking my call. I've just graduated from the University of Texas, and I'm looking to begin a career in social research and data analysis. I've had a chance to work while in school and develop more of the skills required for this kind of career. I have strong

Exhibit 4.1
NETWORK CONTACT RECORD

Name: (Be certain your spelling is correct.)

Title: (Pick up a business card to be certain of the correct title.)

Employing organization: (Note any parent company or subsidiaries.)

Business mailing address: (This is often different from the street address.)

Business E-mail address: _____

Business telephone number: (Include area code and alternative numbers.)

Business fax number: _____

Source for this contact: (Who referred you, and what is their relationship to

the contact?)

Date of call or letter: (Use plenty of space here to record multiple phone calls

or visits, other employees you may have met, names of

secretaries/receptionists, and so forth.)

Content of discussion: (Keep enough notes here to remind you of the substance

of your visits and telephone conversations in case some

time elapses between contacts.)

Follow-up necessary to continue working with this contact: (Your contact may

request that you send him or her some materials or direct

you to contact an associate. Note any such instructions or

assignments in this space.)

Name of additional networker: (Here you would record the names and phone numbers

Address: of additional contacts met at this employer's site. Often

you will be introduced to many people, some of whom

may indicate a willingness to help in your job search.)

E-mail: _____

Phone: _____

Fax: _____

Name of additional networker: _____

Address: _____

E-mail: _____

Phone: _____

Fax: _____

Name of additional networker: _____

Address: _____

E-mail: _____

Phone: _____

Fax: _____

Date thank-you note written: (May help to date your next contact.)

Follow-up action taken: (Phone calls, visits, additional notes.)

Other miscellaneous notes: (Record any other additional interaction you think may be

important to remember in working with this networking

contact. You will want this form in front of you when

telephoning or just before and after a visit.)

interpersonal skills, experience with data analysis and research report writing, and have completed a summer internship that utilized these skills in a city planning office. I've also developed a pretty strong customer-service orientation and have a good sense of how important it is to identify the information needs of clients.

Mr. Jenkins, I'm calling because I'd still like to learn more about the human resources field. I'm hoping you'll have the time to sit down with me for about half an hour and discuss

> your perspective on careers in personnel with me. There are
> so many possible employers to approach, and I am seeking
> some advice on which might be the best bet for my particu-
> lar combination of skills and experiences.
>   Would you be willing to do that for me? I would greatly
> appreciate it. I am available at your convenience.

It very well may happen that your employer contact wishes you to communicate by E-mail. The infomercial quoted above could easily be rewrit-
ten for an E-mail message. You should "cut and paste" your résumé right into
the E-mail text itself.

Other effective self-promotion tools include portfolios for those in the arts,
writing professions, or teaching. Portfolios show examples of work, photo-
graphs of projects or classroom activities, or certificates and credentials that
are job related. There may not be an opportunity to use the portfolio during an interview, and it is not something that should be left with the organization. It is designed to be explained and displayed by the creator. However,
during some networking meetings, there may be an opportunity to illustrate
a point or strengthen a qualification by exhibiting the portfolio.

Beginning the Networking Process

Set the Tone for Your Communications
It can be useful to establish "tone words" for any communications you
embark upon. Before making your first telephone call or writing your first
letter, decide what you want the person to think of you. If you are networking
to try to obtain a job, your tone words might include descriptors such as *genuine, informed,* and *self-knowledgeable.* When you're trying to acquire information, your tone words may have a slightly different focus, such as *courteous,
organized, focused,* and *well-spoken.* Use the tone words you establish for your
contacts to guide you through the networking process.

Honestly Express Your Intentions
When contacting individuals, it is important to be honest about your reasons for making the contact. Establish your purpose in your own mind and
be able and ready to articulate it concisely. Determine an initial agenda,
whether it be informational questioning or self-promotion, present it to your
contact, and be ready to respond immediately. If you don't adequately pre-

pare before initiating your overture, you may find yourself at a disadvantage if you're asked to immediately begin your informational interview or self-promotion during the first phone conversation or visit.

Start Networking Within Your Circle of Confidence

Once you have organized your approach—by utilizing specific researching methods, creating a system for keeping track of the people you will contact, and developing effective self-promotion tools—you are ready to begin networking. The best way to begin networking is by talking with a group of people you trust and feel comfortable with. This group is usually made up of your family, friends, and career counselors. No matter who is in this inner circle, they will have a special interest in seeing you succeed in your job search. In addition, because they will be easy to talk to, you should try taking some risks in terms of practicing your information-seeking approach. Gain confidence in talking about the strengths you bring to an organization and the underdeveloped skills you feel hinder your candidacy. Be sure to review the section on self-assessment for tips on approaching each of these areas. Ask for critical but constructive feedback from the people in your circle of confidence on the letters you write and the one-minute infomercial you have developed. Evaluate whether you want to make the changes they suggest, then practice the changes on others within this circle.

Stretch the Boundaries of Your Networking Circle of Confidence

Once you have refined the promotional tools you will use to accomplish your networking goals, you will want to make additional contacts. Because you will not know most of these people, it will be a less comfortable activity to undertake. The practice that you gained with your inner circle of trusted friends should have prepared you to now move outside of that comfort zone.

It is said that any information a person needs is only two phone calls away, but the information cannot be gained until you (1) make a reasonable guess about who might have the information you need and (2) pick up the telephone to make the call. Using your network list that includes alumni, instructors, supervisors, employers, and associations, you can begin preparing your list of questions that will allow you to get the information you need. Review the question list that follows and then develop a list of your own.

Questions You Might Want to Ask

1. In the position you now hold, what do you do on a typical day?
2. What are the most interesting aspects of your job?

3. What part of your work do you consider dull or repetitious?
4. What were the jobs you had that led to your present position?
5. How long does it usually take to move from one step to the next in this career path?
6. What is the top position to which you can aspire in this career path?
7. What is the next step in *your* career path?
8. Are there positions in this field that are similar to your position?
9. What are the required qualifications and training for entry-level positions in this field?
10. Are there specific courses a student should take to be qualified to work in this field?
11. What are the entry-level jobs in this field?
12. What types of training are provided to persons entering this field?
13. What are the salary ranges your organization typically offers to entry-level candidates for positions in this field?
14. What special advice would you give a person entering this field?
15. Do you see this field as a growing one?
16. How do you see the content of the entry-level jobs in this field changing over the next two years?
17. What can I do to prepare myself for these changes?
18. What is the best way to obtain a position that will start me on a career in this field?
19. Do you have any information on job specifications and descriptions that I may have?
20. What related occupational fields would you suggest I explore?
21. How could I improve my résumé for a career in this field?
22. Who else would you suggest I talk to, both in your organization and in other organizations?

Questions You Might Have to Answer

To communicate effectively, you must anticipate questions that will be asked of you by the networkers you contact. Review the following list and see if you can easily answer each of these questions. If you cannot, it may be time to revisit the self-assessment process.

1. Where did you get my name, or how did you find out about this organization?
2. What are your career goals?
3. What kind of job are you interested in?
4. What do you know about this organization and this industry?

5. How do you know you're prepared to undertake an entry-level position in this industry?
6. What course work have you done that is related to your career interests?
7. What are your short-term career goals?
8. What are your long-term career goals?
9. Do you plan to obtain additional formal education?
10. What contributions have you made to previous employers?
11. Which of your previous jobs have you enjoyed the most and why?
12. What are you particularly good at doing?
13. What shortcomings have you had to face in previous employment?
14. What are your three greatest strengths?
15. Describe how comfortable you feel with your communication style.

General Networking Tips

Make Every Contact Count. Setting the tone for each interaction is critical. Approaches that will help you communicate in an effective way include politeness, being appreciative of time provided to you, and being prepared and thorough. Remember, *everyone* within an organization has a circle of influence, so be prepared to interact effectively with each person you encounter in the networking process, including secretarial and support staff. Many information or job seekers have thwarted their own efforts by being rude to some individuals they encountered as they networked because they made the incorrect assumption that certain persons were unimportant.

Sometimes your contacts may be surprised at their ability to help you. After meeting and talking with you, they might think they have not offered much in the way of help. A day or two later, however, they may make a contact that would be useful to you and refer you to that person.

With Each Contact, Widen Your Circle of Networkers. Always leave an informational interview with the names of at least two more people who can help you get the information or job that you are seeking. Don't be shy about asking for additional contacts; networking is all about increasing the number of people you can interact with to achieve your goals.

Make Your Own Decisions. As you talk with different people and get answers to the questions you pose, you may hear conflicting information or get conflicting suggestions. Your job is to listen to these "experts" and decide what information and which suggestions will help you achieve *your* goals. Only implement those suggestions that you believe will work for you.

Shutting Down Your Network

As you achieve the goals that motivated your networking activity—getting the information you need or the job you want—the time will come to inactivate all or parts of your network. As you do, be sure to tell your primary supporters about your change in status. Call or write to each one of them and give them as many details about your new status as you feel is necessary to maintain a positive relationship.

Because a network takes on a life of its own, activity undertaken on your behalf will continue even after you cease your efforts. As you get calls or are contacted in some fashion, be sure to inform these networkers about your change in status, and thank them for assistance they have provided.

Information on the latest employment trends indicates that workers will change jobs or careers several times in their lifetime. Networking, then, will be a critical aspect in the span of your professional life. If you carefully and thoughtfully conduct your networking activities during your job search, you will have a solid foundation of experience when you need to network the next time around.

Interviewing

Certainly, there can be no one part of the job search process more fraught with anxiety and worry than the interview. Yet seasoned job seekers welcome the interview and will often say, "Just get me an interview and I'm on my way!" They understand that the interview is crucial to the hiring process and equally crucial for them, as job candidates, to have the opportunity of a personal dialogue to add to what the employer may already have learned from the résumé, cover letter, and telephone conversations.

Believe it or not, the interview is to be welcomed, and even enjoyed! It is a perfect opportunity for you, the candidate, to sit down with an employer and express yourself and display who you are and what you want. Of course, it takes thought and planning and a little strategy; after all, it *is* a job interview! But it can be a positive, if not pleasant, experience and one you can look back on and feel confident about your performance and effort.

For many new job seekers, a job, any job, seems a wonderful thing. But seasoned interview veterans know that the job interview is an important step for both sides—the employer and the candidate—to see what each has to offer and whether there is going to be a "fit" of personalities, work styles, and attitudes. And it is this concept of balance in the interview, that both sides have important parts to play, that holds the key to success in mastering this aspect of the job search strategy.

Try to think of the interview as a conversation between two interested and equal partners. You both have important, even vital, information to deliver and to learn. Of course, there's no denying the employer has some leverage, especially in the initial interview for recruitment or any interview scheduled by the candidate and not the recruiter. That should not prevent the interviewee from seeking to play an equal part in what should be a fair exchange of information. Too often the untutored candidate allows the interview to become one-sided. The employer asks all the questions and the candidate simply responds. The ideal would be for two mutually interested parties to sit down and discuss possibilities for each. This is a conversation of significance, and it requires preparation, thought about the tone of the interview, and planning of the nature and details of the information to be exchanged.

Preparing for the Interview

The length of most initial interviews is about thirty minutes. Given the brevity, the information that is exchanged ought to be important. The candidate should be delivering material that the employer cannot discover on the résumé, and in turn, the candidate should be learning things about the employer that he or she could not otherwise find out. After all, if you have only thirty minutes, why waste time on information that is already published? The information exchanged is more than just factual, and both sides will learn much from what they see of each other, as well. How the candidate looks, speaks, and acts are important to the employer. The employer's attention to the interview and awareness of the candidate's résumé, the setting, and the quality of information presented are important to the candidate.

Just as the employer has every right to be disappointed when a prospect is late for the interview, looks unkempt, and seems ill-prepared to answer fairly standard questions, the candidate may be disappointed with an interviewer who isn't ready for the meeting, hasn't learned the basic résumé facts, and is constantly interrupted by telephone calls. In either situation there's good reason to feel let down.

There are many elements to a successful interview, and some of them are not easy to describe or prepare for. Sometimes there is just a chemistry between interviewer and interviewee that brings out the best in both, and a good exchange takes place. But there is much the candidate can do to pave the way for success in terms of his or her résumé, personal appearance, goals, and interview strategy—each of which we will discuss. However, none of this preparation is as important as the time and thought the candidate gives to personal self-assessment.

Self-Assessment
Neither a stunning résumé nor an expensive, well-tailored suit can compensate for candidates who do not know what they want, where they are going,

or why they are interviewing with a particular employer. Self-assessment, the process by which we begin to know and acknowledge our own particular blend of education, experiences, needs, and goals, is not something that can be sorted out the weekend before a major interview. Of all the elements of interview preparation, this one requires the longest lead time and cannot be faked.

Because the time allotted for most interviews is brief, it is all the more important for job candidates to understand and express succinctly why they are there and what they have to offer. This is not a time for undue modesty (or for braggadocio either); it is a time for a compelling, reasoned statement of why you feel that you and this employer might make a good match. It means you have to have thought about your skills, interests, and attributes; related those to your life experiences and your own history of challenges and opportunities; and determined what that indicates about your strengths, preferences, values, and areas needing further development.

A common complaint of employers is that many candidates didn't take advantage of the interview time; they didn't seem to know why they were there or what they wanted. When candidates are asked to talk about themselves and their work-related skills and attributes, employers don't want to be faced with shyness or embarrassed laughter; they need to know about you so they can make a fair determination of you and your competition. If you don't take advantage of the opportunity to make a case for your employability, you can be certain the person ahead of you has or the person after you will, and it will be on the strength of those impressions that the employer will hire.

If you need some assistance with self-assessment issues, refer to Chapter 1. Included are suggested exercises that can be done as needed, such as making up an experiential diary and extracting obvious strengths and weaknesses from past experiences. These simple assignments will help you look at past activities as collections of tasks with accompanying skills and responsibilities. Don't overlook your high school or college career office. Many offer personal counseling on self-assessment issues and may provide testing instruments such as the *Myers-Briggs Type Indicator (MBTI)*, the *Harrington-O'Shea Career Decision-Making System (CDM)*, the *Strong Interest Inventory (SII)*, or any other of a wide selection of assessment tools that can help you clarify some of these issues prior to the interview stage of your job search.

The Résumé

Résumé preparation has been discussed in detail, and some basic examples of various types were provided. In this section we want to concentrate on how best to use your résumé in the interview. In most cases the employer will have seen the résumé prior to the interview, and, in fact, it may well have been the quality of that résumé that secured the interview opportunity.

An interview is a conversation, however, and not an exercise in reading. So, if the employer hasn't seen your résumé and you have brought it along to the interview, wait until asked or until the end of the interview to offer it. Otherwise, you may find yourself staring at the back of your résumé and simply answering "yes" and "no" to a series of questions drawn from that document.

Sometimes an interviewer is not prepared and does not know or recall the contents of the résumé and may use the résumé to a greater or lesser degree as a "prompt" during the interview. It is for you to judge what that may indicate about the individual performing the interview or the employer. If your interviewer seems surprised by the scheduled meeting, relies on the résumé to an inordinate degree, and seems otherwise unfamiliar with your background, this lack of preparation for the hiring process could well be a symptom of general management disorganization or may simply be the result of poor planning on the part of one individual. It is your responsibility as a potential employee to be aware of these signals and make your decisions accordingly.

If you find that the interviewer is reading from your résumé rather than talking with you, you can steer the interview back to a dialogue by saying something like, "Ms. Taylor, if you'd like I can elaborate on the experience I gained working on a community mental health outreach program." Doing this will give you an opportunity to convey more information about your particular strengths and values, and will reengage your interviewer.

By all means, bring at least one copy of your résumé to the interview. Occasionally, at the close of an interview, an interviewer will express an interest in circulating a résumé to several departments, and you could then offer the copy you brought. Sometimes, an interview appointment provides an opportunity to meet others in the organization who may express an interest in you and your background, and it may be helpful to follow up with a copy of your résumé. Our best advice, however, is to keep it out of sight until needed or requested.

Appearance

Although many of the absolute rules that once dominated the advice offered to job candidates about appearance have now been moderated significantly, conservative is still the watchword unless you are interviewing in a fashion-related industry. For men, conservative translates into a well-cut dark suit with appropriate tie, hosiery, and dress shirt. A wise strategy for the male job seeker looking for a good but not expensive suit would be to try the men's department of a major department store. They usually carry a good range of sizes, fabrics, and prices; offer professional sales help; provide free tailoring; and have associated departments for putting together a professional look.

For women, there is more latitude. Business suits are still popular, but they have become more feminine in color and styling with a variety of jacket and skirt lengths. In addition to suits, better-quality dresses are now worn in many environments and, with the correct accessories, can be most appropriate. Company literature, professional magazines, the business section of major newspapers, and television interviews can all give clues about what is being worn in different employer environments.

Both men and women need to pay attention to issues such as hair, jewelry, and makeup; these are often what separates the candidate in appearance from the professional workforce. It seems particularly difficult for the young job seeker to give up certain hairstyles, eyeglass fashions, and jewelry habits, yet those can be important to the employer who is concerned with your ability to successfully make the transition into the organization. Candidates often find the best strategy is to dress conservatively until they find employment. Once employed and familiar with the norms within your organization, you can begin to determine a look that you enjoy, works for you, and fits your organization.

Choose clothes that suit your body type, fit well, and flatter you. Feel good about the way you look! The interview day is not the best time for a new hairdo, a new pair of shoes, or any other change that will distract you or cause you to be self-conscious. Arrive a bit early to avoid being rushed, and ask the receptionist to direct you to a restroom for any last-minute adjustments of hair and clothes.

Employer Information

Whether your interview is for graduate school admission, an overseas corporate position, or a position with a local company, it is important to know something about the employer or the organization. Keeping in mind that the interview is relatively brief and that you will hopefully have other interviews with other organizations, it is important to keep your research in proportion. If secondary interviews are called for, you will have additional time to do further research. For the first interview, it is helpful to know the organization's mission, goals, size, scope of operations, and so forth. Your research may uncover recent areas of challenge or particular successes that may help to fuel the interview. Use the "What Do They Call the Job You Want?" section of Chapter 3, your library, and your career or guidance office to help you locate this information in the most efficient way possible. Don't be shy in asking advice of these counseling and guidance professionals on how best to spend your preparation time. With some practice, you'll soon learn how much information is enough and which kinds of information are most useful to you.

Interview Content

We've already discussed how it can help to think of the interview as an important conversation—one that, as with any conversation, you want to find pleasant and interesting and to leave you with a good feeling. But because this conversation is especially important, the information that's exchanged is critical to its success. What do you want them to know about you? What do you need to know about them? What interview technique do you need to particularly pay attention to? How do you want to manage the close of the interview? What steps will follow in the hiring process?

Except for the professional interviewer, most of us find interviewing stressful and anxiety-provoking. Developing a strategy before you begin interviewing will help you relieve some stress and anxiety. One particular strategy that has worked for many and may work for you is interviewing by objective. Before you interview, write down three to five goals you would like to achieve for that interview. They may be technique goals: smile a little more, have a firmer handshake, be sure to ask about the next stage in the interview process before leaving. They may be content-oriented goals: find out about the company's current challenges and opportunities; be sure to speak of your recent research, writing experiences, or foreign travel. Whatever your goals, jot down a few of them as goals for each interview.

Most people find that in trying to achieve these few goals, their interviewing technique becomes more organized and focused. After the interview, the most common question friends and family ask is "How did it go?" With this technique, you have an indication of whether you met *your* goals for the meeting, not just some vague idea of how it went. Chances are, if you accomplished what you wanted to, it improved the quality of the entire interview. As you continue to interview, you will want to revise your goals to continue improving your interview skills.

Now, add to the concept of the significant conversation the idea of a beginning, a middle, and a closing and you will have two thoughts that will give your interview a distinctive character. Be sure to make your introduction warm and cordial. Say your full name (and if it's a difficult-to-pronounce name, help the interviewer to pronounce it) and make certain you know your interviewer's name and how to pronounce it. Most interviews begin with some "soft talk" about the weather, chat about the candidate's trip to the interview site, or national events. This is done as a courtesy to relax both you and the interviewer, to get you talking, and to generally try to defuse the atmosphere of excessive tension. Try to be yourself, engage in the conversation, and don't try to second-guess the interviewer. This is simply what it appears to be—casual conversation.

Once you and the interviewer move on to exchange more serious information in the middle part of the interview, the two most important concerns become your ability to handle challenging questions and your success at asking meaningful ones. Interviewer questions will probably fall into one of three categories: personal assessment and career direction, academic assessment, and knowledge of the employer. The following are some examples of questions in each category:

Personal Assessment and Career Direction
1. How would you describe yourself?
2. What motivates you to put forth your best effort?
3. In what kind of work environment are you most comfortable?
4. What do you consider to be your greatest strengths and weaknesses?
5. How well do you work under pressure?
6. What qualifications do you have that make you think you will be successful in this career?
7. Will you relocate? What do you feel would be the most difficult aspect of relocating?
8. Are you willing to travel?
9. Why should I hire you?

Academic Assessment
1. Why did you select your college or university?
2. What changes would you make at your alma mater?
3. What led you to choose your major?

4. What subjects did you like best and least? Why?
5. If you could, how would you plan your academic study differently? Why?
6. Describe your most rewarding college experience.
7. How has your college experience prepared you for this career?
8. Do you think that your grades are a good indication of your ability to succeed with this organization?
9. Do you have plans for continued study?

Knowledge of the Employer

1. If you were hiring a graduate of your school for this position, what qualities would you look for?
2. What do you think it takes to be successful in an organization like ours?
3. In what ways do you think you can make a contribution to our organization?
4. Why did you choose to seek a position with this organization?

The interviewer wants a response to each question but is also gauging your enthusiasm, preparedness, and willingness to communicate. In each response you should provide some information about yourself that can be related to the employer's needs. A common mistake is to give too much information. Answer each question completely, but be careful not to run on too long with extensive details or examples.

Questions About Underdeveloped Skills

Most employers interview people who have met some minimum criteria of education and experience. They interview candidates to see who they are, to learn what kind of personality they exhibit, and to get some sense of how this person might fit into the existing organization. It may be that you are asked about skills the employer hopes to find and that you have not documented. Maybe it's grant-writing experience, knowledge of the European political system, or a knowledge of the film world.

To questions about skills and experiences you don't have, answer honestly and forthrightly and try to offer some additional information about skills you do have. For example, perhaps the employer is disappointed you have no grant-writing experience. An honest answer may be as follows:

No, unfortunately, I was never in a position to acquire those skills. I do understand something of the complexities of the grant-writing process and feel confident that my attention to detail, careful reading skills, and strong writing would make grants a wonderful challenge in a new job. I think I could get up on the learning curve quickly.

The employer hears an honest admission of lack of experience but is reassured by some specific skill details that do relate to grant writing and a confident manner that suggests enthusiasm and interest in a challenge.

For many students, questions about their possible contribution to an employer's organization can prove challenging. Because your education has probably not included specific training for a job, you need to review your academic record and select capabilities you have developed in your major that an employer can appreciate. For example, perhaps you read well and can analyze and condense what you've read into smaller, more focused pieces. That could be valuable. Or maybe you did some serious research and you know you have valuable investigative skills. Your public speaking might be highly developed and you might use visual aids appropriately and effectively. Or maybe your skill at correspondence, memos, and messages is effective. Whatever it is, you must take it out of the academic context and put it into a new, employer-friendly context so your interviewer can best judge how you could help the organization.

Exhibiting knowledge of the organization will, without a doubt, show the interviewer that you are interested enough in the available position to have done some legwork in preparation for the interview. Remember, it is not necessary to know every detail of the organization's history but rather to have a general knowledge about why it is in business and how the industry is faring.

Sometime during the interview, generally after the midway point, you'll be asked if you have any questions for the interviewer. Your questions will tell the employer much about your attitude and your desire to understand the organization's expectations so you can compare them to your own strengths. The following are some selected questions you might want to ask:

1. What are the main responsibilities of the position?
2. What are the opportunities and challenges associated with this position?
3. Could you outline some possible career paths beginning with this position?
4. How regularly do performance evaluations occur?
5. What is the communication style of the organization? (meetings, memos, and so forth)
6. What would a typical day in this position be like for me?

7. What kinds of opportunities might exist for me to improve my professional skills within the organization?
8. What have been some of the interesting challenges and opportunities your organization has recently faced?

Most interviews draw to a natural closing point, so be careful not to prolong the discussion. At a signal from the interviewer, wind up your presentation, express your appreciation for the opportunity, and be sure to ask what the next stage in the process will be. When can you expect to hear from them? Will they be conducting second-tier interviews? If you are interested and haven't heard, would they mind a phone call? Be sure to collect a business card with the name and phone number of your interviewer. On your way out, you might have an opportunity to pick up organizational literature you haven't seen before.

With the right preparation—a thorough self-assessment, professional clothing, and employer information—you'll be able to set and achieve the goals you have established for the interview process.

Networking or
Interview Follow-Up

Quite often there is a considerable time lag between interviewing for a position and being hired or, in the case of the networker, between your phone call or letter to a possible contact and the opportunity of a meeting. This can be frustrating. "Why aren't they contacting me?" "I thought I'd get another interview, but no one has telephoned." "Am I out of the running?" You don't know what is happening.

Consider the Differing Perspectives

Of course, there is another perspective—that of the networker or hiring organization. Organizations are complex, with multiple tasks that need to be accomplished each day. Hiring is a discrete activity that does not occur as frequently as other job assignments. The hiring process might have to take second place to other, more immediate organizational needs. Although it may be very important to you, and it is certainly ultimately significant to the employer, other issues such as fiscal management, planning and product development, employer vacation periods, or financial constraints may prevent an organization or individual within that organization from acting on your employment or your request for information as quickly as you or they would prefer.

Use Your Communication Skills

Good communication is essential here to resolve any anxieties, and the responsibility is on you, the job or information seeker. Too many job seekers and networkers offer as an excuse that they don't want to "bother" the organization by writing letters or calling. Let us assure you here and now, once and for all, that if you are troubling an organization by over-communicating, someone will indicate that situation to you quite clearly. If not, you can only assume you are a worthwhile prospect and the employer appreciates being reminded of your availability and interest. Let's look at follow-up practices in the job interview process and the networking situation separately.

Following Up on the Employment Interview

A brief thank-you note following an interview is an excellent and polite way to begin a series of follow-up communications with a potential employer with whom you have interviewed and want to remain in touch. It should be just that—a thank-you for a good meeting. If you failed to mention some fact or experience during your interview that you think might add to your candidacy, you may use this note to do that. However, this should be essentially a note whose overall tone is appreciative and, if appropriate, indicative of a continuing interest in pursuing any opportunity that may exist with that organization. It is one of the few pieces of business correspondence that may be handwritten, but always use plain, good-quality, standard-size paper.

If, however, at this point you are no longer interested in the employer, the thank-you note is an appropriate time to indicate that. You are under no obligation to identify any reason for not continuing to pursue employment with that organization, but if you are so inclined to indicate your professional reasons (pursuing other employers more akin to your interests, looking for greater income production than this employer can provide, a different geographic location), you certainly may. It should not be written with an eye to negotiation, for it will not be interpreted as such.

As part of your interview closing, you should have taken the initiative to establish lines of communication for continuing information about your candidacy. If you asked permission to telephone, wait a week following your thank-you note, then telephone your contact simply to inquire how things are progressing on your employment status. The feedback you receive here should be taken at face value. If your interviewer simply has no information, he or she will tell you so and indicate whether you should call again and when. Don't be discouraged if this should continue over some period of time.

If during this time something occurs that you think improves or changes your candidacy (some new qualification or experience you may have had), including any offers from other organizations, by all means telephone or write to inform the employer about this. In the case of an offer from a competing but less desirable or equally desirable organization, telephone your contact, explain what has happened, express your real interest in the organization, and inquire whether some determination on your employment might be made before you must respond to this other offer. An organization that is truly interested in you may be moved to make a decision about your candidacy. Equally possible is the scenario in which they are not yet ready to make a decision and so advise you to take the offer that has been presented. Again, you have no ethical alternative but to deal with the information presented in a straightforward manner.

When accepting other employment, be sure to contact any employers still actively considering you and inform them of your new job. Thank them graciously for their consideration. There are many other job seekers out there just like you who will benefit from having their candidacy improved when others bow out of the race. Who knows, you might at some future time have occasion to interact professionally with one of the organizations with which you sought employment. How embarrassing it would be to have someone remember you as the candidate who failed to notify them that you were taking a job elsewhere!

In all of your follow-up communications, keep good notes of whom you spoke with, when you called, and any instructions that were given about return communications. This will prevent any misunderstandings and provide you with good records of what has transpired.

Following Up on the Network Contact

Far more common than the forgotten follow-up after an interview is the situation where a good network contact is allowed to lapse. Good communications are the essence of a network, and follow-up is not so much a matter of courtesy here as it is a necessity. In networking for job information and contacts, you are the active network link. Without you, and without continual contact from you, there is no network. You and your need for employment are often the only shared elements among members of the network. Because network contacts were made regardless of the availability of any particular employment, it is incumbent upon the job seeker, if not simple common sense, to stay in regular communication with the network if you want to be considered for any future job opportunities.

This brings up the issue of responsibility, which is likewise very clear. The job seeker initiates network contacts and is responsible for maintaining those contacts; therefore, the entire responsibility for the network belongs with him or her. This becomes patently obvious if the network is left unattended. It very shortly falls out of existence because it cannot survive without careful attention by the networker.

You have many ways to keep the lines of communication open and to attempt to interest the network in you as a possible employee. You are limited only by your own enthusiasm for members of the network and your creativity. However, you as a networker are well advised to keep good records of whom you have met and contacted in each organization. Be sure to send thank-you notes to anyone who has spent any time with you, whether it was an E-mail message containing information or advice, a quick tour of a department, or a sit-down informational interview. All of these thank-you notes should, in addition to their ostensible reason, add some information about you and your particular combination of strengths and attributes.

You can contact your network at any time to convey continued interest, to comment on some recent article you came across concerning an organization, to add information about your training or changes in your qualifications, to ask advice or seek guidance in your job search, or to request referrals to other possible network opportunities. Sometimes just a simple note to network members reminding them of your job search, indicating that you have been using their advice, and noting that you are still actively pursuing leads and hope to continue to interact with them is enough to keep communications alive.

The Internet has opened up the world of networking. You may be able to find networkers who graduated from your high school or from the college you're attending, who live in a geographic region where you hope to work, or who are employed in a given industry. The Internet makes it easy to reach out to many people, but don't let this perceived ease lull you into complacency. Internet networking demands the same level of preparation as the more traditional forms of networking.

Because networks have been abused in the past, it's important that your conduct be above reproach. Networks are exploratory options; they are not backdoor access to employers. The network works best for someone who is exploring a new industry or making a transition into a new area of employment and who needs to find information or to alert people to his or her search activity. Always be candid and direct with contacts in expressing the purpose of your E-mail, call, or letter and your interest in their help or information about their organization. In follow-up contacts keep the tone professional and direct. Your honesty will be appreciated, and people will respond as best they can if your qualifications appear to meet their forthcoming needs. The network does not owe you anything, and that tone should be clear to each person you meet.

Feedback from Follow-Ups

A network contact may prove to be miscalculated. Perhaps you were referred to someone and it became clear that your goals and his or her particular needs did not make a good match. Or the network contact may simply not be in a position to provide you with the information you are seeking. Or in some unfortunate situations, the party may become annoyed by being contacted for this purpose. In such a situation, many job seekers simply say "Thank you" and move on.

If the contact is simply not the right connection, but the individual you are speaking with is not annoyed by the call, it might be a better tactic to express regret that the contact was misplaced and then tell the person what you are seeking and ask for his or her advice or possible suggestions as to a next step. The more people who are aware that you are seeking employment, the better your chances of connecting, and that is the purpose of a network. Most people in a profession have excellent knowledge of their field and varying amounts of expertise in areas tangent to their own. Use their expertise and seek some guidance before you dissolve the contact. You may be pleasantly surprised.

Occasionally, networkers will express the feeling that they have done as much as they can or provided all the information that is available to them. This may be a cue that they would like to be released from your network. Be alert to such attempts to terminate, graciously thank the individual by letter, and move on in your network development. A network is always changing, adding and losing members, and you want the network to be composed only of those who are actively interested in supporting you.

As a sociology major you will have acquired valuable written and oral communication skills. Now that you are looking for a job, the time you have spent writing research papers and giving oral presentations will really pay off, as nearly every career path that might be pursued by a sociology major requires strong communication skills.

Remember that the importance of communicating clearly and effectively extends to every aspect of your job search. Telephone conversations, personal interviews, and written correspondence with network contacts as well as potential employers are opportunities to demonstrate your ability to thoughtfully articulate your ideas, and thus create a favorable impression in those you meet.

7

Job Offer Considerations

For many recent college graduates, the thrill of their first job and, for some, the most substantial regular income they have ever earned seems an excess of good fortune coming at once. To question that first income or to be critical in any way of the conditions of employment at the time of the initial offer seems like looking a gift horse in the mouth. It doesn't seem to occur to many new hires even to attempt to negotiate any aspect of their first job. And, as many employers who deal with entry-level jobs for recent college graduates will readily confirm, the reality is that there simply isn't much movement in salary available to these new college recruits. The entry-level hire generally does not have an employment track record on a professional level to provide any leverage for negotiation. Real negotiations on salary, benefits, retirement provisions, and so forth come to those with significant employment records at higher income levels.

Of course, the job offer is more than just money. It can be composed of geographic assignment, duties and responsibilities, training, benefits, health and medical insurance, educational assistance, car allowance or company vehicle, and a host of other items. All of this is generally detailed in the formal letter that presents the final job offer. In most cases this is a follow-up to a personal phone call from the employer representative who has been principally responsible for your hiring process.

That initial telephone offer is certainly binding as a verbal agreement, but most firms follow up with a detailed letter outlining the most significant parts of your employment contract. You may, of course, choose to respond immediately at the time of the telephone offer (which would be considered a binding oral contract), but you will also be required to formally answer the letter of offer with a letter of acceptance, restating the salient elements of the employer's description of your position, salary, and benefits. This ensures that both parties are clear on the terms and conditions of employment and remuneration and any other outstanding aspects of the job offer.

Is This the Job You Want?

Most new employees will respond affirmatively in writing, glad to be in the position to accept employment. If you've worked hard to get the offer and the job market is tight, other offers may not be in sight, so you will say, "Yes, I accept!" What is important here is that the job offer you accept be one that does fit your particular needs, values, and interests as you've outlined them in your self-assessment process. Moreover, it should be a job that will not only use your skills and education but also challenge you to develop new skills and talents.

Jobs are sometimes accepted too hastily, for the wrong reasons, and without proper scrutiny by the applicant. For example, an individual might readily accept a sales job only to find the continual rejection by potential clients unendurable. An office worker might realize within weeks the constraints of a desk job and yearn for more activity. Employment is an important part of our lives. It is, for most of our adult lives, our most continuous productive activity. We want to make good choices based on the right criteria.

If you have a low tolerance for risk, a job based on commission will certainly be very anxiety-provoking. If being near your family is important, issues of relocation could present a decision crisis for you. If you're an adventurous person, a job with frequent travel would provide needed excitement and be very desirable. The importance of income, the need to continue your education, your personal health situation—all of these have an impact on whether the job you are considering will ultimately meet your needs. Unless you've spent some time understanding and thinking about these issues, it will be difficult to evaluate offers you do receive.

More important, if you make a decision that you cannot tolerate and feel you must leave that job, you will then have both unemployment and self-esteem issues to contend with. These will combine to make the next job search tough going, indeed. So make your acceptance a carefully considered decision.

Negotiating Your Offer

It may be that there is some aspect of your job offer that is not particularly attractive to you. Perhaps there is no relocation allotment to help you move your possessions, and this presents some financial hardship for you. It may be that the health insurance is less than you had hoped. Your initial assignment may be different from what you expected, either in its location or in the duties and responsibilities that comprise it. Or it may simply be that the salary is less than you anticipated. Other considerations may be your official starting date of employment, vacation time, evening hours, dates of training programs or schools, and other concerns.

If you are considering not accepting the job because of some item or items in the job offer "package" that do not meet your needs, you should know that most employers emphatically wish that you would bring that issue to their attention. It may be that the employer can alter it to make the offer more agreeable for you. In some cases it cannot be changed. In any event the employer would generally like to have the opportunity to try to remedy a difficulty rather than risk losing a good potential employee over an issue that might have been resolved. After all, they have spent time and funds in securing your services, and they certainly deserve an opportunity to resolve any possible differences.

Honesty is the best approach in discussing any objections or uneasiness you might have over the employer's offer. Having received your formal offer in writing, contact your employer representative and indicate your particular dissatisfaction in a straightforward manner. For example, you might explain that while you are very interested in being employed by this organization, the salary (or any other benefit) is less than you have determined you require. State the terms you need, and listen to the response. You may be asked to put this in writing, or you may be asked to hold off until the firm can decide on a response. If you are dealing with a senior representative of the organization, one who has been involved in hiring for some time, you may get an immediate response or a solid indication of possible outcomes.

Perhaps the issue is one of relocation. Your initial assignment is in the Midwest, and because you had indicated a strong West Coast preference, you are surprised at the actual assignment. You might simply indicate that while you understand the need for the company to assign you based on its needs, you are disappointed and had hoped to be placed on the West Coast. You could inquire if that were still possible and, if not, would it be reasonable to expect a West Coast relocation in the future.

If your request is presented in a reasonable way, most employers will not see this as jeopardizing your offer. If they can agree to your proposal, they will. If not, they will simply tell you so, and you may choose to continue your candidacy with them or remove yourself from consideration. The choice will be up to you.

Some firms will adjust benefits within their parameters to meet the candidate's need if at all possible. If a candidate requires a relocation cost allowance, he or she may be asked to forgo tuition benefits for the first year to accomplish this adjustment. An increase in life insurance may be adjusted by some other benefit trade-off; perhaps a family dental plan is not needed. In these decisions you are called upon, sometimes under time pressure, to know how you value these issues and how important each is to you.

Many employers find they are more comfortable negotiating for candidates who have unique qualifications or who bring especially needed expertise to the organization. Employers hiring large numbers of entry-level college graduates may be far more reluctant to accommodate any changes in offer conditions. They are well supplied with candidates with similar education and experience so that if rejected by one candidate, they can draw new candidates from an ample labor pool.

Comparing Offers

The condition of the economy, the job seeker's academic major and particular geographic job market, and individual needs and demands for certain employment conditions may not provide more than one job offer at a time. Some job seekers may feel that no reasonable offer should go unaccepted for the simple fear there won't be another.

In a tough job market, or if the job you seek is not widely available, or when your job search goes on too long and becomes difficult to sustain financially and emotionally, it may be necessary to accept an inferior offer. The alternative is continued unemployment. Even here, when you feel you don't have a choice, you can at least understand that in accepting this particular offer, there may be limitations and conditions you don't appreciate. At the time of acceptance, there were no other alternatives, but you can begin to use that position to gain the experience and talent to move toward a more attractive position.

Sometimes, however, more than one offer is received, and the candidate has the luxury of choice. If the job seeker knows what he or she wants and has done the necessary self-assessment honestly and thoroughly, it may be clear that one of the offers conforms more closely to those expressed wants and needs.

However, if, as so often happens, the offers are similar in terms of conditions and salary, the question then becomes which organization might provide the necessary climate, opportunities, and advantages for your professional development and growth. This is the time when solid employer research and astute questioning during the interviews really pays off. How much did you learn about the employer through your own research and skillful questioning? When the interviewer asked during the interview "Do you have any questions?" did you ask the kinds of questions that would help resolve a choice between one organization and another? Just as an employer must decide among numerous applicants, so must the applicant learn to assess the potential employer. Both are partners in the job search.

Reneging on an Offer

An especially disturbing occurrence for employers and career counseling professionals is when a job seeker formally (either orally or by written contract) accepts employment with one organization and later reneges on the agreement and goes with another employer.

There are all kinds of rationalizations offered for this unethical behavior. None of them satisfies. The sad irony is that what the job seeker is willing to do to the employer—make a promise and then break it—he or she would be outraged to have done to him- or herself: have the job offer pulled. It is a very bad way to begin a career. It suggests the individual has not taken the time to do the necessary self-assessment and self-awareness exercises to think and judge critically. The new offer taken may, in fact, be no better or worse than the one refused. You should be aware that there have been incidents of legal action following job candidates' reneging on an offer. This adds a very sour note to what should be a harmonious beginning of a lifelong adventure.

The Graduate School Choice

The reasons for furthering one's education in graduate school can be as varied and unique as the individuals electing this course of action. Many continue their studies at an advanced level because they simply find it difficult to end the educational process. They love what they are learning and want to learn more and broaden their academic exploration.

While you are an undergraduate sociology major you may find yourself completely captivated by a particular area of research. Perhaps you are intrigued by the issues generated by the new sociological studies of cyberspace or are drawn into debates about the most effective programs to address the youth gang problems. It might be that you have decided to go on to graduate school so that you can continue to research, analyze, and write about your own theories and discoveries and those of others. Continuing the intellectual pursuit is a logical choice for those who have thrived on being an undergraduate sociology major.

Or perhaps you are considering graduate school for more so-called "practical" reasons. You've studied the job market and noted that those with graduate degrees have a better chance at getting the jobs you want.

Consider Your Motives

The answer to the question of "Why graduate school?" is a personal one for each applicant. Nevertheless, it is important to consider your motives carefully. Graduate school involves additional time out of the employment market, a high level of critical evaluation, significant autonomy as you pursue your studies, and considerable financial expenditure. For some students in doctoral programs, there may be additional life choice issues, such as relationships, marriage, and parenthood, that may present real challenges while in a program of study. You would be well advised to consider the following questions as you think about your decision to continue your studies.

Are You Postponing Some Tough Decisions by Going to School?

Graduate school is not a place to go to avoid life's problems. There is intense competition for graduate school slots and for the fellowships, scholarships, and financial aid available. This competition means extensive interviewing, résumé submission, and essay writing that rivals corporate recruitment. Likewise, the graduate school process is a mentored one in which faculty stay aware of and involved in the academic progress of their students and continually challenge the quality of their work. Many graduate students are called upon to participate in teaching and professional writing and research as well.

In other words, this is no place to hide from the spotlight. Graduate students work very hard and much is demanded of them individually. If you elect to go to graduate school to avoid the stresses and strains of the "real world," you will find no safe place in higher academics. Vivid accounts, both fictional and nonfictional, have depicted quite accurately the personal and professional demands of graduate school work.

The selection of graduate studies as a career option should be a positive choice—something you *want* to do. It shouldn't be selected as an escape from other, less attractive or more challenging options, nor should it be selected as the option of last resort (i.e., "I can't do anything else; I'd better just stay in school."). If you're in some doubt about the strength of your reasoning about continuing in school, discuss the issues with a career counselor or a faculty member at your school. Together you can clarify your reasoning, and you'll get some sound feedback on what you're about to undertake.

On the other hand, staying on in graduate school because of a particularly poor employment market and a lack of jobs at entry-level positions has proven to be an effective "stalling" strategy. If you can afford it, pursuing a graduate degree immediately after your undergraduate education gives you a year or two to "wait out" a difficult economic climate, while at the same time acquiring a potentially valuable credential.

Have You Done Some "Hands-On" Reality Testing?

There are experiential options available to give some reality to your decision-making process about graduate school. Internships or work in the field can give you a good idea about employment demands, conditions, and atmosphere.

There is no substitute for a period of "hands-on" experience in the career you would like to pursue. You heard it before, but it remains especially true for a sociology major whose work can bring them into a range of challenging and even difficult situations. Suppose, for example, that you are considering going to graduate school to get a degree in clinical sociology. A chance to work closely with someone who has already taken that path will truly open your eyes to the reality of this job. You'll observe firsthand the decisions that must be made every day in order for this professional to best serve his or her clients.

Have You Compared Your Expectations of What Graduate School Will Do for You with What It Has Done for Alumni of the Program You're Considering?

Most colleges and universities perform some kind of postgraduate survey of their students to ascertain where they are employed, what additional education they have received, and what levels of salary they are enjoying. Ask to see this information either from the university you are considering applying to or from your own alma mater, especially if it has a similar graduate program. Such surveys often reveal surprises about occupational decisions, salaries, and work satisfaction. This information may affect your decision.

The value of self-assessment (the process of examining and making decisions about your own hierarchy of values and goals) is especially important in analyzing the desirability of possible career paths involving graduate education. Sometimes a job requiring advanced education seems to hold real promise but is disappointing in salary potential or number of opportunities available. Certainly it is better to research this information before embarking on a program of graduate studies. It may not change your mind about your decision, but by becoming better informed about your choice, you become better prepared for your future.

Have You Talked with People in Your Field to Explore What You Might Be Doing After Graduate School?

In pursuing your undergraduate degree, you will have come into contact with many individuals trained in the field you are considering. You might also have the opportunity to attend professional conferences, workshops, seminars, and job fairs where you can expand your network of contacts. Talk to them all! Find out about their individual career paths, discuss your own plans and hopes, get their feedback on the reality of your expectations, and heed their advice about your prospects. Each will have a unique tale to tell, and each will bring a different perspective on the current marketplace for the credentials you are seeking. Talking to enough people will make you an expert on what's out there.

Are You Excited by the Idea of Studying the Particular Field You Have in Mind?

This question may be the most important one of all. If you are going to spend several years in advanced study, perhaps engendering some debt or postponing some lifestyle decisions for an advanced degree, you simply ought to enjoy what you're doing. Examine your work in the discipline so far. Has it been fun? Have you found yourself exploring various paths of thought? Do you read in your area for fun? Do you enjoy talking about it, thinking about it, and sharing it with others? Advanced degrees often are the beginning of a lifetime's involvement with a particular subject. Choose carefully a field that will hold your interest and your enthusiasm.

If nothing else, do the following:

- Talk and question (remember to listen!)
- Reality test
- Soul-search by yourself or with a person you trust

Finding the Right Program for You: Some Considerations

There are several important factors in coming to a sound decision about the right graduate program for you. You'll want to begin by locating institutions that offer appropriate programs, examining each of these programs and their requirements, undertaking the application process by reviewing catalogs and obtaining application materials, visiting campuses if possible, arranging for letters of recommendation, writing your application statement, and, finally, following up on your applications.

Locate Institutions with Appropriate Programs

Once you decide on a particular advanced degree, it's important to develop a list of schools offering such a degree program. Perhaps the best source of graduate program information is Peterson's. The website (petersons.com) and the printed *Guides to Graduate Study* allow you to search for information by institution name, location, or academic area. The website also allows you to do a keyword search. Use the website and guides to build your list. In addition, you may want to consult the College Board's *Index of Majors and Graduate Degrees*, which will help you find graduate programs offering the degree you seek. It is indexed by academic major and then categorized by state.

Now, this may be a considerable list. You may want to narrow the choices down further by a number of criteria: tuition, availability of financial aid, public versus private institutions, United States versus international institutions, size of student body, size of faculty, application fee, and geographic location. This is only a partial list; you will have your own important considerations. Perhaps you are an avid scuba diver and you find it unrealistic to think you could pursue graduate study for a number of years without being able to ocean dive from time to time. Good! That's a decision and it's honest. Now, how far from the ocean is too far, and what schools meet your other needs? In any case, and according to your own criteria, begin to put together a reasonable list of graduate schools that you are willing to spend time investigating.

Examine the Degree Programs and Their Requirements

Once you've determined the criteria by which you want to develop a list of graduate schools, you can begin to examine the degree program requirements, faculty composition, and institutional research orientation. Again, using resources such as Peterson's website or guides can reveal an amazingly rich level of material by which to judge your possible selections.

In addition to degree programs and degree requirements, entries will include information about application fees, entrance test requirements, tuition, percentage of applicants accepted, numbers of applicants receiving financial aid, gender breakdown of students, numbers of full- and part-time faculty, and often gender breakdown of faculty as well. Numbers graduating in each program and research orientations of departments are also included in some entries. There is information on graduate housing; student services; and library, research, and computer facilities. A contact person, phone number, and address are also standard information in these listings.

It can be helpful to draw up a chart and enter relevant information about each school you are considering in order to have a ready reference on points of information that are important to you.

Undertake the Application Process

Program Information. Once you've decided on a selection of schools, obtain program information and applications. Nearly every school has a website that contains most of the detailed information you need to narrow your choices. In addition, applications can be printed from the site. If, however, you don't want to print out lots of information, you can request that a copy of the catalog and application materials be sent to you.

When you have your information in hand, give it all a careful reading and make notes of issues you might want to discuss via E-mail, on the telephone, or in a personal interview.

> If you are drawn to a career that involves working in the field, it's of paramount importance that you subject yourself to some reality testing. You'll be able to find out what skills you have, which ones need to be developed, and what aspects of your academic preparation you rely on. Internships and co-op experiences speed that process up and prevent the frustrating and expensive process of investigation many graduates begin only after leaving school.

What is the ratio of faculty to the required number of courses for your degree? How often will you encounter the same faculty member as an instructor?

If the program offers a practicum or off-campus experience, who arranges this? Does the graduate school select a site and place you there, or is it your responsibility? What are the professional affiliations of the faculty? Does the program merit any outside professional endorsement or accreditation?

Critically evaluate the catalogs of each of the programs you are considering. List any questions you have and ask current or former teachers and colleagues for their impressions as well.

The Application. Preview each application thoroughly to determine what you need to provide in the way of letters of recommendation, transcripts from undergraduate schools or any previous graduate work, and personal essays. Make a notation for each application of what you will need to complete that document.

Additionally, you'll want to determine entrance testing requirements for each institution and immediately arrange to register for appropriate tests. Information can be obtained from associated websites, including ets.org (GRE, GMAT, TOEFL, PRAXIS, SLS, Higher Education Assessment), lsat .org (LSAT), and tpcweb.com/mat (MAT). Your college career office should also be able to provide you with advice and additional information.

Visit the Campus if Possible

If time and finances allow, a visit, interview, and tour can help make your decision easier. You can develop a sense of the student body, meet some of the faculty, and hear up-to-date information on resources and the curriculum. You will have a brief opportunity to "try out" the surroundings to see if they fit your needs. After all, it will be home for a while. If a visit is not possible but you have questions, don't hesitate to call and speak with the dean of the graduate school. Most are more than happy to talk to candidates and want them to have the answers they seek. Graduate school admission is a very personal and individual process.

Arrange for Letters of Recommendation

This is also the time to begin to assemble a group of individuals who will support your candidacy as a graduate student by writing letters of recommendation or completing recommendation forms. Some schools will ask you to provide letters of recommendation to be included with your application or sent directly to the school by the recommender. Other graduate programs will provide a recommendation form that must be completed by the recommender. These graduate school forms vary greatly in the amount of space provided for a written recommendation. So that you can use letters as you need to, ask your recommenders to address their letters "To Whom It May Concern," unless one of your recommenders has a particular connection to one of your graduate schools or knows an official at the school.

Choose recommenders who can speak authoritatively about the criteria important to selection officials at your graduate school. In other words, choose recommenders who can write about your grasp of the literature in your field of study, your ability to write and speak effectively, your class performance, and your demonstrated interest in the field outside of class. Other characteristics that graduate schools are interested in assessing include your emotional maturity, leadership ability, breadth of general knowledge, intellectual ability, motivation, perseverance, and ability to engage in independent inquiry.

When requesting recommendations, it's especially helpful to put the request in writing. Explain your graduate school intentions and express some of your thoughts about graduate school and your appreciation for their support. Don't be shy about "prompting" your recommenders with some suggestions of what you would appreciate being included in their comments. Most recommenders will find this direction helpful and will want to produce a statement of support that you can both stand behind. Consequently, if your interaction with one recommender was especially focused on research projects, he or she might be best able to speak of those skills and your critical thinking ability. Another recommender may have good comments to make about your public presentation skills.

Give your recommenders plenty of lead time in which to complete your recommendation, and set a date by which they should respond. If they fail to meet your deadline, be prepared to make a polite call or visit to inquire if they need more information or if there is anything you can do to move the process along.

Whether you are providing a graduate school form or asking for an original letter to be mailed, be sure to provide an envelope and postage if the recommender must mail the form or letter directly to the graduate school.

Each recommendation you request should provide a different piece of information about you for the selection committee. It might be pleasant for letters of recommendation to say that you are a fine, upstanding individual, but a selection committee for graduate school will require specific information. Each recommender has had a unique relationship with you, and his or her letter should reflect that. Think of each letter as helping to build a more complete portrait of you as a potential graduate student.

Write Your Application Statement

Here's your chance to thoughtfully lay out your reasons for wanting to go on to graduate school. It's an opportunity to explore your feelings about this decision. And a statement that conveys your understanding of the challenges and your commitment will be an important factor in the decision process of the graduate school admissions committee.

An excellent source to help in writing this essay is *How to Write a Winning Personal Statement for Graduate and Professional School*, by Richard J. Stelzer. It has been written from the perspective of what graduate school selection committees are looking for when they read these essays. It provides helpful tips to keep your essay targeted on the kinds of issues and criteria that are important to selection committees and that provide them with the kind of information they can best utilize in making their decision.

Follow Up on Your Applications

After you have finished each application and mailed it along with your transcript requests and letters of recommendation, be sure to follow up on the progress of your file. For example, call the graduate school administrative staff to see whether your transcripts have arrived. If the school required your recommenders to fill out a specific recommendation form that had to be mailed directly to the school, you will want to ensure that they have all arrived in good time for the processing of your application. It is your responsibility to make certain that all required information is received by the institution.

Researching Financial Aid Sources, Scholarships, and Fellowships

Financial aid information is available from the academic department to which you apply and from the university's graduate school. Some disciplines provide full tuition and a monthly stipend for graduate students. These decisions are made in the specific academic department. It is important that you ask about the availability of this type of financial support. If it is not available, you may be eligible for federal, state, and/or institutional support. There are lengthy forms to complete, and some of these will vary by school, type of school (public versus private), and state. Be sure to note the deadline dates on each form.

There are many excellent resources available to help you explore all of your financial aid options. Visit your college career office or local public library to find out about the range of materials available. Two excellent resources are Peterson's website (petersons.com) and its book *Peterson's Grants for Graduate and Post Doctoral Study*. Another good reference is the Foundation Center's *Foundation Grants to Individuals*. These types of resources generally contain information that can be accessed by indexes including field of study, specific eligibility requirements, administering agency, and geographic focus.

Evaluating Acceptances

If you apply to and are accepted at more than one school, it is time to return to your initial research and self-assessment to evaluate your options and select the program that will best help you achieve the goals you set for pursuing graduate study. You'll want to choose a program that will allow you to complete your studies in a timely and cost-effective way. This may be a good time to get additional feedback from professors and career professionals who are familiar with your interests and plans. Ultimately, the decision is yours, so be sure you get answers to all the questions you can think of.

Some Notes About Rejection

Each graduate school is searching for applicants who appear to have the qualifications necessary to succeed in its program. Applications are evaluated on a combination of undergraduate grade point average, strength of letters of recommendation, standardized test scores, and personal statements written for the application.

A carelessly completed application is one reason many applicants are denied admission to a graduate program. To avoid this type of needless rejection, be sure to carefully and completely answer all appropriate questions on the application form, focus your personal statement given the instructions provided, and submit your materials well in advance of the deadline. Remember that your test scores and recommendations are considered a part of your application, so they must also be received by the deadline.

If you are rejected by a school that especially interests you, you may want to contact the dean of graduate studies to discuss the strengths and weaknesses of your application. Information provided by the dean will be useful in reapplying to the program later or applying to other, similar programs.

PART TWO

THE CAREER PATHS

9

Path 1: Teaching with an Advanced Degree

Your own sociology professors have probably inspired as well as informed you during your undergraduate years. You've seen them in action: lecturing and grading papers, pursuing their own research, and fulfilling other academic roles. Perhaps one of your college teachers has already suggested that you consider pursuing your education with the goal of receiving an advanced degree and seeking work as a professor yourself. It is a natural progression, as more than two-thirds of the sociologists working in this country teach in colleges and universities. And life in academia reaches beyond the classroom, as many sociologists are also involved in research, consulting, and other aspects of public life.

Teaching is certainly an appealing career choice. To pursue ideas and theories, accumulate and disseminate information, and influence the intellectual development of countless students over the years provides many rewards. In the classroom, learning occurs for instructors as well as students. Most teachers readily admit they enjoy being students themselves, and good teachers come to the classroom as ready to learn from students as students arrive hoping to learn from their teachers. Good teachers maintain a regular program of professional development, adding to their body of knowledge, continuing to learn new classroom techniques, and improving their teaching methods.

The life of an academic provides for a nice balance between time spent working independently and time spent with others. Hours are spent reviewing literature, writing lectures, and grading papers and exams. At the same time, however, the life of a teacher allows for a great deal of intellectual exchange. Collaboration on research projects, team teaching, institutional committees, and projects combine and recombine faculty colleagues and students as they move toward common goals.

Faculty members may share anecdotes about techniques that have or have not worked in the classroom, and many also share an interest in the growth and development of particular students they have interacted with through the years. Students often come back and visit the teachers who have been huge inspirations in their lives, and that brings its own rewards to the teachers they visit.

Talk to any sociology professor you know and he or she will tell you a surprising fact about the profession and teachers. They don't teach sociology, they teach students! The art of teaching and the skills required to handle the dynamics of student interaction are as important as knowledge of the course content. Your classroom will be populated with many students majoring in sociology. Their responses to your presentations are important factors in their ongoing commitment to this major. You'll also have many non-sociology majors who are taking your course as a general education requirement or for a minor. Students of diverse ages, cultural backgrounds, and biases sit in your class with dramatically different degrees of interest in the subject and the teacher. With all those variables, simply having a love of sociology yourself is not enough; commitment to teaching is essential.

Over and over again, the college teaching candidate will encounter the phrase "strong commitment to teaching is essential." You will be expected to demonstrate that commitment to the classroom with recommendations by those who have observed your teaching, student and peer evaluations of your classroom, and, more frequently, by teaching a sample instructional unit to faculty during an on-campus job interview.

Teaching requires more than knowledge skills in a subject area. The world is full of extremely knowledgeable people who, for one reason or another and quite often inexplicably, cannot transmit that knowledge to others.

Planning for learning outcomes is a good example of a critical teaching skill. Teaching sociology within an established college curriculum means your course content must correspond to departmental goals and course outlines. A written course description will be in the catalog. To cover this body of learning within a set time period requires judicious planning of the material. What will be done each day? How much time is to be allowed between assignments, readings, and labs? What materials should be required and what others should only be recommended? Scores of decisions must be made about how material will be introduced and presented and about how you will evaluate your students.

Now consider, also, that students learn in different ways; some are auditory learners who enjoy listening and gain most of their information in this way. They may not learn as much from printed materials as from oral lectures and discussions in class. They may need to audiotape your lecture in lieu of taking notes if this process is too awkward for them. For others, auditory learning is less successful and they prefer a visual approach with board work, videos, handouts, their own notes, diagrams, books, and many visual materials. They retain these images and can call them up to remember the material.

Some need to participate through role plays, team projects, and other activities that physically involve them. They learn best this way. These are kinesthetic learners, and they are often forgotten in planning and curriculum design. The professional teacher ensures that his or her class is satisfying the learning styles of all the students through judicious combinations of modalities in teaching. Professional teachers have analyzed their own teaching styles and have sought to incorporate teaching styles that come less naturally to them to ensure they reach all their students.

What happens in a classroom is not static. The classroom is an emotionally charged environment for the student and instructor. For students, issues of self-esteem and competency frequently surface. Students are exploring their self-image—their capabilities, values, and achievements. A good teacher understands this and encourages a risk-free environment of mutual appreciation and participation. Both teacher and student are allowed to make mistakes and move on. The teacher strives to assist in establishing congruence between the student's self (who I know I am right now), the ideal self (who I want to be), and the learning environment being created in the classroom.

Issues of competency, self-esteem, and self-worth are closely associated with the basics of evaluation and grading. Grades are an expected and required part of many institutional academic settings. Establishing fair and consistent standards for evaluating your students and assigning grades is a significant challenge to many teachers who otherwise feel perfectly competent in the teaching role. Fair and intellectually respectable test design and construction is an art and science deserving of a teacher's attention. Students often complain about grading practices in teachers they, in every other respect, feel positively about.

You will be called upon to fill other roles, too. Animating the class and inspiring attention and commitment to the material are all required in teaching. One factor in this is the teacher's enthusiasm. Another factor is teaching style, including the effective use of ancillary materials and the ability to relate this material and other course elements to a student's life.

Sociologists study human society and social behavior by examining the groups and social institutions that people form. These include families, tribes, communities, and governments, as well as a variety of social, religious, political, and business organizations. Sociologists study the behavior and interaction of groups, trace their origin and growth, and analyze the influence of group activities on individual members. Some sociologists are concerned primarily with the characteristics of social groups and institutions. Others are more interested in the ways individuals are affected by the groups to which they belong. There are actually numerous areas of possible specialization available to sociologists. Further on in this chapter, we'll examine an extensive list of areas of specialization.

Each class is not only an opportunity to teach the subject sociology, but to teach students how to learn, as well. Routinely, you should be helping students learn how to question, how to record information, how to be selective in focusing their research, and how to retain information.

Most of all, an instructor will evaluate and, by example, develop the student's capacity for self-evaluation through careful, caring feedback about both in- and out-of-class work. The instructor's own example of preparation, organization, personal appearance, evaluation standards, student interest, and enthusiasm will remain an example long after the memory of the actual class content may have faded.

Teachers are very frequently cited as important factors in our choices of careers. Very often teachers will remember one or two of their teachers who were strong influences on their decisions to teach. Much of that influence was a result of the teacher's presence in the classroom: serving as a model of someone enjoying what he or she was doing and doing it skillfully. This teacher was professional and correct yet remained natural and approachable. We could watch and listen and think, "Yes, that is what I want to do."

Definition of the Career Path

Teaching at a college or university requires a master's or doctoral degree. There are more opportunities for those students who have continued on to the doctoral level, particularly at the more prestigious public and private universities. However, depending on one's area of specialization, one can also find many instances in which a master's degree is sufficient. This is due to the fact that when hiring teachers, academic institutions are also interested in finding candidates who have expertise in a certain area of sociology. Thus many faculty position descriptions are specific in the research interests they hope an applicant will bring to their campus.

Areas of Specialization

Teachers of sociology can focus their research and teaching efforts in at least one of many different areas. The following list is by no means inclusive:

Community sociology	Minority groups
Complex organizations	Poverty
Computer applications in social science	Small group processes
	Social change
Courtship and marriage	Social control
Criminology	Social policy
Cross-cultural studies	Social problems
Delinquency	Social stratification
Deviance	Social theory
Dynamics of human populations	Sociolinguistics
Environmental sociology	Sociology of cyberspace
Ethnic studies	Sociology of law
Gender/sexuality	Sociology of race
General sociology	Statistics methods
Gerontology	Substance abuse
Health/illness sociology	Urban sociology
History of sociology	Urban rural sociology
Immigration intervention strategies	Youth services

You may be familiar with some of these areas of specialization from your undergraduate survey courses; others may be completely foreign. It can be a bewilderingly long list, and even if some of these specialties do seem interesting, you are probably asking yourself "How do you become knowledgeable about these areas?" The answer, in most cases, is in the early days of your graduate degree work. Your graduate work will expose you to a number of other graduate students, each of whom has his or her own perspective on the study of sociology and personal research interests. The intellectual sharing that goes on during graduate programs will stimulate your own reading and research into many of these specialty areas. Your graduate faculty members will also have specific areas of interest in which they actively research and publish the results of that research and fieldwork.

You may enter a doctoral program that does not necessarily require a stopping-off point at the master's level. Doing this represents a major commitment of your time, your finances, and your belief in the resources of your graduate school.

You may decide to begin your graduate work with a master's degree and then reevaluate your position before launching yourself on the doctoral course. This allows you to receive some credential for your first two years of graduate work and provides a resting place from which you can survey the future. Do you want to stop out for a year or two and work with your master's degree, continue on immediately in the same institution for your doctoral degree, or change schools?

For many, university affiliation changes between the master's and doctoral degrees. This change may be due to a desire for a particular field of study, the wish to work with a new group of sociology professionals, or taking advantage of the resources (scholarly, financial, or geographic) of a new graduate school.

Teaching with a Master's Degree

While most teaching positions at colleges and universities require a doctorate, there are many college positions for the master's level degree holder in sociology. The *Chronicle for Higher Education*, the weekly newspaper reporting on higher education issues, provides the most complete listing of faculty, staff, and leadership position openings for colleges and universities in the United States and some foreign countries. Here you will find listings for positions that accept the master's degree in sociology, including jobs at state universities, community colleges, technical colleges, and private colleges, as well as for nonacademic positions. Review the following job description, which presents specific demands for area expertise within sociology as well.

> **Sociology.** Master's in sociology. Experience teaching in a community college preferred. Ability to teach Introduction to Sociology and other courses such as Social Problems, Urban Sociology, Race and Ethnicity, Gerontology, etc.; development of additional courses in this discipline preferred.

You can find similar positions, even those requiring a high level of specialization, in satellite campuses of state colleges that offer two-year degrees or in colleges with smaller enrollments. With a master's degree, it is possible to have a rewarding career teaching sociology at the college level. Two-year programs and community college work can provide a long and productive career within the same institution or provide the opportunity for a lateral move to a similar type of institution. At the same time, however, it is important to caution you that if you are interested in moving from that type of institution to a four-year college or university, it may be difficult without an advanced degree, despite the fact that you may have years of teaching experience.

There are also some jobs teaching at the four-year college level with a master's degree in sociology. Nevertheless, the trend in these schools, the expectation, and the market demand would be for the doctoral degree, and it is that degree that will provide the most security of both employment and employment opportunities for a teaching career at the college and university level.

Teaching with a Doctoral Degree

Those students who pursue a doctorate in sociology will find wider opportunities in the world of academia. Yet even at this level, competition is keen.

The road to a doctorate is fairly long and arduous. It is hard work, requiring sustained effort and commitment. And despite fellowships and teaching assistantships, it can also be expensive. Many doctoral students juggle heavy academic demands with jobs that leave them fatigued and not always able to meet all of their financial needs. At the same time, undergraduate friends may be well along in their careers and beginning to raise families or enjoy the other benefits of being established in a career. This can be frustrating to the doctoral student who is also several years older than when he or she began, perhaps tired of being the student and wanting to get started on a real job. Both men and women in doctoral programs have to make decisions about relationships, marriage, children, and other significant events that will impact on their pursuit of the Ph.D.

Along the way, you'll meet some wonderful people: fellow graduate students and faculty from your own department and other academic areas. Some of these friends and colleagues will remain friends the rest of your life. Even colleagues separated by long distances with only an E-mail connection have the opportunity to revisit at conferences and symposia. In a long teaching career, it is not uncommon to change employers, and you may find yourself crossing paths with old friends.

Building and maintaining this network of relationships can play an important role in your job search after you have earned your Ph.D. and even later in your career. Your friends and colleagues provide you with the ability to learn of position openings early and to marshal the necessary support, recommendations, and documentation you may need to successfully compete for jobs and tenure.

The Earned Doctorate Versus ABD

Many graduate students begin their search for placement before having completed their Ph.D. While some openings require that you already have your dissertation completed and your doctoral degree in hand, some advertisements will encourage the application of All But Dissertation (ABD) candidates who have not yet but are soon to complete their degree work.

A position requiring an earned doctorate will pay more than an ABD position and will lead more directly and quickly to possible tenure and promotion. The ABD candidates will also have to decide how they will finish their degrees (the dissertation often being the most time-consuming aspect of their academics) and hold down full-time jobs.

Especially in sociology, because of the sensitive nature of the material being presented, college and universities of even modest size are going to seek the most credentialed and skilled faculty they can find and afford. Larger and more prestigious schools with significant research agendas will be even more demanding of the backgrounds of their faculty.

You'll have opportunities to write, teach, and perhaps publish all before you finish your degree. Take advantage of these opportunities when you can. As the advertisements suggest, these qualifications may be desired. However, it is possible to become overly involved in some of these areas to the detriment of degree progress.

Beyond the Degree: Other Qualities of Teachers of Sociology

There are many issues important for both master's and doctoral degree holders:

- Teaching effectiveness
- Research, publications, and presentations
- Cultural sensitivity
- Community service

Position descriptions, such as those found in scholarly publications, allow the sociology graduate considering a teaching career to approach the hiring process with eyes wide open! A close reading of these advertisements indicates not only the degree of specialization that is demanded, but also the institutional values for teaching, publication, community outreach, and collaboration that must be demonstrated and met. Getting a college teaching position requires much, much more than a doctoral degree.

Teaching Effectiveness

Job announcements often include a request for documentation of teaching success. Graduate teaching assistantships obtained while working on your doctoral degree provide this experience. Many students acquire this experience from part-time faculty, lecturer, or adjunct faculty positions taken at other colleges or programs while engaged in doctoral studies. Summaries of student teaching evaluations that you received while gaining this experience can be used to document teaching success.

Research, Publications, and Presentations

Some institutions of higher learning emphasize the teaching role and do not put excessive demands on faculty to "publish or perish." But other institutions do value research and publications very highly and there exists a determined effort by faculty to find good research projects and then publish them.

More important is that regardless of the posture of your institution vis-à-vis research and publications, as a teacher you should have an interest in sharing what you know with a larger audience, perhaps through writing books, articles, or monographs. Or you may prefer public presentations at seminars, workshops, and conferences.

When being considered for promotion and tenure, your record of sharing your technical and professional expertise will be examined.

Cultural Sensitivity

Some teaching advertisements make demands for cultural sensitivity, perhaps prompted by the location of the particular school. They may have a student body that is already highly diverse. The hiring institution should always make a sincere attempt to increase sensitivity and awareness of whatever diversity exists on the campus.

Profound cultural sensitivity and awareness is insistent and pervasive throughout teaching communities, but especially focused in sociology classrooms where the subject is apt to be individual and group behaviors.

If you were teaching in a multicultural class with an Asian complement, it would be highly inappropriate—and a good example of cultural bias—to indicate in a class discussion on symptomatic behavior that a failure to make direct and sustained eye contact with a physician was significant. Many Asian cultures do not make direct eye contact to strangers and, even more seldom, to authority figures.

Gender-biased language, ignorance of cultures and customs, inconsiderate choice of texts or illustrative materials from a diversity perspective only serves to impugn your teaching and undermine your credibility. It is in your best interest to broaden your horizons and ensure that your classroom is an inclusive and welcoming one.

Community Service

Colleges and universities have always been part of the larger communities in which they reside. Faculty and staff are often called upon to contribute to the school's community. These contributions can take many forms, including anything from participating in annual cleanup days to allowing local organizations to use space for special events.

Because of the very nature of sociology, the need and opportunities for sociology faculty to engage in outreach is very great. Local counseling hotlines may need staffers or someone to train them. Local homeless shelters or halfway houses often need skilled volunteers to take client histories or do referrals with other helping agencies. Teen drop-in sex-information clinics, local civic groups needing speakers, a variety of board of trustee opportunities—all of these could benefit from the sociology faculty member's involvement and attention.

How Long Does It Take to Get a Ph.D.?

There has been considerable discussion in academic circles of the number of individuals who begin doctoral programs and do not see them through to completion. In fact, Neil Rudenstine, a former president of Harvard University, coauthored a book on the issue of improving and tightening up the time requirements to earn a Ph.D., particularly in the humanities and social sciences.[1] His research clearly demonstrated that the timeline between initiating the Ph.D. degree and earning it (elapsed time-to-degree[2]), in candidates earning a social science degree (which includes sociology), was 7.5 years. Not all students who begin a Ph.D. program complete it, so a correspondingly high rate of mortality goes along with this issue of time-to-degree.

Doctoral work comes at a time in many young people's lives where, after sixteen or more years of education, no matter how fascinating the advanced study, distractions occur. These might be relationships, a desire to begin a family, economic pressures to leave school and earn an income, or simply fatigue. Consequently, the dropout rate for students has been high, especially when doctoral programs are not sufficiently explicit about requirements and the time it takes to complete a degree.

Working Conditions

The working conditions for college sociology teachers may vary somewhat according to the institution, but there is enough commonality of experience that we can make some generalizations. Many people consider a college teaching environment one of the most attractive work settings imaginable. There is less need to appease a number of outside publics. There are no school boards to satisfy, no parents, no parent-teacher groups. Students are there voluntarily, and the upper-level classes are populated with sociology majors who love their subject and are interested in doing the work required to succeed in their courses.

Work Schedule

The actual teaching time in a college or university setting involves about six to twelve class hours taught per week. At an institution that focuses on faculty research, the teacher would be responsible for teaching two to three courses that each meet two to three hours per week. Schools that emphasize teaching rather than research require instructors to teach three to four courses for a total of nine to twelve hours of class meetings per week. These class hours and some mandated office hours for advising students and general advisees are the principle requirements for attendance on the faculty member's part. They hardly tell the whole story of the work schedule because they do not include the many, many hours that most faculty members put into doing scholarly research, an important component of an academic career. Depending on their schedule in a given academic term, they might be found working as many as thirty hours a week investigating and writing research articles and books.

Another less well-known aspect of academic life is the number of faculty members who work part-time for the college or university. In 2000, about three out of ten college and university faculty worked part-time. These instructors, sometimes referred to as "adjunct faculty," have other, primary jobs in government, private industry or services, and nonprofit research.[3]

A college day is certainly not a rigid routine. Class schedules are the fixed element; beyond those, much is up to the involvement and activity level of the individual faculty member. Certainly, it can be busy and long. The college teacher may feel institutional and professional pressures to fulfill certain roles, but the actual election of how to do that is up to the individual. There will be classes, office hours, meetings, and research work to do. Because college campuses are often wonderful centers of art, music, and intellectual exchange, there are frequently events to attend in the evening. Faculty members may act as advisors to fraternities, sororities, campus newspapers, or clubs, all of which will certainly add hours to the workday.

Administrative Duties

In some departments the role of chair of the department is rotated, and all faculty are expected to serve a term. In other institutions, the chair is a hotly contested office.

Department chair duties involve overseeing the scheduling of each semester's courses and assigning faculty responsibility for those course offerings. They may include hiring part-time faculty and adjuncts to meet demand or replace faculty on sabbatical. It may involve negotiations with other administrators for additional classroom space.

Supervision of the department budget is the chair's responsibility and this includes monitoring expenditures for supplies, special events, faculty development, and travel. There is often intense faculty lobbying for travel and professional development funds from the chair, who must try to exercise impartiality and discretion in administering these funds.

Department meetings are called and run by the chair, who also sets the meeting agenda. Meeting frequency is often a function of the size of a department, and they may be as frequent as every week for a department of twelve members. In the largest departments, a meeting will occur at least once a month.

Many colleges and universities hold a council of chairs to address issues such as curriculum change, general education requirements, faculty standards, and other interrelated issues.

Committee Work

Committee work is also important, as the faculty at most colleges are the governing and rule-making bodies who determine and vote on governance and program changes. Committee work can be issue oriented, such as a commission on the status of women or a female faculty pay-equity survey. It may be programmatic, such as a committee to study the core curriculum for undergraduates or to devise a new graphic arts major. Or it may be related to credentials, as in a committee set up to prepare materials for an accreditation visit.

Some committees—such as academic standards, curriculum review, promotion and tenure, planning, and administrator review—are permanent, though the members may change on a rotating schedule. Other committees are formed for a limited time or until completion of some task. These ad hoc committees are essential and are one vehicle for guiding the direction of the school. For the faculty, having the support of all the faculty and a constant supply of fresh and interested members helps to ensure all voices are heard and many different opinions considered in making what are often long-reaching decisions.

Facilities and Support

Facilities, including laboratories, tend to be excellent for college faculty. Often adequate-to-excellent support staff are available to process materials, do copying, and prepare testing materials. A private office is usually provided and there may be quite a varied menu of faculty privileges. Computers are usually provided for writing, research, library access, and data manipulation.

Teaching Introductory Courses

Most advertisements also indicate that the successful candidate will be teaching general sociology classes. Teaching Introduction to Sociology classes is generally part of the teaching load of new college sociology faculty. Many of these students will be taking Introduction to Sociology because it is a college requirement for graduation and part of a general-education core curriculum and not because they are sociology majors or have deliberately chosen the course. In offering this course, the sociology department performs a service to the entire college. Of course, for many students, regardless of how they found their way to the class, this introductory course may prove to be an exciting introduction to a field of study they had not previously considered. Many undecided students base their choice of major on the introduction provided by these generally required courses. Even senior faculty will teach at least one offering of Introduction to Sociology, though as you become more senior in the faculty you can take on courses more directly related to your interests and educational background.

Scholarly Research

In addition to courses and advising, scholarly research is an expectation even at those colleges for whom tenure is not based on publication. All colleges want their faculty to contribute to the scholarly dialogue in their disciplines; this is reviewed by chairs of departments and academic deans periodically throughout one's career. It may be a determining element in granting tenure or promotion to that faculty member and may influence issues such as salary negotiations and merit increases.

Tenure

An added protection is the granting of tenure to established professors who have documented significant teaching histories and excellent student reviews, publications, campus committee work, and outreach to the community. The granting of tenure gives professors an additional degree of job security and further supports their expression of academic freedom. It must be kept in mind that colleges and universities have strict guidelines for promotion and tenure. At many schools, faculty members are under significant pressure to write, do research, deliver papers at professional meetings, and become involved in outreach to the community and in college service in order to rise in academic rank or even hold their positions.

Tenure means a lifetime appointment at a given university. But with higher education struggling to cut costs, even this once sacred cow is under scrutiny. Given current economic straits, administrators often must cut budgets, and one easy way is by replacing retiring tenured faculty or departmental tenured faculty with cheaper, nontenured personnel. The fewer tenure budget lines on the accounting sheet, the more flexible the budget.

Training and Qualifications

Most four-year colleges and universities require that job candidates possess a doctorate in sociology and usually will, in addition, look for specialized areas of research, publication, or prior teaching and/or clinical experience. Occasionally, a college will hire a faculty member on a nontenured basis with less than a doctoral degree, but generally, the larger the institution, the less likely this will be the case. Salary and assignments may be affected by lack of an earned doctorate.

If hired without an earned doctoral degree, the contract at hiring may stipulate how much time can elapse before the degree must be earned. The difficulty here would be finishing the degree (for many the dissertation is the most challenging and time-consuming aspect of the degree) while holding down a full-time job. This certainly needs to be considered in your negotiations. You might set a tentative date for Ph.D. completion, to be reviewed and finalized after your first year of teaching.

Seasoned scholars work with students at the very senior levels of graduate work for both master's and doctoral degrees. These scholars enhance their own unique areas of expertise as students pursue their degrees. Classes may be very small at this level, even at a large university, and the work is highly collaborative. At this level, your teaching work may be reduced to allow for pure research and writing in your areas of interest and scholarship, and you are likely to be called upon frequently to speak to professional and scholarly groups about that research.

Earnings

According to the National Education Association (NEA), in 2000 the average faculty salary in sociology positions in four-year colleges or universities was $54,471 at public institutions and $53,242 at private institutions. Overall, the average salary for college and university faculty in that same year was $56,022, with higher salaries going to such disciplines as engineering and public health. Academic salaries also vary from state to state, with the highest-paid positions in California and Alaska. Assistant professors earned, on average, $44,999; instructors (which would include the ABD candidate) earned an average of $34,912.[4]

In the world of academia, however, the bottom line is not always the most important factor in choosing a particular position. College and university professors also negotiate with their employers for flexible teaching schedules and paid sabbaticals, which provide time for doing their own independent scholarly research. Also, many college and university faculty are also able to take advantage of the unique benefits of academic life, such as using research and athletic facilities, tuition waivers for their children, and travel and research budgets.

Career Outlook

The decline in the traditional college-age population, which began in the early 1980s, has halted. The population of eighteen- to twenty-four-year olds began increasing in 1996, leading to a corresponding need for an increase in the number of college-level teachers. In addition, a significant number of adults are returning to college, and the enrollment of foreign-born students is on the rise, particularly in California, Texas, Florida, New York, and Arizona. Moreover, the faculty who were hired during the 1960s and 1970s to teach the baby boom generation are now approaching retirement age, opening up a large number of faculty positions. While the number of candidates receiving doctorate degrees is expected to only rise by about 4 percent, competition for tenure-track university appointments will remain very intense.

One interesting development is the growth of distance learning, particularly over the Internet. This method of learning appeals to those who live in remote areas, or whose family and work responsibilities prohibit them from enrolling in full-time programs. The U.S. Army is also exploring offering distance learning opportunities to enlisted men and women. The new technological developments, however, will only be as useful as the information that can be imparted via these new methods, leading to a demand for online teachers at both traditional colleges and universities as well as at new online institutions.[5]

Strategy for Finding the Jobs

Acquiring the educational credentials to become a professor of sociology requires years. But once you've taken it this far, you will certainly want to employ an equally intelligent and thorough strategy towards finding the right job. This strategy should include being prepared to relocate, getting your curriculum vitae in shape, using well-established job listings such as the *Chronicle of Higher Education*, networking with faculty colleagues, and attending professional meetings. Be sure to enhance your strategy as you decide on the area of sociology you will specialize in by talking with mentors and career development professionals.

Be Open to Relocating

Acquiring a college teaching position in sociology nearly always means that you will have to relocate to an institution other than where you received your degree. Higher education has limited openings at any one time. You increase your opportunities for securing a teaching post as you expand the boundaries of where you will consider relocating.

Like many graduate students, you may have enjoyed some part-time teaching employment at your degree-granting institution. Occasionally, an opportunity to teach as an adjunct faculty member for a limited period might be available. Adjunct positions are often used to staff introductory courses or to complement shortages during national searches for permanent full-time faculty. Adjunct or part-time work is a wonderful experience and will be an excellent recommendation or means to a recommendation to an institution considering your application. It is seldom, however, a guarantee of earning a full-time spot at your own school.

Most sociology departments have budget lines dedicated to full-time, tenured faculty. That means that faculty who are hired in those budget lines are hired with the expectation they will become a permanent part of the faculty and earn tenure and promotion when they are qualified.

Consequently, though there may be schools you would enjoy teaching at or areas of the country where you would prefer to live, the supply and demand of college professorships clearly dictate that you must follow the demand and relocate.

Though it may be disappointing to feel your job search is completely dictated by marketplace demands, if you talk to some of your own faculty mentors you will learn how it was for them in their job search. Most of them have relocated as well. In my conversations with faculty colleagues, time and again, they will mention their real pleasure at discovering a new area of the country, bringing new activities, experiences, and professional and personal relationships, as they have moved with their careers. College communities the world over tend to be centers of exchange, with speakers, arts events, celebrations, and a year-round calendar of activities for people of all ages and interests. Because of the college population, many have good shopping and excellent services. Most college communities are wonderful places in which to live, raise a family, and retire.

Sources for Academic Job Listings

The *Chronicle of Higher Education* is the weekly, national publication that lists junior college, four-year college, and university teaching positions in sociology. Many of these advertisements are large display ads that detail in full the requirements and duties of the positions advertised. This publication is widely available on college campuses, and usually many offices have individual subscriptions. Your career center, department office, and college library will all have copies you can review each week.

The *Chronicle's* job advertisements are also available online, and entire electronic editions are often accessible on public campus computer networks, thus making it easy to print out copies of announcements that interest you.

Network with Your Future Colleagues

Perhaps the most important foundation for finding a college-level position will be the faculty colleague contacts you make as you pursue your advanced degree. The well-established network becomes very active when schools are filling positions. Many search committees rely on the personal recommendations of friends or former teaching associates as the best sources of information on candidates.

This is a referral network, not a placement service. Your colleagues will be suggesting your name as an applicant. There are no guarantees, and all positions at this level must go through a search committee and interviews. Nevertheless, a request from a faculty colleague to apply for a teaching vacancy is a strong beginning.

For this reason, it's important to ensure that your faculty mentors and colleagues are well aware of your teaching and research interests and your geographic preferences so they can speak in your behalf when they hear of an opening that might suit your research background and teaching experience.

Attend Conferences and Other Professional Meetings

Academic conferences, professional meetings, and seminars (on your own campus as well as at other institutions) allow you to meet and listen to representatives from many institutions. You become aware of research initiatives and many of the current issues in academe. Familiar faces will begin to appear as you continue on the conference circuit. Don't hesitate to submit your own proposals for presentations. These are good opportunities to share your scholarship and demonstrate your willingness to do outreach.

Interviews are also often conducted at professional meetings. Job openings for which interviews are being held are posted in a conspicuous place at the conference registration table. As a graduate student, many of these conferences are available to you at substantially reduced fees, and you should take advantage of them for the professional content and the opportunity to meet representatives from the departments of other higher education institutions.

Possible Employers

While it's certainly helpful to have a network of colleagues who are keeping their ears tuned for news of job openings, the positions themselves are always advertised. There is no hidden job market, and the listings are usually widely distributed. Here are resources that can provide the names of potential employers.

- **Directories.** There are several directories that will help you identify schools where you could teach sociology. These compendiums contain far too many listings for even the most ambitious mass mailing, but will help you locate schools by size, number of faculty, geographic location, and so forth. They include *Peterson's Guide to Two-Year*

Colleges, Peterson's Guide to Four-Year Colleges, Peterson's Guides to Graduate Study, and *The College Board Index of Majors and Graduate Degrees.*

- **Career office postings.** Career offices often carry national job vacancy listings which include teaching positions. Some of these listings include *Current Jobs for Graduates in Education* and *Current Jobs for Graduates,* as well as the *Chronicle of Higher Education.* Many career offices also receive individual job posting fliers directly from institutions looking to hire sociology faculty. Be sure to find out if your institution receives these notices.
- **Sociology department postings.** Sometimes when a hiring institution is seeking to fill a position under pressures of time, they will send notices of openings to every school offering a graduate program in sociology. Be sure to find out where the sociology department posts these notices at your school. Often you'll find them on a bulletin board near the department chair's office or the department secretary's desk.
- **Professional associations.** In addition, be sure to carefully review the list of professional associations for teachers of sociology later in this chapter. For several associations there is a line labeled "Job Listings" and any activities that the association undertakes to assist its members in finding employment are shown. These include professional meetings for sharing résumés, newsletters that contain job openings or positions wanted, and advertising space in journals.

Possible Job Titles

Job titles for positions relating to teaching and research in sociology will be fairly standard: teacher or researcher. Position descriptions will list areas of educational and research specialization required for the position. In both teaching and research, a specialization can be developed in one of the following fields.

Clinical sociology	Organizational sociology
Comparative sociology	Phenomenological sociology
Educational sociology	Political sociology
Historical sociology	Sociolinguistics
Industrial sociology	Sociological jurisprudence
Microsociology	Visual sociology

Professional Associations

The primary information resource for someone considering a career in teaching sociology at the college or university level is the American Sociological Association. Students are eligible to join at reduced rates, and by doing so they can begin the ever-important tasks of networking and gaining an insight on working as a professional in this field. Review the other associations to see if you feel they can assist you in your job search.

Alpha Kappa Delta
Southwestern Texas State University
Department of Sociology
San Marcos, TX 78666
Members/Purpose: Honorary society—men and women, sociology.
   Sponsors undergraduate paper competitions, holds research symposia.
Publications: Handbook, newsletter, *Sociological Inquiry.*

American Sociological Association
1307 New York Ave. NW, Suite 700
Washington, DC 20005
Members/Purpose: Sociologists, social scientists, and others interested in
   research, teaching, and application of sociology; graduate and
   undergraduate sociology students who are sponsored by a member of the
   association.
Publications: *American Sociological Association—Annual Meeting Proceedings,*
   American Sociological Association—Directory of Departments, American
   Sociological Association—Directory of Members, Guide to Graduate
   Departments of Sociology, Journal of Health and Social Behavior.

Association of Black Sociologists
College of Urban, Labor, and Metropolitan Affairs
Urban Health Program
Faculty/Administration Building
656 W. Kirby, Room 3249
Detroit, MI 48202
Members/Purpose: Purposes are to promote the professional interests of
   black sociologists; promote an increase in the number of professionally
   trained sociologists; help stimulate and improve the quality of research
   and the teaching of sociology; provide perspectives regarding black
   experiences as well as expertise for understanding and dealing with

problems confronting black people; protect professional rights and safeguard the civil rights stemming from executing the above objectives.
Publications: *ABS Newsletter, Race and Society, Roster of Membership*

Association for Humanist Sociology
John Jay College of Criminal Justice
899 Tenth Ave.
New York, NY 10019
Members/Purpose: Sociologists, social scientists, social workers, and others interested in humanistic sociology. Provides a forum for sociologists concerned with the value-related aspects of sociological theory, research, and professional life. Seeks to extend the boundaries of humanist sociology by exploring connections between sociology and other disciplines.
Publications: *The Humanist Sociologist, Humanity and Society*

Association for the Sociology of Religion
3520 Wiltshire Dr.
Holiday, FL 34691-1239
Members/Purpose: Works to encourage study and research in the sociology of religion and to promote the highest professional and scientific standards for research and publication in the sociology of religion.
Publications: *Directory, News and Announcements, Sociological Analysis*

Committee on the Status of Women in Sociology
c/o American Sociological Association
1307 New York Ave. NW, Suite 700
Washington, DC 20005
Members/Purpose: A standing committee of the American Sociological Association. Primary task is to monitor and further the status of women in the sociological profession.

Honors Program Student Association of the American Sociological Association
Sociology Department
John Carroll University
University Heights, OH 44118
Members/Purpose: Individuals who have completed the Honors program of the American Sociological Association. Facilitates communication among members; assists sociology students.
Publications: *Honors Student Handbook, Network*

International Association of Family Sociology
Northern Illinois University
Department of Sociology
DeKalb, IL 60115-2854
Members/Purpose: Seeks to improve the study of marriage and family and to increase the effective application of research results. Fosters personal and professional contacts among family sociologists, other family professionals and professional organizations. Encourages information exchange and cross-cultural, interdisciplinary research in the field.
Training: Holds international and regional seminars
Publications: *International Journal of Sociology in the Family* (newsletter)

National Education Association (NEA)
1201 16th St. NW
Washington, DC 20036
Members/Purpose: Professional organization and union of elementary and secondary school teachers, college and university professors, administrators, principals, counselors, and other concerned with education.
Publications: *ESP Journal, ESP Progress* (handbook), *NEA Today*

Population Association of America (PAA)
8630 Fenton St., Suite 722
Silver Spring, MD 20910-3812
Members/Purpose: Professional society of individuals interested in demography and in its scientific aspects.
Publications: *Demography* (quarterly), *Directory of Members, PAA Affairs* (quarterly), newsletter

Rural Sociological Society
Department of Sociology
Room 510, Armtzen Hall
Western Washington University
Bellingham, WA 98225-9081
Members/Purpose: Promotes the development of rural sociology through research, teaching, and extension work.
Publications: *Directory of Members, The Rural Sociologists, Rural Sociology*

Sociological Practice Association
Anne Arundel Community College
Division of Social Sciences
101 College Pkwy.
Arnold, MD 21012-1895
Members/Purpose: Promotes the application of sociology to individual and
social change and advances theory, research, and methods to this end;
develops opportunities for the employment and use of clinically trained
sociologists; provides a common ground for sociological practitioners,
allied professionals, and interested scholars and students.
Training: Promotes training and educational opportunities to further
sociological practice.
Publications: *Clinical Sociology Review, Practicing Sociologist, Sociological
Practice*; *Using Sociology: An Introduction from the Clinical Perspective*

Sociological Research Association
c/o American Sociological Association
1307 New York Ave. NW, Suite 700
Washington, DC 20005
Members/Purpose: Persons, elected from membership of the American
Sociological Association, "who have made significant contributions to
sociological research, other than a doctoral dissertation, and who
maintain an active interest in the advancement of sociological
knowledge."

10

Path 2: Human Services

Community Organizations and
Social Service Agencies

At most colleges and universities you are certain to see notices on bulletin boards and in the school newspaper calling for volunteers to help staff local community organizations and social service agencies. Perhaps you have dedicated some of your free time to these organizations, maybe helping out with a mentoring program at the local public grade school or answering phones at the student crisis center. Even if your schedule hasn't allowed for it, as a sociology major you are probably already tuned in to the many causes and issues affecting the community. They must grab your attention because they so closely mirror the material you are studying. Indeed, perhaps your choice of sociology as a major grew out of a concern with the many social issues facing our communities and our nation at large.

The issues that engage sociologists are clearly manifested in these "real world" organizations. It's only logical that you would consider how you could explore these issues by seeking employment in an organization that serves the societal groups that you have studied. Consider the courses that you took in your degree program. They probably included topics such as:

Aging and society	Sociology of mental health
Rural sociology	Ethnicity
Cultural ecology	Social deviance
Criminology	The family

This brief list of typical courses from the sociology major is a good place to start a job search relevant to the issues you studied.

You can forge a fascinating and challenging career in any of the thousands of human services agencies that segment society according to health, deviance, age, ethnicity, religion, and any number of other characteristics. While it may, admittedly, take a master's degree or higher to work as a professional sociologist, you can find a meaningful job as a working sociologist in many of these organizations. Such entry-level jobs can launch rich careers whether you stay in agency work for a lifetime or move on after a few years to acquire additional education.

Great Jobs for Sociology Majors has five career paths that keep you working on issues directly related to the subjects you enjoyed so much in college. The human services path gives you an opportunity to select fieldwork that any sociologist would appreciate.

The Yellow Pages: A Surprising Resource

Put down this book for a moment and go and find the yellow-page telephone directory. Look up "Social and Human Service Organizations." You'll find a significant number of listings, even in the slimmest of local directories. Many you'll recognize immediately, such as the American Red Cross or your state legal assistance fund. You'll also find variety of local and state family planning groups and counseling offices and domestic violence halfway houses. You may also notice additional agency names, which, though unfamiliar to you, you'll find intriguing. For example, your state may have an assistive technology and equipment center or a program of academic excellence to motivate inner-city youth. Other organizations are centered on issues such as helping people with AIDS, housing difficulties, or those in need of fuel assistance. There will be programs offering abortion counseling or general counseling services for young people. Many agencies help people with disabilities.

If you look in a larger city or metropolitan directory, or do a search on the Internet, you'll find a staggering number of human service agencies listed. You will be surprised at how narrowly focused some of the programs are. In fact, the headings will begin to remind you of the chapters of your Introduction to Sociology text: Mental Health, Religion, Children's Services, Vocational Services, Elderly Person's Services.

You might also be astonished to see the sheer number of organizations listed under these particular headings. So, while you may be very interested to know there are social service workers concentrating on housing assistance issues, you may be even more surprised to see the large number of organizations listed under that heading. Each may have a very different mission.

Some organizations may serve to organize residents, others may find housing for the homeless, others may seek to repair and maintain the homes of the elderly who can no longer do their own and have limited incomes. Some organizations may use local youth to revitalize apartment buildings, providing them with meaningful work experience and housing at the same time.

These listings read like an index of our social concerns, our social structure, and our social conscience. They are clear signs of what is happening in our society. In the needs they express and in the provision of an agency to help meet those needs, they express society's response to these situations. It's fair to say that the size and breadth of these listings have as much to do with the size of the community as they do with the concern the community expresses for others and the determination of those committed to the public good to found organizations and agencies to help.

Major Social Concerns in Our Communities

So the choice of issues is a rich one. Each organization presents its own set of issues. Community organizations and agencies for women present an excellent example. A women's organization may be information oriented, perhaps teaching about breast cancer detection or osteoporosis. It may be about role modeling, matching young women from disadvantaged homes with more mature women who can provide some friendship and support. It may be an activist group, seeking to end discrimination in rate of pay or sexual harassment in the workplace. Another group's goal may be to offer support for women who have lost a child, husband, or companion. The group may address sexual identity or gender role issues, such as groups for lesbians or transsexuals. The focus of women-oriented organizations is not exhausted by this short list.

Each group makes demands on the skills and talents of the workers serving them and challenges them to an ongoing development of their skills and talents. The following is a list of some of our nation's social concerns, with capsule descriptions of relevant issues and statistics. For each an actual job description is included that indicates that a candidate with a sociology undergraduate degree would be welcomed.

Youth

Growing unemployment, dysfunctional families, and school systems that have difficulty coping—all contribute to a continuing delinquency problem among young people. Issues such as crime, vandalism, drug and alcohol abuse, prostitution, early pregnancy, and gangs are covered widely in the media, making them prominent issues of social concern. For example, one of the most troubling developments is the astronomical rise in juvenile gangs. In the 1970s, nineteen states reported having gang problems, primarily in the larger cities. By the end of the 1990s, every single state and the District of Columbia were reporting gang activity. Moreover, gangs are no longer limited to large cities. Whereas in the 1970s the average population of a city with gangs was 182,000, by the end of the century the average population of an affected city was 34,000.[1]

Our penal institutions are generally not very oriented toward or successful with rehabilitation. And many job-training programs have discovered the need for providing extensive follow-through for graduates in order to ensure employment. Working with juvenile offenders presents great challenges but also the possibility of large rewards for those working with them.

Many young people today, however, are working hard to stay on track and need community organizations and other support systems to help them stay focused. After-school programs, counseling services, vocational training, sports, and recreation programs are appearing all over the country to satisfy this very real and positive need.

Poverty

Despite the wealth and resources of the United States, poverty remains a serious social issue, affecting millions of individuals and families. In 1999, the government's official poverty rate was $8,501 for an individual and $13,290 for a household of three. The number of persons who were officially impoverished in 1999 was 32.3 million, representing 11.8 percent of the nation's population. However, 16.9 percent of the children in this country lived in poverty.[2] Add to this the large number of the "working poor," wage-earners whose income is perhaps above the official poverty rate but still inadequate to meet their families' needs. Homeless shelters in large cities not only must meet the needs of destitute individuals, but must also provide shelter to families that have been forced from their homes.

Poverty is not their only problem. Alcoholism, drug abuse, illness, and a host of other social ills are also factors in chronic poverty, the treatment of which requires additional skills and knowledge on the part of the social service worker. The social service worker is not alone as an agent for change. Federal programs for jobs, housing, employment, and numerous preventative initiatives try to help, as does an enormous network of other helping professionals.

Substance Abuse

Substance abuse remains a complex and challenging problem with a multitude of related issues. For the community and social service worker, addiction is a problem that requires the combined forces of both the medical community and helping professionals of social services. In 1999, the Substance Abuse and Mental Health Services Administration's Drug Abuse Warning Network (DAWN) reported an estimated 554,932 admissions to hospital emergency rooms nationwide that involved drug abuse, up 2 percent from 1998. Cocaine was the drug most frequently involved.[3] The cost to the nation goes beyond care and treatment of drug takers, however. Max Frankel, in the *New York Times Magazine*, writes, "The direct, recognizable cost of this [drug] war is probably in excess of $100 billion a year."[4] Society also pays a price in terms of the overall safety of our communities, as addiction often involves crime, particularly theft, to support the substance habit.

Drug and alcohol abuse destroys relationships, and rebuilding one's life from addiction is often a long, difficult journey. Self-help programs, halfway houses, and other services in a community provide vital therapies for the recovering addict.

Alcoholism. Alcoholism remains largely hidden to the majority of the public, but the community and social service worker is all too aware of the extent of alcoholism and the great sadness and pain it can bring to families, relationships, employment, and most importantly, to alcoholics themselves. According to the National Institute of Alcohol Abuse and Alcoholism, the most recent estimated economic cost of alcoholism in 1998 was $185 billion. Of this, some 70 percent of the cost was attributed to lost productivity, including losses from alcohol-related illness, premature death, and crime. Approximately $7.5 billion is spent each year on treating alcohol abuse and dependence.[5] We are learning more about treatment methods, the impact on children of alcoholic parents, and the role heredity may play in the predisposition to alcoholism. Considerable work is being done on several frontiers for alcoholics and their problems but it remains an enormous social challenge.

Law Enforcement

Crime is a real concern for every citizen of this country. The good news is that the crime rate began falling in the last years of the twentieth century, falling by 5 percent in 1998 and 6.8 percent in 1999. Among violent crimes, murder fell by 8.5 percent in 1999, robbery by 8.4 percent, and forcible rape by 4.3 percent. Meanwhile, motor vehicle theft was down by 7.7 percent and burglary decreased by 10 percent.[6] Unfortunately, the fluctuations in the economy could cause a rise in the beginning of the twenty-first century. And even with a decline, however, the destruction of lives and property remains a disturbing characteristic of our society. The price of justice is also high. At the end of 1999, the total number of individuals under the jurisdiction of federal or state adult correctional authorities was a record high 1,366,721.[7] These populations present issues revolving around punishment versus rehabilitation. Community and social service workers are involved, some at prison sites, others assisting with reentry to the community.

Numerous citizen activist groups and agencies are appearing that self-police neighborhoods, crack down on drug activity in specific locales, or ensure housing projects are safe for residents. Organizers and coordinators help these groups in setting reasonable goals, raising funds, and focusing the efforts of volunteers to best achieve desired aims.

In this area, you'll probably work alongside criminologists. Criminology was an early offshoot of sociology that has now become its own discipline. Criminologists often have strong backgrounds in sociology. They help plan and direct juvenile and adult crime-prevention projects.

Mental Health

While public education has begun to remove the stigma associated with mental illness, there remains much to be done to create an atmosphere of greater understanding and acceptance of people suffering from mental disorders. According to the National Institute of Mental Health, an estimated 22.1 percent of Americans eighteen or older suffer from a diagnosable mental disorder in any given year. In other words, more than 44 million people are living with illnesses such as a major depression, bipolar disorder, schizophrenia, and obsessive-compulsive disorder. Left untreated, these diseases can be life-threatening. In 1997, 30,535 people died from suicide in the United States. The vast majority, more than 90 percent, who killed themselves had a diagnosable mental disorder, such as depression. Similarly, the mortality rate among people with anorexia is a problem that is primarily affecting women. As many as 3.7 percent of women suffer from anorexia during the course of their lifetimes. The mortality rate among people with anorexia has been estimated at 56 percent a year, which is about twelve times higher than the annual death rate due to all causes of death among females age fifteen to twenty-four.[8]

Mental illness exacts an enormous cost from the economy of the country, both in days missed at work and poor performance due to illness. One positive result of increased public awareness is the increase in the numbers and types of treatment sites available.

An Aging Population

One of the most significant developments is the aging of the American population. During the last decade of the twentieth century, the number of Americans sixty-five and older increased by 10.6 percent, compared to an increase of 9.1 percent for those under sixty-five. In 1999, there were 20.2 million older women and 14.3 million older men. But the increase of the 1990s was just the tip of the iceberg, because the real boom in the elderly population will come when those born after the Great Depression, an era of suppressed birth-rate, begin to reach retirement age. While senior citizens now constitute 12.7 percent of the population, projections by the U.S. Bureau of the Census indicate that they will make up 20 percent of the population by the year 2030. The actual number may be as high as 70 million, more than twice the current senior population.[9] This new generation of seniors is healthier, more active, and more interested in maintaining their activity level than ever before. They want city and town recreation programs to accommodate their needs, they use the YMCA and YWCA, and they belong to a number of activist organizations designed to lobby for their interests.

Though more physically active than their predecessors, with age comes an increased need for physical therapy, transportation services, counseling for depression and emotional difficulties, and help coping with necessary changes such as living situations and diet. Although some elderly individuals can afford to reside in planned communities, others live alone or in a variety of other settings. Some are in hospitals, nursing homes, or facilities that care for people with mental illnesses, including Alzheimer's disease.

Investigate the Wide Range of Populations and Issues Served by Social Service and Community Organizations

This chapter has addressed only a few of the many social issues receiving the attention of social services organizations. Many other population groupings are served and issues are addressed. The listing of types of services that follows only scratches the surface of the possibilities available to the graduate looking to enter the community organization and social service field. Go down the list and think about which issues you are interested in. These are fields that can be emotionally as well as intellectually demanding, and each area is worth your exploration. Your local library or college career center can provide you with supplemental information. In addition, at the end of this chapter a number of professional organizations are listed that can provide helpful information.

Abortion alternatives counseling	Gay, lesbian, and bisexual
Abortion counseling	organizations and services
Adoption services	Halfway houses
Athletic services	Health services
Battered spouses' and children's	Home care services
services	Homeless persons' services
Blind organizations and services	Housing assistance
Charity services	Human services
Child counseling	Immigrant assistance
Children's services	Legal counseling
Chronic disease services	Medical relief services
Communicable diseases counseling	Mental health services
and services	Men's services
Community services	Philanthropic services
Consumer services	Pregnancy counseling and prevention
Credit counseling	information
Crime victim services	Pregnancy and maternity services
Crisis intervention services	Rape crisis services
Day care assistance	Religious organizations
Deaf and hearing impaired services	Sex information and counseling
Developmentally disabled persons'	Single parents' services
services	Suicide prevention services
Divorce counseling	Tenants' services
Drug abuse and prevention services	Travelers' assistance
Educational information services	Vocational services
Ethnic organizations and services	Volunteer services
Family and individual services	Women's services
Foster care services	Youth services

The Role of the Sociology Major in Human Services

Clearly there is the need for perceptive and sensitive employees who can bring their education in sociology to the table. The challenge for those who enter this field is to learn what these various organization actually do. It's even more important to discover what roles are available for a sociology major with an undergraduate degree. For the sociology major interested in community and social service, the problem is not who will hire you or where you can work but how to choose among the many types of agencies that do exist. Each is a world of specialized information, unique support networks, relationships with referral agencies, informational and financial resources, and dedicated professionals and paraprofessionals working to improve the human condition.

To best understand where you might fit in this jigsaw puzzle of agencies and organizations, it will help if you

- Understand the goals and missions of social service work
- Realize your value to the service-agency labor pool
- Analyze the demands of actual job listings
- Consider your strengths against job demands

Social and community service connects people with the information and tools they need to cope with and surmount the challenges facing them. Community workers help to bring harmony to strained lives, enrich lives that may be impoverished in various respects, and teach people the skills and techniques to become capable of self-advocacy and self-sufficiency.

Any profession that deals with humanity and the infinite number of human issues from birth to death cannot be limited to workers of one educational preparation, one kind of knowledge, or one kind of experience. When issues as diverse as sexual abuse, disease, mental and physical disabilities, housing, insurance, education, crime, and alcoholism are part of the daily menu of problems presented to social service agencies, they obviously require an array of talents.

HELP WANTED: SOCIAL SCIENCE MAJORS INVITED TO APPLY

The field of community and social service draws from many academic backgrounds. The sociology major is of course an important resource. The fields of psychology, religion, counseling, medicine, health and nutrition, home economics, child care, law enforcement, political science, mental health, criminal justice, and, of course, social work also provide skilled workers. It is a networking, communicating, bridge-building, role-modeling, counseling, and mentoring partnership role that the social service worker plays in connecting clients with the many services and agencies providing assistance.

Definition of the Career Path

Looking at a current group of entry-level community and social service want ads, the skills and attributes they all have in common are the ability to

Meet immediate needs	Work with volunteers
Assess a wide range of conditions	Network and interact with
Build a knowledge base	multidisciplinary teams
Keep accurate records	Research and retrieve information
Provide counseling and referrals	

Because each job and each agency presents unique circumstances, the priorities of these job components vary with the position and the setting. Consider what your strengths are (you should refer back to the self-assessment you completed in Part One) in determining how to choose the setting in which you may work most effectively.

Responding to Immediate Needs

In many situations, there are immediate and demanding needs to be met, such as shelter, food, and health care. Some clients can be assisted quickly, many others, very slowly. Sadly, many clients cannot be helped at all. Those who work in this field, therefore, find that the rewards are found in reaching and assisting those clients who can be helped. Community organization and social service workers who remain in the trenches make a contribution each day helping those who, if left alone, might not be able to do things for themselves.

Outreach Social Worker: B.A. to work on mobile van outreach team providing assessment/linkage service to homeless in Queens. Exp. in mental health/homeless issues; driver's license.

Assessing a Wide Range of Conditions

The types of human conditions seen in various settings are described in the advertisements. You can expect to become quite adept at recognizing the signs of alcoholism, delirium tremens, diabetes, hypothermia, malnutrition, or addiction and will become skilled at assessing your client's self-help skills and willingness to change.

Contributing to a Greater Understanding of the Issues

Reading this, you undoubtedly have begun to appreciate the time and focus the entry-level community organization or social service workers must bring to the job. All the while, as they improve their job performances (their ability to help), they are acquiring valuable information, knowledge, and skills for working with the population they are serving. A knowledge base builds almost imperceptibly, aided by in-service training, conferences, seminars, and a daily schedule of clients with their individual case histories. Case workers find their understanding of the system expanding, and the bureaucratic and legal aspects of assistance and support become clearer and more workable. Laws and pending legislation can vary dramatically state by state, and even within states there can be differences in implementation. To be an effective community and social service agency worker you must understand the system you are in and act as a guide in helping your client secure needed services. To do this well requires making contacts and connections, most often in the process of working with individual clients and learning how things work in your locality.

Though you provide helping skills yourself, much of your work depends on making connections with others and in advocating for your client the support and assistance he or she is eligible for. Understanding and learning that takes time and experience.

> **Director of Preventive/Wellness Services:** Successful candidates will have some prior experience in wellness programming development and be able to interface with the medical community of preventive initiatives. Bachelor's degree required with solid interpersonal and communication skills.

Record Keeping

While all of this is going on, the community and social service worker must keep excellent records and may sometimes be responsible for determinations of financial assistance or other forms of aid. You may be called upon to explain local, state, or federal regulations or procedures to your clients and may actively assist them in their efforts to secure assistance.

Many new entrants into the field of social service are overwhelmed by the amount of paperwork and telephone work. Hours and hours of each day are spent chasing people down by telephone or processing paperwork. Carrying out administrative duties can certainly create doubts about the "service" in social and community service work.

Record keeping is a natural by-product of the funding structure of many social service agencies, and it is probably best to realize now that many workers in this field spend their careers seeking the right balance between client services and administrative work.

Counseling

Counseling is a process of connection and deep human involvement between two people. Though there are many formal schools of counseling theory and technique, all counselors ultimately evolve a counseling technique that works for them and for their clients. Often, for the clientele of the community and social service worker, the deeply empathic listening attention of the counselor is, in and of itself, therapeutic. Clients who have a caring listener who values them as individuals and to whom they can talk about their problems can be at the beginning of a road to healthier living.

Providing Referrals

Connecting clients to agencies and sources for everything from housing to day care is often a first step in the helping and rehabilitative process. Some clients need counseling and subsequent referral to drug-abuse or other treatment programs before other initiatives can successfully be undertaken.

An adult client with cerebral palsy may need help connecting with someone who can advocate for him finding appropriate and accessible housing. You may refer this same client to another agency that can provide help in wheelchair maintenance or physical therapy. The client may need some assistance in applying for food stamps or in obtaining transportation to and from the store. Any given client may need referrals to a variety of support services.

The job involves interviewing clients to assess the scope and severity of their problems, to clarify their specific needs, and to determine how those needs might best be met. The community organization and social service agency worker then begins to organize all the necessary agencies, individuals, information, and resources to create some positive change.

Networking

As a new entrant in the field you are sure to build a network of contacts that you will be able to count on for help in serving your clients. This could take a variety of forms: help with solving a legal problem, help in finding long-term housing, help in locating job training programs, employment, and sources for food, clothing, medical help, etc. You will become very aware of the complexity of factors influencing every individual client's situation, and the social fabric that contributes to their problems and the difficulties in solving them.

Research and Information Retrieval

The work of sociologists is intricately connected to that of many other professionals, including psychologists, physicians, economists, statisticians, urban and regional planners, political scientists, anthropologists, law enforcement and criminal justice officials, and social workers.

Sociologists and statisticians work together to analyze the significance of data. This research role is so important that it comprises one of the major career paths in this book (Chapter 13, "Path 5: Social Research and Data Analysis").

The results of sociological research have helped educators, lawmakers, administrators, and others interested in resolving social problems and formulating public policy. Some of the significant issues addressed by these sociologists include abortion rights, high school dropouts, homelessness, and latchkey children.

Though research may not be the dominant part of your job in human services work, it will most certainly be a skill you will need to use at some point in your job. Every day you'll encounter questions. "How many senior citizens live in town?" or "How many indigent poor are there in the state?" are typical of the simple inquiries that can have you working overtime if your research skills are rusty.

Many larger human service agencies have research departments that hold job prospects for the new sociology graduate. Health sociologists have done dramatic research work on the AIDS virus and were part of the research team at the Center for Disease Control in Atlanta that discovered the first cluster of sexually transmitted cases of AIDS.

Sociology in Social Work

You will have noticed that in the many examples of job ads you would often be competing with social work graduates for the same position. It might be that you've already encountered some confusion among your friends or relatives who think you are getting a social work degree. The explanation of the relationship between the two will be instructive to you as you build confidence for the job search.

Sociology forms the body of knowledge that the social action work of social work is founded upon. Both fields are deeply concerned with certain values that lie embedded in the culture. Social work is interested in this body of knowledge and theory only insofar as the discovery and interpretation of those facts allow it to assist in doing something about the social problems of individuals and groups.

As a newly graduated sociology major, it's only natural to look at those jobs where you can direct your learning toward results-oriented outcomes— the fields of social services. As you progress in your career, and if you happen to add to your education, you may want to return to the field of sociological theory and research.

The short selection of job listings previously provided should give you some sense of the diversity of work present in social services, not only in the kinds of activities a social service worker engages in, but also in the kinds of problems that affect the people they work with and the age and gender mix of those populations. The breadth and scope of social service work through an agency or community organization and its initiatives results in an equally broad scope in the selection of candidates for social service jobs.

What you took special notice of were the fairly generalized degree demands: in most cases, a bachelor's degree or a sociology degree or some reasonably related degree. Most employers, for obvious reasons, would prefer previous experience so that job candidates understand the job and the issues of the people they will be working with.

While the generalized requirements may please some, others may be skeptical. Why don't they demand a social work degree? How can they be so loose in job qualifications when the work is so important? The answers lie in the nature of social service work. It is enormously demanding, many would say taxing, of the social service worker's energy, patience, time, and physical resources. Although the field has an incredibly wide range of pay for similar jobs, depending upon the employment setting, high salaries have not been a tradition of the community and social service field. The short answer may be that hiring officials who fill tough jobs paying less than top wages must draw from a wide pool of applicants.

There's another equally valid reason. When you look at the spectrum of problems social workers must wrestle with and the diversity of the human canvas that is placed before them, it is difficult to know where the talent may lie to help alleviate some of the struggle. Certainly, we have social workers who have studied the issues and earned a degree in the subject on the bachelor's, master's, and doctoral level. Others come to these same issues and concerns with as much to offer, but a different yet equally valuable preparation in their academic areas and life experiences.

A wonderful book, now sadly out of print but still widely available in academic libraries, is *Sociology in Social Work* by Peter Leonard from the University of Liverpool. He explains the natural and vital relationship between sociology and social work and offers his outlook on the future of the relationship and the use of sociological knowledge in social work.

Opportunities for Professional and Personal Growth in Human Services

If you are seriously contemplating a career in community and social services, you have probably asked yourself whether you will be able to sustain a lifelong career in this field. Perhaps you are worried about burning out, becoming overwhelmed by the magnitude of the social problems facing many of your fellow citizens. Will you become less effective as you continue in this field, becoming disinterested or hardened when faced with a particular set of problems, or simply not being able to handle the deluge of individuals seeking your assistance?

As you begin your career you can do three specific things that will help you successfully deal with these issues over time. First of all, think about whether the skills you are using and the knowledge base you are building can be transferred to other populations and settings. Second, think about preparing for advancement. And third, take care of your own needs.

Transferring Your Skills and Knowledge
One way to prevent burnout is to change your work setting from time to time. Successful changes happen as a result of being aware of which skills and knowledge are valued in a given workplace. Some of the skills and knowledge you acquire as you begin your career will be directly transferable to a different situation, while other skills and knowledge will not relate as well to other settings. Look for the common threads! A position assisting homeless adults will provide some good experience in working with an older population, and that work can relate to a number of other more stable elder-care situations. Or, work in adult substance abuse might prove a good basis for a move to an adolescent substance abuse clinic. A move from a facility servicing homeless adults to a residential center caring for child victims of sexual or physical abuse would, however, be more difficult to make. The type

of facility and the type of client have changed, so fewer skills and less knowledge is transferable.

Preparing for Advancement

You can advance in community and social service work by building upon your knowledge base and helping skills. That, by necessity, suggests working with a particular population and learning the resources that exist for that group until you are proficient. Job growth might then come in the form of more supervisory responsibility for other caregivers, management control of a facility, or advanced or specialized education in your field.

Taking Care of Your Own Needs

It's no mystery why community and social service workers burn out. It's a tough, tough job, and some professionals simply get weary of the obstacles put in their clients' way or the backsliding that occurs among people they have strived to help.

You may get tired, you may get cynical, or you may want a job that is less physically and emotionally draining. Changing the population you work with is certainly one technique, especially if many of the issues are familiar to you. Growing within your specialty and taking an administrative or management position is yet another option.

Whatever you decide to do, make it an active choice. Don't let your career just "happen." You don't want your boss to one day take you aside and suggest that you're overextended, tired, and no longer effective. Take your own career pulse from time to time, and ask yourself how you truly feel about the work you are engaged in. If you feel you need something different, make it your choice. Community and social service is a noble calling with rich rewards, but it makes equally insistent demands on your time and energy.

Working Conditions

Community organization and social service agency employees at every level of expertise (doctorate, master's, bachelor's, and paraprofessional) are employed in a number of different settings. The setting, in large part, dictates the types of activities in which social service workers are engaged, the jobs and duties they have, the types of clients and client needs they will encounter, and the ways in which they will practice their social service profession.

Some specific issues to consider include

- Population served
- Source of funding for agency/service
- Working hours
- Specific issues of the clientele
- Personal safety

Population Served

Your interest in people—why they behave as they do, how they form groups, and how they work out conflicts—has been what drew you to work in community and social services. Many agencies serve specific age populations, so if you feel the age of your clientele is an important condition, be sure to target the appropriate agencies.

Some services are structured for particular age groups, so activities, programs, and atmosphere all combine to say to the client "This is a for-you service." The Elderhostel program for active seniors is a fine example of an organization that responds to active seniors who want learning to be lifelong and who retain a curiosity and enthusiasm about the world around them. Shelters for adolescent males or after-school drop-in counseling centers are other good examples of age-targeted programs. Other services are age blind and are built around a health condition (osteoporosis), disease entity (AIDS), physical activity (swimming), and so forth. HIV is age blind, and services supporting those clients span all ages and genders.

Source of Funding for Agency/Service

The stability of funding is an important consideration for any helping service. Funds that are not stable, that perhaps need to be renewed each year, can create a sense of impermanence. This can affect staff morale and impact on the timely delivery of services if refunding is irregular.

Other agencies may have relatively stable funding but require significant development work to continually raise money. You will be called upon to assist in fund-raising efforts in these circumstances. While necessary to continued viability, this fund-raising work can often be an additional burden on already overworked staff.

Some grant-funded programs ultimately end, or program funding slowly drops and programs are disbanded, leaving workers to seek new employment. Funding sources can also impact the physical facilities, location, supplies, services, and quality of staff.

Working Hours

Community and social service jobs differ from some other jobs because of the hours. Service providers work many different shifts and schedules, especially in the areas of homelessness, drug and substance abuse, and sheltered care.

You may have standard rotating eight-hour shifts, or you may have three full days on and four days off. You may have sleep-in accommodations but need to be available twenty-four hours. There are also the more traditional thirty-seven-hour weeks. You'll need to consider this aspect of your work carefully and think about how various jobs will impact on your personal life, your relationships, your outside interests, and your overall well-being.

Specific Issues of the Clientele

Some substance abusers steal to support their habits. Adolescent men and women have unprotected sex before marriage. The list of problems and behaviors goes on and on. These behaviors are probably inconsistent with your own values and behavior.

But your clients need help, not judgment. It is important for you, as you explore possible work settings, to ascertain how you feel about the issues of the people you choose to work with. Compassion, caring, a sense of humor, and hopefulness are what your clients need, not lecturing, censorship, or condemnation. You need to consider this as you explore various jobs. With which kinds of issues and clients will you be able to work more effectively?

Personal Safety

When people encounter hardships and struggles in their lives, it can have pronounced effects on their temperaments. Anger, hostility, and violence may lie close to the surface, and from time to time, there certainly are incidences involving threats to the personal safety of community and social service workers.

Most professionals would assure you this is not a dominant concern in their workday lives. They exercise caution in their client relationships, they share their concerns with coworkers, and they activate response systems, including police, if threats occur. In some settings, such as abortion clinics, overnight shelters, or disaster-relief situations, tempers flare and outbreaks of violence may occur. In most cases, personnel have been trained to deal with this and are able to act effectively to minimize the risk of danger to all involved.

Think about your own ability to tolerate conflict and mediate possible violence. Consider your personal, physical characteristics and the population you are interested in serving. It's a good idea to talk to professionals now serving in these areas for greater insight into issues of physical safety in their jobs.

There is no better way to find out the real story behind a career than to talk with people who are already engaged in the profession. Talking to people in the field will provide a reality check that no amount of reading can give you.

Training and Qualifications

Social service and community work is so diverse that it would be foolish to try to create a comprehensive list or menu of necessary personal characteristics. The long list that follows is just suggestive of many of the personal characteristics that people in this profession draw upon to some extent or another. The counseling techniques that may be effective in establishing rapport with young, unwed mothers may not serve the social service worker as well when dealing with the chronically mentally ill. But many of these qualities are helpful across the board in a variety of social and community service positions. The sociology major considering a career in community and social service needs to review this list and rate him- or herself on these criteria.

Maturity	Communication
Concern for others	Teacher
Responsibility	Idealistic
High standards	Ethical
Sense of humor	Sensitivity
Good with people	Mutual respect
Dedication	Listener
Speaking skills	Productive
Discretion	Realistic
Objectivity	Innovative
Independence	Writer
Stability	Thoughtful
Empathy	Responsive
Resilience	

Concern for Others

To engage the client and to assess the situation, the social service worker needs empathy, sensitivity, and an ability to establish and maintain rapport. One also needs to appreciate the wonderful diversity present among people.

Working with frustrated adolescents may require talking with them for quite a while before they begin to open up and talk to you about their problems. Elderly patients may share their fears and concerns more easily if you begin by letting them show you a family album or some favorite pictures.

Appropriate Detachment

To be effective, however, the social service worker relies on his or her maturity and ability to remain removed (or detached) from the client's problems. The community and social service professional will find no paucity of clients and many problems to deal with that can seem almost insurmountable. The work goes on and on, and sometimes progress is very slow.

For that reason, professionals need to pace themselves. They need to respect their own limitations and what they can accomplish. If you are exhausted, overwrought, or allowing clients to call you at home or interfere with your personal life, you will eventually self-extinguish. What help can you be to the system if you are suffering from burnout?

True professionals know their limitations and understand the importance of leaving work at work. They appreciate their own needs for rejuvenation and restoration each day to be able to return and do effective work. Clients may have problems you can help with, but you must continually remind yourself that the client's problems are not your problems.

Ability to Work the System

Workers in human service agencies must be quick studies in political systems to be able to marshal the necessary resources to help solve clients' problems. Referral networks and sources of financial aid and housing entitlements all have their hierarchies, paperwork, and influential personalities. To do your best for your clients is to understand not only how the system should work, but how it, in fact, does work.

Flexibility

Flexibility is another key personal trait needed in community and social service work. Work hours or shifts may change constantly, the physical location where you carry out your duties may move, and even the members of your team may constantly change because of different schedule rotations. Assess your ability to be happy with the level of flexibility required in the positions you are considering.

Professional Qualifications

There are both preprofessional and professional positions in community and social service work, largely determined by degree level and type. Preprofessional positions are those nondegree or associate-degree positions in which job holders act as aides or assistants to social and community service workers. Professional positions are those in which the individual has at least a bachelor's degree in sociology, social work, psychology, or some other human service field that will satisfy the social service agencies.

Licensure/Certification. Workers in the community and social services field have come under increasing public scrutiny. As in any area of human endeavor, there have been scandals and examples of unethical behavior. Laws and regulations surrounding the provision for services have increased exponentially, and many professional organizations publish detailed ethical guidelines for their members.

In addition to advanced degree attainment as an outward mark of professionalism, many states will require you to have licenses and/or certification to do some types of work. Licensure is the process by which states ensure that you have attained certain educational and/or experiential standards, often involving some type of written examination. These standards help the public know the individual has met some state-mandated criterion for professionalism. Licensing boards also have the authority to discipline unethical or fraudulent practitioners by revoking their licenses.

Certification through professional organizations promotes standards of education, practice, accountability, discretion, ethics, and visibility. Certification can involve testing or the documentation of professional development and years of practice. It is often issued for a limited period of time.

Certification by the Sociological Practice Association (SPA) is required for some positions in clinical sociology and applied sociology, especially at the doctoral level.

See your career office or talk with state officials for information on licensure and your applicable professional associations for certification information.

Knowledge of Other Languages. Frequently, an urban metropolitan job announcement in social and community service will express the desire for fluency in Spanish, Chinese, Vietnamese, Cambodian, or another language, because of the expanding immigrant communities in our cities. While the record of assimilation, especially in language acquisition, among these new citizens is remarkable, new arrivals and the elderly often cannot be effectively serviced without being able to communicate in their native tongues.

Earnings

According to the Bureau of Labor Statistics, in 2000 the median annual earnings of social and human services assistants was $22,300. The middle 50 percent earned between $17,820 and $27,930. Wages may vary slightly depending on the work site and the geographic region of the country. Because these figures may be lower than you anticipated, be sure to complete the "Calculate Your Economic Needs" portion of the self-assessment in Chapter 1 to verify that you will be able to meet your basic economic needs.

Career Outlook

Regrettably, the problems that face society do not abate. Each generation seems to encounter new and more challenging issues, such as the spread of AIDS and acts of violence. In addition, natural disasters, fires, and other uncontrollable events occur without warning and also do tremendous damage to people's lives and well-being. Solving problems requires a core of services and other support mechanisms.

The cost of affordable health care, housing, and food should be controllable, but remain out of reach for many people, and with dire consequences. Community and social service workers will continue to be needed to help connect these people with available services.

Some economic trend analysts predict a growing number of people, even moderate- to high-income earners, losing employment to technology and overseas competition. Many of these individuals, while technically middle class, find they are precariously close to destitution following such job loss. In spite of their education, socioeconomic class, and information resources skills, these people are particularly ill-equipped to know and discover social services resources. They will depend on community and social service workers to help them.

Given these, as well as other trends, the U.S. Department of Labor, Bureau of Labor Statistics projects that human services workers will grow by 54 percent from 2000 to the year 2010. This classification of worker is listed in the Winter 2002 *Occupational Outlook Quarterly* as one of the top ten fastest growing occupations in the United States. Fast-growing occupations generally have good employment prospects and conditions favorable for advancement.

Human service workers are expected to grow much faster than average because of increases in programs and provisions for the elderly, disabled, and mentally ill. Excellent opportunities for qualified people will be available because of the high job turnover caused by the demanding nature of the work and relatively low pay.

Strategy for Finding the Jobs

It's never to early to begin your job search. What's more, much of the quest to land the right job in human services can be started even before you've finished your class work and polished your résumé. There are six tasks you can undertake to enhance your job search:

1. Determine which community and social concerns interest you the most.
2. Identify your own personal qualifications.
3. Familiarize yourself with the required professional qualifications.
4. Build skills and gain direct experience with the population you want to focus on.
5. Network with professionals working in the field.
6. Relate your sociology background to what the employer needs.

Undertaking these activities, together with the other phases of the job search outlined in Part One of this book, will put you on the right track as you begin to establish your career and make the most of your sociology degree.

Possible Employers

You have an enormous variety of options when it comes to potential employers. You might want to begin your investigations by looking into these groupings:

- Nonprofit agencies
- Medical health organizations
- Federal/state/local governmental agencies

- Corrections and rehabilitation
- Insurance companies
- Religious organizations
- Retirement homes/communities

Exploring the different types of employment opportunities will bring you that much closer to discovering the best fit for your career goals.

Nonprofit Agencies

Nonprofit agencies offer an incredibly wide array of community and social services, and each hires workers to provide, oversee, administer, and manage these services. They need you, the sociology major, on their staffs. Whether you're working in consumer services, aid to the homeless, or immigration assistance, your skills in counseling, record keeping, and referral will be critical to your success.

Help in Locating These Employers. There are several books devoted to the search for a job in the nonprofit world. These include *Jobs and Careers with Non-Profit Organizations,* by Ronald L. Krannich and Caryl Rae Krannich, and *Making a Living While Making a Difference,* by Melissa Everett. If you would like to look at actual job postings, one of the best places to start is with Access Non-Profit Jobs Clearinghouse. At any given time there are nearly one thousand current job listings with nonprofit organizations on their Access website (accessjobs.org).

Medical/Health Organizations

These types of facilities serve a range of clients and assist them with issues relating to, among others: alcohol and chemical dependency, rape, family planning, hospice care, health, and AIDS. The knowledge and skills you've built could be put to use in any of these settings. If, for instance, you were an AIDS outreach worker and your clients were deaf Americans, you would use your specialized knowledge in working with this type of client to educate them about the disease and help them receive available media as well as other services.

Help in Locating These Employers. Be sure to look at *Careers in Health Care, Medical and Health Information Directory, America's Top Medical and Human Services Jobs, Encyclopedia of Medical Organizations and Agencies,* and *Mental Health and Social Work Career Directory* to gain valuable insights into working in the medical/health field. These references will provide specific information on job listings and potential employers that you will be able to use to enhance your job search.

Federal/State/Local Governmental Agencies

About one-fourth of what the U.S. Department of Labor calls human services workers, which includes some community and social service workers, are employed by state and local governments in hospitals and outpatient mental health centers, in departments of human services (mental health divisions), and in facilities for people with mental retardation and developmental disabilities.

The diversity of possible employment roles and situations is considerable in this category. Providing counseling to the families of enlisted military personnel, doing in-home visits for the infirm elderly to ensure service provision, case managing in a mental health facility, and coordinating educational benefits for women on welfare are just a few of the possibilities.

Help in Locating These Employers. Two resources to start with are *The Book of U.S. Government Jobs*, by Dennis V. Damp, and *Guide to America's Federal Jobs. The Complete Guide to Public Employment* and *America's Federal Jobs* provide additional specifics about weaving your way through the maze of public employment. Be sure to also review actual federal job listings posted on the government's own website at usajobs.gov.

Corrections and Rehabilitation (Federal, State, Local)

Social services workers in corrections and rehabilitation at all governmental levels may have job titles such as child welfare caseworker, clinical psychologist, corrections counselor, parole officer, recreation leader, or social group worker. Sociology majors who have taken related course work or have an academic minor in a field such as criminal justice, and have also gained direct work experience (internship, part-time job, summer job, volunteer work) are eligible for many of these types of positions.

Help in Locating These Employers. Several books provide a starting point for your exploration of a career in corrections and rehabilitation. *Opportunities in Law Enforcement and Criminal Justice Careers* and *Criminal Justice Careers Guidebook* are excellent starting points. Be sure to network with authorities in the relevant state and local agencies to get the latest information on hiring needs and employment application procedures. The U.S. Department of Justice has information regarding careers in this field on their website, usdoj.gov.

Insurance Companies

Many health insurers provide managed health care services to their members, and they employ sociology majors to fill positions in customer service, claims, and provider relations. You probably won't meet face to face with your clients, but you will assist them in obtaining the physical and mental health services they are entitled to.

For a large employee benefit program you might serve as a telemarketing resource, using computerized directory information to provide referrals to individuals seeking assistance. This is a sophisticated position, requiring excellent listening and questioning skills to determine need, and critical thinking skills to determine a number of appropriate treatment options.

Help in Locating These Employers. *Peterson's Job Opportunities Health and Science* and *Career Opportunities in Banking, Finance, and Insurance* both provide useful information on starting a career in the insurance industry. The Health Insurance Association of America, Washington, D.C., also publishes a directory of members, which includes accident and health insurance firms. Contact the human resources department at those companies where you believe you might want to work and determine their application procedures.

Religious Organizations

Many religious organizations offer services to the community and provide trained and qualified personnel to assist those who ask for help. The organization may provide some type of center where youth can come to use a gym or settlement house where homeless people can come to sleep. Not all of the workers have specific religious training, although many of them do.

Help in Locating These Employers. Three resources that identify service agencies include: *The Catholic Almanac*, the *Yearbook of American and Canadian Churches*, and the *American Jewish Year Book*. You will also want to review the *National Directory of Churches, Synagogues and Other Houses of Worship*; separate editions cover different part of the country. Contact those organizations with a query letter requesting information regarding employment.

Retirement Homes or Communities

If you are interested in working in a retirement home or community, you can follow several different paths. You may be interested in a counseling role, in which case job titles might include social worker, leisure counselor, or rehabilitation counselor. Or you may want to play an administrative role, in which case the job titles to look for are housing project manager, site coordinator, or administrator.

Help in Locating These Employers. The American Association of Homes and Services for the Aging publishes a directory of members, which has the makings of an excellent networking resource if you would like to talk to directors about beginning a career in social services for the elderly. *The Mental Health and Social Work Career Directory* also contains valuable information relating to careers in gerontology that the sociology major may be interested in pursuing. Don't overlook a handy resource—your local yellow pages directory. It lists retirement and life-care communities and homes in specific geographic regions that you can contact about employment prospects.

Possible Job Titles

You will see a wide variety of job titles associated with community and social services. Sometimes the word counselor is in the job title, and oftentimes these are considered entry-level positions. For those workers who have more experience through part-time or summer employment, or an internship, the term coordinator might be used. More experienced workers who have case management experience or who are responsible for supervision of other workers, facilities, or budgets will often have the term manager, director, or supervisor in their job title. Review the titles shown below and look for job listings that match your level of experience.

Care manager	Historian
Case worker	Hospital administrator
Child care worker	Housing coordinator
City manager	Labor relations specialist
Community services specialist	Medical records worker
Community support clinician	Mental retardation and mental health
Consultant	counselor
Counseling coordinator	Occupational career counselor
Criminologist	Parent counselor/educator
Demographer	Prevention counselor
Educator	Project manager
Environmental organizer	Program coordinator
Family counselor	Program director
Fund-raising assistant director	Program manager
Gerontologist	Public administrator

continued

Public assistance worker	Social worker
Public health supervisor	Substance abuse counselor
Public relations manager	Survey worker
Research assistant	Women's counselor
Recreation worker	Youth specialist
Rural health outreach worker	

Professional Associations

Because community and social services work takes place in a variety of settings, just an introduction to a variety of possible professional associations is provided here. Contact those that have titles or work with populations you are interested in. Use the *Encyclopedia of Associations* or other references cited to get additional information about the goals and activities of these associations.

American Association of the Deaf-Blind
814 Thayer Ave., Suite 302
Silver Spring, MD 20910

American Association of Homes and Services for the Aging
901 E St. NW, Suite 302
Washington, DC 20004-2011

American Association on Mental Retardation
444 N. Capitol St. NW, Suite 846
Washington, DC 20001-1512

American Association of Retired Persons
601 E St. NW
Washington, DC 20049

American Board of Examiners in Crisis Intervention
Association Headquarters
2750 E. Sunshine
Springfield, MO 65804

American Council of the Blind
1155 15th St. NW, Suite 1004
Washington, DC 20005

American Foundation for Suicide Prevention
120 Wall St., Floor 22
New York, NY 10005-4001

American Society of Criminology
1314 Kinnear Rd., Suite 212
Columbus, OH 43212

American Society of Directors of Volunteer Services
American Hospital Association
One Franklin St.
Chicago, IL 60606

Association for Career and Technical Education
1410 King St.
Alexandria, VA 22314

Center for Immigrants' Rights
48 St. Mark's Pl., 4th Floor
New York, NY 10003

Consumer Federation of America
1424 16th St. NW, Suite 604
Washington, DC 20036

Disability Rights Education and Defense Fund
2212 6th St.
Berkeley, CA 94710

Health Education Resource Organization
101 W. Read St., Suite 825
Baltimore, MD 21201

Hospice Foundation of America
777 17th St., No. 401
Miami Beach, FL 33139

Housing Assistance Council
1025 Vermont Ave. NW, Suite 606
Washington, DC 20005

Men's Defense Association
17854 Lyons
Forest Lake, MN 55025

National Abortion Federation
1755 Massachusetts Ave. NW, Suite 600
Washington, DC 20036

National Adoption Center
1500 Walnut St., Suite 701
Philadelphia, PA 19102

National Association for Crime Victims Rights
P.O. Box 16161
Portland, OR 97216-0161

National Association of Developmental Disabilities Councils
1234 Massachusetts Ave. NW, Suite 103
Washington, DC 20005

National Association of Public Child Welfare Administrators
c/o American Public Welfare Association
810 1st St. NE, Suite 500
Washington, DC 20002-4267

National Association of Social Workers
750 1st St. NE, Suite 700
Washington, DC 20002-4241

National Association of State Alcohol and Drug Abuse Directors
808 17th St. NW, Suite 410
Washington, DC 20006

National Charities Information Bureau
19 Union Square West, 6th Floor
New York, NY 10003-3395

National Child Day Care Association
1501 Benning Rd. NE
Washington, DC 20002-4599

National Coalition Against Domestic Violence
P.O. Box 18749
Denver, CO 80218-0749

National Coalition for the Homeless
1012 14th St. NW, Suite 600
Washington, DC 20005-3406

**National Council on Child Abuse and
Family Violence**
1155 Connecticut Ave. NW, Suite 400
Washington, DC 20036

National Legal Aid and Defender Association
1625 K St. NW, Suite 800
Washington, DC 20006-1604

National Lesbian and Gay Health Education Foundation
1407 S St. NW
Washington, DC 20037

National Mental Health Association
1021 Prince St., 2971
Alexandria, VA 22314

National Organization for Women
733 15th St. NW, Second Floor
Washington, DC 20005

Single Parent Resource Center
31 East 28th St., Floor 2
New York, NY 10016-7923

U.S. Conference of City Human Services Officials
1620 I St. NW
Washington, DC 20006

World Medical Relief
11745 Rosa Parks Blvd.
Detroit, MI 48206

Young America's Foundation
110 Elden St.
Herndon, VA 20170

Path 3: Human Resources Management

As a sociology major, you've focused on human society and social behavior in groups and institutions. You've looked at how individuals adapt to a wide range of situations, and how groups of individuals coalesce to form social units. And perhaps while you've been in college you have also worked part-time and had a chance to observe firsthand some of the theories play out in a real-world environment. Sociology is obviously relevant to the human resource management function of many organizations. Human resources is the department that most often brings us into the institution when we are hired. It is where we often seek job growth, training, or conflict resolution. And it is the department most often given the task of managing workplace change. All of these issues and how workers react to them are central to the concerns of sociologists.

You are well aware from following the news of difficulties that often arise in today's workplace. With a little reflection you should see the implications for human resources professionals. In times of recession, the human resource staff is very often responsible for handling the layoffs and terminations; on the bright side, when the economy improves they are in the position to make certain that the right people are found for various positions. Despite progress, episodes of discriminatory behavior toward women, minorities, homosexuals, and other groups still occur. As the population of our country becomes even more heterogeneous, human resources professionals must build organizations from an increasingly diverse ethnic, racial, and religious population. There are corresponding challenges to assimilation, inclusion, and tolerance. Human resources professionals try to create understanding and, hopefully, appreciation and enjoyment of this diversity.

Reading the newspaper should also make you aware of the large number of lawsuits between employers and employees. Issues of harassment, discrimination, illegal firing and layoffs, and workplace injury or stress have exponentially escalated in the last five years and have resulted in additional challenges for those working in the human resources area. Each lawsuit puts a special burden on human resource departments. Parties in a lawsuit may request documentation that includes personnel files, records of vacation or sick days, training opportunities, formal commendations or reprimands, and many other kinds of legitimate requests for data from the human resource department. Very recently, historical E-mail files have come under scrutiny as a possible source of documentation. These document requests can add a tremendous burden to an already busy office.

Potential employees are more aggressively interested in the economic health of their employers. They are concerned, too, about the possibility of being fired or laid off. Employees are not so naive as to think they will be with the same firm for all of their lives. They also recognize the possibility that the organization may be bought, or moved, or fail. Many of them want to know from human resources what contingency plans are in effect in any of these situations. Will there be severance pay, outplacement services, counseling, relocation assistance, or transfers to a branch office?

The possibility of job loss and/or frequent job change (something many trend analysts feel is the new reality for the employee of the future) means workers will be more aggressive in extracting not only benefits but also training and development from current employers. Employees as a group may demand resource acquisitions (gym or weight room, diet counseling, blood pressure checks, ergonomic consultations) and an accounting from the organization's management on money spent on staff development. As workers realize a need to be always ready to acquire new skills in preparation for new jobs, they will be more aggressive in using every benefit opportunity. Employees' use of benefits increases the work of human resources as well as the cost to the organization. Later in this chapter, in the "Working Conditions" section, you will find an expanded discussion of the training and development role human resource professionals must play.

Health-care issues dominate the press, and as the United States moves slowly toward more comprehensive health care, there will be a dramatic impact on employers and employees. Workers who previously could not leave their jobs for fear of jeopardizing health benefits because of their own or a family member's preexisting condition will now be assured coverage. Part-time workers will not necessarily lose coverage under new plans. These changes may indicate that we will see greater worker mobility and less loyalty than in the past, as employees are not benefit-tied to a particular employer. Since out-processing a former employee and in-processing and training new talent is costly, human resources professionals have much to be concerned about if worker mobility is no longer tied to health benefits.

Organizations are subtly affected in a positive way by the core of long-term employees who have experienced some history with the organization and have learned to work together as a team. If that team breaks up beyond a critical point, some of that efficiency and networking will be lost, and that hurts the organization's ability to function as effectively.

Definition of the Career Path

If you are still working toward your degree, take every opportunity to add elective courses that would be most relevant to a human resources function. These would include courses such as Sociologists at Work, Introduction to General Psychology, Methods of Social Research, Applied Sociology, and Aging and Society. The anthropology courses in a combined anthropology/sociology degree program would not hold as much relevance for a career in human resources, but the workplace as a social organization would be directly reflected in your sociology courses.

If you've already graduated, your academic program in sociology has also helped you build a critical set of transferable skills that are highly valued in human resources. You mastered them in the context of studying sociology, but now you must make them relevant to the human resources employer. These skills include your ability to analyze, evaluate, draw conclusions, interview, manage time, write, manage projects, master computer technology, and to plan. Each of these skills is critical to functioning effectively in human resources.

"Human resources" is an apt description, as this area of the organization manages the resource of human productivity for the organization. Sociology could be an excellent preparation for a career in this area if you understand how you will use your degree in a human resource job.

Working Conditions

In examining working conditions in the human resources area, it's best to look at the overall mission of a human resources department and how that, in turn, affects the activities of the department.

Major human resources functions include

- Staffing and placement
- Salary administration
- Employee benefits administration
- Training and development
- Data management

Staffing and Placement

A healthy organization is one that assimilates new employees in a way that enhances productivity. One of the primary tasks of the human resource department is to help bring new workers into a company as others retire, change jobs, get promoted, or move away.

In most organizations, the ultimate hiring decision is made by the department needing staff. Those within a department are best equipped to judge whether a candidate is qualified for the job they seek to fill. Human resources departments, however, often serve as gateways to the departments: collecting applications, assembling the candidates' files, and performing credential checks and background investigations. They might conduct training workshops for supervisors and their staff on how to conduct interviews fairly and objectively. Except in situations where the demand for lower-level employees is heavy, the human resources department seldom makes hiring decisions, except for a human resources employee.

Once an employee is hired, however, it is usually the responsibility of the human resources department to provide new employee orientation. This may include an actual tour of the employer's facility and will surely include a lengthy discussion of rules and regulations, policies and procedures, benefits and compensation. Most organizations publish an employee manual, and it is often provided at this initial meeting. This is a prime opportunity for the human resources professional to interact positively with an employee.

But employers' needs for employees change over time. The marketplace may create new demands, products, and services. Outside economic conditions can create internal changes. Whatever the reason, most organizations are seldom static in terms of staffing needs, and the human resources professional is frequently being asked to assess department needs for new personnel or to examine an area suspected of having an excess of workers. Consulting for this purpose, the human resources worker needs to understand the department and the various roles its workers play so he or she can effectively offer solutions to staffing issues. The result could be transfers of employees to other departments or even layoffs or termination. Because personnel costs often represent the largest consistent expense of an organization, the human resources' role here is critical to the financial success of an organization.

The sociology major will have little difficulty in bringing his or her sociology studies to bear on the employment and placement activities of the organization. Issues of self-esteem, job definition and structure, and an employee's entry into a new organization are all significant employee issues. Your sensitivity to these issues will help you when working with department managers to define job parameters, when planning for interviewing procedures that give each candidate a fair chance, and when arranging to help a new employee make a successful transition into a new job.

Salary Administration

The largest percentage of many organizations' budgets goes toward pay and benefits. It follows that human resource professionals dedicate a great deal of energy toward salary administration.

Basic salaries, opportunities for wage increases, and deductions for various benefits are of crucial importance to all employees. After all, pay is a basic need. Money guarantees the possibility of satisfying many of our needs, such as housing, food, and security. Understanding this, a sociology major will recognize how important it is to educate workers on their pay, on how it works, and the reasons for any changes in pay schedules.

A sociology major in human resources can understand that many people define their work by their salary level, that people make comparisons to others of similar employment level, and that people are on the alert for any discrepancies or hints of discrimination. Wages and salary are a sensitive and complex issue. The ramifications of these behaviors to the human resource department are significant. Many human resource departments are regularly researching the salaries paid by similar organizations for comparable jobs. If there are potential issues of inconsistency within one's own organization, those inconsistencies should be either eliminated or determined to be reasonable.

Employee Benefits Administration

One of the first things a new employee does on the job is meet with the human resource department to fill out the forms for health insurance and other benefits. Providing the right benefits is critical, as is maintaining costs.

No human resources office is open for any length of time before the paperwork involved in the administration of benefits begins to accumulate. Requests for tuition reimbursement; workers' compensation; dental, medical, and optical care; pension planning; and 401(k)s pile up. The specific list varies from organization to organization as each offers a unique blend of employee benefits. Often, the benefits menu changes depending upon the status of the employee. Full-time employees receive a full complement of benefits, and those who work less than full time often have their benefits prorated according to their percent-time worked or may receive no benefits.

It adds up to a mountain of paperwork. Some employees have horror stories to tell of how human resources mismanaged one of their benefit claims, but far more will speak of excellent benefits and administrators who are sensitive and discreet in the processing of the ever-present forms.

Furthermore, new benefits are always emerging. Some of the newest ones include spousal benefits for same-sex partnerships and supplemental health allowances for individuals requiring special diets and food supplements. With the current governmental initiatives in health care, the area of benefits administration should remain vital and volatile. For example, many firms are now understanding and dealing with the issues of drug and alcohol abuse among their workers and are developing programs that refer these employees for counseling and treatment to off-site employee assistant programs. Usually, these employees continue working or return to full employment following a course of treatment.

Employers realize, moreover, that the physical and mental health of their employees plays a key role in productivity. When an organization provides exercise rooms, or has a professional making mental health referrals, it knows it will see sharply reduced absenteeism, fewer claims on employee health and benefit programs, and increased productivity because of these efforts. So, while the human resources promotional literature emphasizes enhanced benefits to the employee, the real rewards are savings in dollars and cents for the employer.

Benefits administration could be a deeply rewarding job for the sociology major, especially today, as organizations become ever more sensitive to human needs and the relationship between satisfying those needs and work productivity. You can hardly function well at work if you're worried about the hospitalization costs for your child's chronic illness. Sociology majors employed in human resources work will have many opportunities to review benefit options and consider new proposals that might directly answer employees' needs.

Training and Development

The training and development function in human resources provides continuing education opportunities for employees. This training may be developed and delivered in-house by staff trainers, it may be purchased with a contract for a speaker or workshop facilitator, or it may involve sending employees off-site to attend educational conferences and symposia.

Depending on the number of employees and the size of the human resources department, training and development may be conducted in-house or contracted out to other professionals. In most cases, it is a combination. In-house human resources professionals will offer workshops year-round on issues as diverse as retirement planning, safe driving, employee safety and health precautions, and using employee benefits effectively. Workshops on stress management and promotion opportunities may be provided along with new supervisor training programs. Outside professionals may be called in to do cholesterol tests and education programs, self-examination and mammograms clinics, as well as multicultural and diversity workshops. You will find challenges and satisfaction in developing and delivering staff training programs. Workers value good on-the-job training and will often let you know it. Many issues are facing the workplace from AIDS and the Americans with Disabilities Act (ADA) to sexual harassment. Staff development and training not only builds a sense of employee cohesion and camaraderie, but it can also be a quick and deliberate response to critical issues facing the workplace and its employees. Some training programs are established and remain in place with modifications, only as needed, for years.

The sociology major looks out over the range and variety of employees in an organization and realizes that each person is at a different stage in his or her developmental life and career. Some are young and ambitious, eager for change and growth, and able to be flexible with their time and lives. Others are embarking on relationships or starting families and have chosen, for the present time, to concentrate their energies on these aspects of their lives. Some may be continuing their education, while others may be anticipating slowing down their schedules, working less, and easing into retirement. Each individual is in a different place in work life, chronological age, and personal development as well as in commitment to the organization and the job, and your appreciation of these differences can spark ideas and strategies for wonderful and varied training and development programs.

The organization in general and the human resources worker in particular are primarily concerned with three types of development which create a cohesive workforce and achieve organizational missions and goals: 1) training and development, or developing key competencies in workers that enable them to carry out their duties, 2) organizational development, which primarily focuses on helping groups manage change, and 3) career development, which involves helping employees manage their careers within and beyond the organization.

Job Development. Most workers want to be proud of what they accomplish in their jobs, but they may need additional training to be able to work at their full potential. A computer data-entry worker may need to learn database management. A new supervisor may need to develop some conflict negotiation skills. In any of these kinds of situations, the human resources professional is responsible for ensuring that workers either come into the organization with the skills they need to do the assigned work or that mechanisms are available (courses, cross training, self-tutoring programs) to allow the worker to develop those competencies.

Organizations today are very interested in the concept of cross training—teaching workers to perform a variety of tasks. Workers learn each other's jobs, thus making their work more interesting and varied as well as allowing for greater flexibility in staffing and hiring.

Organizational Development. Organizations are undergoing stressful levels of change to maintain their strategic advantage in the marketplace. Whether the organization is a nonprofit that coordinates emergency relief efforts or a for-profit manufacturer producing the latest in computer chip technology, both require employees who can handle changing needs. The human resources department can help effect these changes through hiring procedures, employee training, and employee transitions within the organizations.

Many organizations are increasing their contacts outside of the United States. Foreign travel for management and visitors from abroad have become commonplace in many workplaces. The need for some bilingual employees, increased technology for overseas communication, and adjusting work hours to better coordinate with foreign markets are all competitive realities if an organization is to stay viable. Human resources helps to plan and implement these changes in a productive and nonthreatening manner.

Career Development. Job seekers face an ever-changing marketplace, one that demands flexibility to be able to handle organizational change. Human resources personnel may help employees take concrete and specific steps to manage their own careers within the organization, allowing each person to use a greater range of his or her skills and abilities to accomplish organizational goals.

Data Management. Record keeping and retrieval are critical in human resources work. That's why you'll see ads similar to this:

> **Records Management Supervisor:** Bachelor's degree in human resource management or a human service area for records management of a busy manufacturing environment human resources office.

Requests for a history of workers' compensation claims, average salary increases for middle management, or any of a number of other data on employees frequently come in to the human resources department. Staff personnel need to be comfortable analyzing and providing data that will be useful to management in making staffing and other strategic decisions.

The ADA, contract negotiations and arbitration, the Equal Employment Opportunity initiatives, fair wages standards, and Occupational Safety and Health Administration (OSHA) guidelines as well as an organization's own internal grievance process all provide enormous amounts of paperwork.

Excellent record keeping skills with an eye to data retrieval are required to meet these information needs. This is one of the many reasons why a human resources office is often very concerned with paperwork and administration. In fact, many entry-level employees are disappointed to discover the human resources position involves as much paperwork (or more) as it does interactions with people.

As a sociology major, you should be able to handle the data required in the job, because you've not only had to complete numerous research reports in your studies, but you have probably created some data yourself, which you had to transform into meaningful information.

Who Are You Really Working for in Human Resources?

Probably the most vexing question for many human resources professionals is, "Do I serve the organization or the worker?" In the overwhelming majority of circumstances the answer is he or she serves the organization and seeks to maintain the expectations of management. In areas such as job design, pay grades and classifications, promotion and job enhancement, training and development, benefits administration, and the arbitration of grievances and employee policies, human resources professionals are not advocates of the employee but rather representatives of the employer, exercising that employer's mandates in the administration of the workforce.

On the other hand, human resource professionals can also serve as advocates for the employees. Workers do grow in their jobs, often because of the policies and encouragement of human resources professionals. As a result, they may need to be reclassified to a higher rank. Human resources personnel design creative and innovative programs for workers that not only impact their work performance and relationships but can also influence other aspects of their lives. Human resources programs, depending on their size and breadth, can touch on life changes: parenthood, retirement, aging, and many other personal and family challenges.

None of this programming is done, however, without keeping in mind a strong sense of the organization's overall mission and the impact of these programs on the budget and use of human resources personnel. Human resource activities do not drive the organization; they support its principal mission and goals.

If you are seriously interested in pursuing this career path, however, it is important to sit down and talk with a human resources professional about the negative or stressful aspects of the field. The human resource worker faces the anger of employees frustrated with benefits administration, changes in work conditions, salary negotiations, or promotion opportunities. You may be privileged to hear a human resources professional share what it's like to listen to the complaints and humiliation of a discharged employee who must be accompanied by a human resource official as he packs up his office and is escorted from the building. On occasion, there is the challenge of having to remove an employee with the help of security personnel. To have the full picture of this job, you need to hear both the positive and the negative.

Suitable Qualifications

The foregoing discussion of human resources functions suggests many of the skills and attributes that will be important to a new human resources professional. But there are others that are important as well, including communications skills, public presentation skills, computer literacy, and data analysis.

Communications Skills
In both oral and written communication, human resources professionals need to be very careful of the accuracy, tone, and nuance of their language.

Most of the issues dealt with in human resources departments are immensely important to employees, and work conditions can be vital to an employee's sense of self-esteem and identity. Change, even the suggestion of change, can provoke great anxiety among some employees. How such change is presented is crucial to the success of any plan. Strong—make that excellent—communications skills will be required for maximum effectiveness.

For example, let's say your firm has decided to purchase a new telephone system that requires each employee to key in his or her own identification number for every call. Prior to this, phone charges have been anonymously lumped by department for each extension number. The unwritten policy has been that reasonable numbers of personal phone calls (for example, calls home to your spouse) were OK. Now, with a new caller ID number, many employees will be concerned about the loss of that privilege. Realizing this is a concern, you may want to specifically address it in your memo and reassure employees that a reasonable number of personal calls is still acceptable.

One-on-one conferences, small group and department meetings, memoranda, and policies and procedures manuals all need to contain clear and direct language that will enable all staff members to understand and carry out organizational policies. If time allows, you might, as a new human resources employee, take on the project of collecting and reviewing literature and human resource publications from other public organizations for sensitive and clear language. Analyzing the communications styles of these other publications should provide ideas for improving your own organizational communicating efforts.

Public Presentation Skills

"Platform skills" is another term frequently used for the ability to speak before groups in an organized manner.

Because many human resources programs affect large groups of employees, it is often more efficient to present material to large groups. Professional staff need to have excellent public presentation skills including the ability to plan, organize, and write a workshop or seminar; design and execute effective and appropriate visual materials; and design and execute forms for evaluation. Technical competency with audiovisual materials including slide projectors, VCRs, video recording equipment, and overhead projectors is certainly a plus.

If you've had experience with presentation and audiovisual aids in college, be sure to feature that on your résumé or in a cover letter. Skilled presenters are always in demand, especially when they are comfortable with technology that can be used to improve retention and communication.

As with all administrative units, the use of computers in a human resources department is pervasive. Database management skills are crucial for data analysis and retrieval, as are word-processing skills that are used for employee communications. Many departments produce their own brochures and information pieces, and they rely on staff to create the newsletters to be distributed to employees.

Just as it is safe to assume that all human resources staff at every level employ some degree of computer use in this field, it is likewise a safe assumption that the entry-level candidate with strong computer skills stands a markedly increased opportunity for employment compared to the candidate who has neglected this technical competency.

Have you included your computer and data management courses on your résumé? If not, be sure to mention them in your cover letter or during an interview. Reading about human resources, you've become aware of the vast amounts of data and detail that are going to be stored electronically. It's ironic, but true, that to perform your human resources task in a very human, connected manner with your employees, you need to be proficient with computer technology.

If you have a chance to meet and talk with a human resources professional (perhaps an alumni meeting arranged through your career office), ask about data technology. Ask about the expectations of the employer for computer skills. What should you have for an entry-level position and how much will you gain on the job? How much of the day's work is on the computer? Is there a human resources data analyst on the staff? Who inputs data? A discussion about computer technology will help you understand the importance of these skills in a human resources department.

Data Analysis

Earlier in this chapter, under "Working Conditions," the critical role of data management was discussed. Data analysis allows the human resource professional to interpret and explain the meaning of the data. In effect, data analysis transforms otherwise meaningless data into useful information. To the hackneyed statement of many young job candidates for human resources positions that they're "a people person," most hiring professionals might chuckle and say most days they could use a good data analyst! The reality is, as with so many issues, somewhere in the middle of those two extremes lies the ideal candidate. An effective human resources department needs to provide management with good data analysis.

For every human interaction, be it a one-on-one meeting, a public presentation to a department or group of employees, or new staff orientation and briefing, a great deal of time is spent reading, analyzing, and discussing data concerning staff. Overtime and associated costs, sick days, temporary help expenditures, vacation scheduling and conflicts, and use of benefits all need to be monitored and understood.

You know from your methods of sociological research course that data can reveal trends and indicate problems. You bring to your human resource job an ability to build a bridge from anonymous cold data to the real, live human interactions the data represents. Often, your time spent in reading the early warning signs in data can lead you right out of your office into the satisfying human interaction of conferences and meetings as you seek answers to questions and solutions to problems.

Earnings

How much you will earn as a human resource professional will depend on your place of employment and level of experience. According to the *Occupational Outlook Handbook* published in 2000, the median annual earnings of human resource managers were $59,000. The lowest 10 percent earned less than $33,600, and the highest 10 percent earned more than $104,020. Training and development specialists earned a median annual salary of $40,830.

Even in a troubled economy, the base salaries in this field continue to increase faster than the national average. A survey sponsored by the Society for Human Resource Management and published by the consulting firm William M. Mercer, Inc. revealed that those in this field are also receiving incentive pay—often in the form of stock options—indicating the crucial role they play in the success of their organizations.

This same survey showed that those human resource professionals received the highest pay, with median salaries of $99,200, followed by compensation managers at $86,000. But the compensation for human resource generalists is also rising, and in 2000 the median salary for this role was $49,000.[1]

Career Outlook

The number and types of positions in human resources vary dramatically, depending on the size of the organization, the current state of its fiscal health, and the emphasis the organization puts on its employees and their welfare. Human resources is not a revenue-producing department. Unlike the sales forces, for example, whose high working expenses (travel, meals, and accommodations) are offset by the generation of income for the firm, the human resources department is pure administration and is seen as overhead. Consequently, it is often earmarked during difficult economic times for trimming its staff or not rehiring empty positions to ensure greater profitability. The training and development division of many human resources departments is frequently the first target of such staff trimming.

Sociology majors looking for the most promising entry-level jobs in human resources would do best to select from among mid- to larger-size organizations and the largest corporations. While many small, entrepreneurial firms are enjoying profitability and growth, they seldom have the developed human resource function of the larger corporations.

Court rulings in recent years that affect the workplace, on issues such as occupational safety and health, equal employment opportunity, and family leave, will increase the demand for human resource workers. Moreover, companies hoping to avoid costly court cases will call on their own internal human resource departments to mediate labor-management disputes. And given the changing demographics of the United States, employees who have special skills in international human resources management will be needed.

Strategy for Finding the Jobs

Fortunately, human resource departments of whatever size are usually the easiest departments to locate in an organization! Most organizations, even the smallest, have someone designated to answer the telephone when the caller asks for personnel. Since locating human resource activity will not represent a challenge, your strategic efforts will focus more on how to handle each contact you make with a potential employer.

Human resources positions, especially entry-level ones, are filled by graduates who come from a variety of academic disciplines. So, expect that the level of competition for these positions will be keen. A job search in this field should revolve around the following suggestions. First, begin as early as you can in your college career to build a portfolio of expertise in human resources. Suggestions for doing so are discussed in the following sections. Second, you must be ready to explain to a potential employer how your sociology education has prepared you to work effectively in this field. Both your résumé and your interview comments must highlight the relevance of a sociology major to human resources. Finally, you will then need to identify employment settings that seem like a good fit for you to begin your human resources career.

Gain Experience While Still in College

Whenever possible, make sure to register for courses that are directly related to human resources. If there is a business school at your university, you might look into auditing courses in personnel or human/industrial relations or taking a minor in one of these areas. In addition, you should make an effort to obtain some actual "hands-on" experience in the field, perhaps in the form of a for-credit internship.

Don't neglect your own college or university personnel office and inquire about internships there. Though there may be issues of confidentiality and discretion regarding student employees, generally these offices have numerous projects where you could make a contribution and learn more about the human resource function at the same time.

In addition to appropriate classes, you should try to be on the lookout for material focusing on current societal trends that affect the functions and mission of a human resources department, and issues the human resources professional faces.

Keep Track of Societal Trends. This chapter has provided a basic outline of this profession, but how it plays out in the field varies dramatically by organization, product or service, and even by geographic region. For example, many of our newer, cutting-edge technological firms have instituted some of the newest—and often controversial—employee benefit programs. Many have proven comfortable with employees working from home part of the week, flextime, and loose organizational structures. Such policies might not succeed in a more traditional organization with a less sophisticated or less educated employment pool. A continued reading of business periodicals and the business section of newspapers will help you to become conversant with trends that affect the current state of human resources administration.

Learn the Legal Issues. Becoming more knowledgeable about the legal issues that increasingly dominate human resource management is an important part in preparing yourself for positions in this field. Some of the topics you'll want to be familiar with include:

- OSHA
- Pension planning
- 401(k)s
- Medical claims/syndromes
- Ergonomics
- Arbitration

- Labor relations
- Negotiations
- Contracts
- Sexual harassment

You needn't become an expert on these topics, but they are important issues to human resources professionals, and your job search will be far more successful if you can demonstrate an awareness of and appreciation for these challenges. By doing so, you can overcome any hesitancy an employer may feel due to your lack of actual human resource experience. Your willingness to educate yourself is, in and of itself, a strong employment consideration.

Use your summer or part-time employment to find out as much as you can about working in human resources. If you cannot find employment in that area, working in an organization that has a professional human resource management department can be useful. You can network with the director or manager of personnel to let him or her know about your interests and to see if he or she can assist you in getting information or making contacts in the field. You may want to invest in a membership in a professional personnel or human resources organization (see end of chapter for suggestions) to further pursue your networking and to begin learning about actual employment opportunities.

Make the Connection Between Sociology and Human Resources

Your sociology degree has helped you develop many skills important in working effectively in human resources. But those skills and that knowledge might not be readily apparent to potential employers. Don't let them guess about how well-qualified you are. Show them on your résumé and in your interview. Point out your relevant training and tell them how you can help accomplish their human resources goals.

Consider Yourself Your First Placement. In the "Possible Employers" section of this path, we describe a wide range of employers. You may be able to picture yourself working in some settings, and you will know immediately that you wouldn't feel comfortable in others. Review the following section and make a decision about where you would like to begin your employment search. You may have to widen the scope, depending on the geographic area where you live and the types of employers you do decide to focus on first. But start with an industry that looks like the best fit.

Possible Employers

Personnel, training, and labor relations specialists and managers are found in every industry, from manufacturing to banking and transportation to health care and education. Some of the possibilities include

Education	Health care
Employment agencies	Manufacturing
Finance and insurance	Service
Government	

Your job search should begin with a review of all types of possible employers. After you have familiarized yourself with the range of possibilities, begin your job search by starting to network with professionals, and then apply for jobs in one or more industries.

Education
The very largest elementary and secondary schools; higher education, including community and two-year colleges; four-year colleges; and universities all hire a variety of workers to help them achieve their educational mission and goals. Whether it is the custodian who keeps the facility in shape, the teacher in the classroom, the support or technical staff member, or the administrator, all are important, and the human resources worker helps find the right person for the right job.

Help in Locating These Employers. Several books have information about preschools, elementary schools, and secondary schools. These include *The Handbook of Private Schools, Patterson's Elementary Education, Patterson's American Education, Peterson's Private Secondary Schools,* and *Peterson's International Directory of University Preparatory Boarding Schools in the U.S. and Canada.* For higher education, be sure to review three of Peterson's references: *Guide to Two-Year Colleges, Guide to Four-Year Colleges,* and *Guides to Graduate Study.* The *Chronicle of Higher Education* contains job listings as well.

Employment Agencies
The importance of employment agencies in the workplace, providing either temporary or permanent hires, is growing dramatically. Rather than hiring

a regular employee, many organizations will instead hire a field staffer (temporary employee) to try out. If all goes well, the staffer may be offered regular employment. In some large organizations, however, the situation creates a schism in the workforce. Often, temporary workers do not receive the same benefits that accrue to regular salaried employees, even though these temporary workers might be working long-term assignments at a given organization. At the same time, the hourly wages for temporary workers—not counting the benefits such as health insurance—is sometimes higher than those filling similar roles at the same company.

The agencies that fill these temporary postings need professionals, including graduates with sociology degrees, on their own staffs. Sociology graduates might start out as service coordinators and be responsible for interviewing and orienting applicants, testing them, and making a decision as to whether the agency wants to work with them. They evaluate job orders, locate and refer qualified applicants, and write job advertisements. In this industry, service coordinators can move into positions in sales, marketing, and management once they have paid their dues as service coordinators.

Help in Locating These Employers. One easy way to begin locating employment agencies is to review the yellow pages for the geographic area where you would like to work. Yellow pages directories are available in many larger public and college libraries. Your local phone company business office may also be able to provide you with some directories for a fee. Look under Employment Agencies, Employment Contractors—Temporary Help, and Employment Service—Employee Leasing. You will probably be surprised at the number of agencies listed. You may also want to contact the American Staffing Association in Alexandria, Virginia, for more information.

Finance and Insurance

This category includes commercial banks, savings institutions, credit unions, mutual fund companies, securities firms, venture capital firms, commodities futures trading companies, and insurance companies. Telecommunications capabilities are changing the way this industry does its work, and some sociology majors will be particularly interested in the impact of this new technology on the workforce. The human resources department in industries with cutting-edge technology will play a valuable role in maintaining worker cohesiveness and job satisfaction.

Help in Locating These Employers. If you would like to begin generating a list of possible employment sites, begin by using these two references:

the *Directory of American Savings and Loan Associations* and the *Financial Institutions Directory*, the latter published by the American Bankers Association. Your career office can provide you with corporate literature on finance and insurance organizations that have recruited at the college or university level, and don't forget to check the yellow pages for organizations in business in your area.

Federal Government

Chapter 12 contains up-to-date information on both the federal hiring process and those departments and agencies most interested in sociology graduates. Because of the nature of the federal job classification system, sociology graduates are considered to be qualified applicants for entry-level human resource generalist positions in the federal workforce. The federal government is the largest employer in the country and, in times of uncertainty, is a source of secure jobs with predictable rates of promotion. The sociology major working in human resources can help screen, process, and train the best candidates for federal government positions and administer operations relating to personnel functions.

The hiring process, as detailed in Chapter 12, has become simpler. Online government job sources, such as usajobs.opm.gov, list thousands of federal openings throughout the United States as well as international positions. You may contact the Office of Personnel Management (OPM) directly and speak with a personnel assistant. OPM has regional offices that are responsible for their area's personnel matters, and you can begin by applying for work at those offices. In addition, you may now contact and directly apply to individual agencies and departments. All federal jobs are assigned a job series number, and personnel management and industrial relations positions fall within the 0201-0299 category, so look for job numbers in this range. OPM addresses are provided at the end of this chapter.

Help in Locating These Employers. In addition to the information provided in Chapter 12, reference books that can familiarize you with the operations of various agencies and their hiring procedures include VGM's *Opportunities in Federal Government Careers*, *The Complete Guide to Public Employment*, and *Government Job Finder*. The *Occupational Outlook Handbook*, published quarterly by the U.S. Department of Labor, frequently profiles job categories in the federal government, opportunities for liberal arts majors, and tips to assist aspiring federal employees. The *OOH* contains information on federal pay scales, tips on application process alternatives, and how to apply to agencies. Addresses for the personnel or human resources functions of the largest executive departments and excepted agencies are given. Contact those you may be interested in working for to determine their hiring procedures.

State and Local Government

State and larger local governments offer human resources positions that help in staffing departments that include corrections, court systems, education, fire protection, health, highway and street construction, housing and community development, hospitals, libraries, natural resources, parks and recreation, police, sanitation, transportation, utilities, and welfare services. Your background in sociology has helped prepare you to process, test, and screen applicants who will be interviewed by the various departments.

Help in Locating These Employers. Begin your search by checking with the personnel or human resources office for the state or local governmental unit you would like to work for. These offices can tell you how they advertise for open positions, and they can provide application forms that may be required. Resources such as VGM's *Opportunities in State and Local Government Careers, Careers in State and Local Government, Government Job Finder,* and *The Complete Guide to Public Employment* detail ways to work this particular system.

Health Care

The dramatically changing face of health care in this country will continue to provide opportunities for human resource professionals. Health-care delivery facilities employ doctors, nurses, technicians, food-service workers, maintenance workers, administrators, managed-care coordinators, social workers, and a host of other types of employees. The human resources professional can play a critical role in filling positions with the right people. If you would like to play an important role in this fast-changing industry, consider health care.

Help in Locating These Employers. You should review several resources as you conduct your job search, including *The American Hospital Association's AHA Guide to the Health Care Field, Gale's Encyclopedia of Medical Organizations and Agencies,* and *Medical and Health Information Directory.* Be sure to directly contact those health organizations you would like to work for, and do some informational interviewing or inquire about their procedure for advertising job openings.

Manufacturing

Whether a company is manufacturing teddy bears, hats and gloves, computer microchips, or trucks and automobiles, human resources personnel have screened, processed, oriented, trained, and/or provided benefits to the labor force. As the United States fights to maintain its competitiveness in manufacturing, it needs competent human resources workers to assemble a well-qualified group of employees.

Help in Locating These Employers. Some resources to start with include *Moody's Industrial Manual, Tower Publishing's Manufacturing Directories, America's Corporate Families,* and the *Directory of American Firms Operating in Foreign Countries.* You'll want to become familiar with the Standard Industrial Coding (SIC) scheme, which groups manufacturers producing similar products, to find environments in which you are interested in working. Contact your local Chamber of Commerce for assistance in identifying manufacturing firms operating in your area.

Service

No matter where you go, whether it's in food retailing, household furniture and appliance sales, clothing sales, travel services, or business and professional services, personnel are available to assist you. Medium- to large-sized organizations have human resources professionals who help them hire people willing to work to support organizational goals and serve customers.

Help in Locating These Employers. Because the service industry is so large, just a few titles that will be useful in your job search will be presented. Be sure to ask the other professionals you are working with, such as career counselors and librarians, for further recommendations. The business reference section of your college library will have a number of directories that you can review. Depending on your interests, you may want to look at *Moody's Transportation Manual, American Bankers Association Financial Institutions Directory, Standard Directory of Advertising Agencies, O'Dwyer's Directory of Public Relations Firms, Ward's Business Directory,* and *Hoover's Handbook of American Business.*

Possible Job Titles

Because human resources workers can be generalists or specialists, depending on the size and complexity of the organization, you will see quite a range of job titles. Consider them all to decide which positions you're qualified to fill or to determine an area that you would like to specialize in.

Affirmative action coordinator	International human resource
Arbitrator	manager
Benefits administrator	Interviewer
Benefits analyst	Job analyst
Benefits manager	Job classification specialist
Compensation manager	Labor relations specialist
Compensation specialist	Management analyst
Education specialist	Mediator
Employee assistance plan manager	Occupational analyst
Employee benefits manager	Personnel administrator
Employee development specialist	Personnel consultant
Employee relations representative	Personnel director
Employee welfare office/manager	Personnel management specialist
Employer relations representative	Personnel officer
Employment interviewer	Personnel staffing specialist
Employment specialist	Position classification specialist
Equal Employment Opportunity	Position classifier
(EEO) representative	Position review specialist
Grievance officer	Recreation specialist
Human resource information systems	Recruiter
specialist	Salary administrator
Human resources coordinator	Service coordinator
Human resources manager	Test development specialist
Human resources specialist	Trainer
Industrial relations manager/director	Training and development manager
Industrial relations specialist	Training specialist

Professional Associations

If you are interested in pursuing a career in human resources there are several associations that serve this group of workers. Review the listings shown below and decide whether any of the groups can provide information relevant to your job search.

American Arbitration Association
335 Madison Ave.
New York, NY 10017-4605
Members/Purpose: Businesses, unions, trade and educational associations, law firms, arbitrators, and other interested individuals
Training: Conducts workshops, seminars, conferences, and skill-building sessions
Publications: *Dispute Resolution Journal, Arbitration and the Law, Arbitration in the Schools, Dispute Resolution Times*
Job Listings: Regional offices sometimes have listings; contact AAA for regional office nearest you.

American Society for Healthcare Human Resources
c/o American Hospital Association
One North Franklin
Chicago, IL 60606
Members/Purpose: To provide effective and continuous leadership in the field of health-care human resources administration
Publications: *Directory of Health Care Human Resources Consultants, The Pulse*
Job Listings: Offers placement service

American Society for Training and Development
1640 King St.
Box 1443
Alexandria, VA 22313-2043
Members/Purpose: Professional association for persons engaged in the training and development of business, industry, education, and government
Training: Maintains database on more than 100,000 public seminars, workshops, and conferences, and on coursework from more than 100 suppliers
Publications: *Info-Line: Practical Guidelines for Human Resource Development Professionals, Training and Development Journal*
Job Listings: Local chapters offer a job bank; see *Training and Development Journal*, classified section.

American Staffing Assocation
277 S. Washington St., Suite 200
Alexandria, VA 22314-3646

Members/Purposes: Companies supplying workers to other firms on a temporary basis

Publications: *Con Temporary Times*, membership directory

College and University Personnel Association
1233 20th St. NW, Suite 301
Washington, DC 20036-1250
Members/Purpose: Professional organization made up of colleges and universities interested in the improvement of campus personnel administration
Training: Sponsors training seminars
Publications: *CUPA News*, directory, various salary surveys
Job Listings: *CUPA News* classified lists upper-management positions.

International Association of Personnel in Employment Security
1801 Louisville Rd.
Frankfort, KY 40601
Members/Purpose: Officials and others engaged in job placement and unemployment-compensation administration through municipal, state, provincial, and federal government employment agencies and unemployment compensation agencies
Training: Conducts workshops and offers professional development program of study guides and tests
Publication: *IAPES News*

International Foundation of Employee Benefit Plans
Box 69
18700 W. Bluemound Rd.
Brookfield, WI 53008-0069
Members/Purpose: Jointly trusteed, public, Canadian, and company-sponsored employee benefit plans; administrators, labor organizations, employer associations, benefit consultants, investment counselors, insurance consultants, banks, attorneys, accountants, actuaries, and others who service or are interested in the field of employee benefit plans
Training: Cosponsors the Certified Employee Benefit Specialist Program, a ten-course college-level study program leading to a professional designation in the employee benefits field
Publications: *Employee Benefits Basics*, *Employee Benefits Practices*, *Employee Benefits Quarterly Job Listings* provides a job service

International Personnel Management Association
1617 Duke St.
Alexandria, VA 22314
Members/Purpose: Public personnel agencies and individuals (personnel workers, consultants, teachers); seeks to improve personnel practices in government
Training: Sponsors seminars and workshops on public personnel administration
Publications: *Agency Issues*, membership directory, *IPMA News*, *Public Employee Relations Library*, *Public Personnel Management*

National Association of Personnel Services
3133 Mt. Vernon Ave.
Alexandria, VA 22305
Members/Purpose: Private employment agencies
Training: Conducts certification program
Publications: *Inside NAPS*, membership directory

National Association of State Personnel Executives
c/o Council of State Governments
2760 Research Park Dr.
P.O. Box 11910
Lexington, KY 40578-1910
Members/Purpose: Personnel directors for state and territorial governments
Publication: *State Personnel View Newsletter*

Society for Human Resource Management
1800 Duke St.
Alexandria, VA 22314
Members/Purpose: Professional organization of human resource, personnel, and industrial relations executives
Publications: *HR Magazine*, *HR News*
Job Listings: See *HR News*

World at Work (formerly American Compensation Association)
14040 N. Northsight Blvd.
Scottsdale, AZ 85260
Members/Purpose: Managerial and professional-level administrative personnel in business, industry, and government responsible for the

establishment, execution, administration, or application of compensation practices and policies in their organization

Training: Organizes almost 300 seminars annually

Publications: *ACA Journal, ACA News, ACA Building Blocks in Total Compensation, ACA*

Job Listings: *ACA Career Bulletin*

12

Path 4: Public Employment

As a sociology major you no doubt have read numerous studies that tie in to the realm of public policy and government services. At the federal, state, and local level, sociologists are engaged in researching social trends, compiling data, facilitating government services, and helping form government policies. In fact, the materials compiled by government agencies are critical to the ongoing work of sociologists in academia as well as in other fields. You've certainly seen federal studies cited in your readings numerous times. Moreover, the federal government is the largest supplier of funding for many social service endeavors and is the architect of countless national programs, including welfare, unemployment, aid to families with dependent children, and other social service organizations. In recent years, state and local governments have increasingly taken on projects and funding for initiatives once shouldered by the federal government. As a result, the bureaucracy for human service workers and social service departments on the state and local level has escalated dramatically.

Public Careers Today

Given the integral connection between government and the realm of sociology, it won't surprise you to find a chapter on this career path. Although you might have expected it, you may still be thinking that a government job is not for you. After all, you've read the bad press that governmental agencies often receive, and perhaps you don't want to be part of that.

As a sociology student, you know enough not to believe everything you hear or read in the papers. Too many generalizations are propagated about governmental agencies. Your education has taught you to look beyond the superficial and discover what's really going on. In this chapter, that's what we'll do. We'll examine the opportunities that exist in every aspect of government and discover exactly what kinds of jobs and work are available. You'll raise your public employment IQ and learn that not only does government present attractive opportunities to the sociology major, but that working for a governmental agency at the federal, state, or local level may also prolong and enhance your career.

Consider the concept of bureaucracy, for example. Your negative image may include concepts such as regimentation, boredom, routine tasks, and lack of advancement. Nothing could be farther from the truth. In fact, it is the overwhelming size of the government bureaucracy that has dictated the need for a correspondingly large bureaucratic structure. This is not, in and of itself, a bad thing. The public sector has led the way in introducing many innovative work concepts. This includes cross training of employees to increase job satisfaction, job sharing for more flexible time schedules, and standardization of qualifications for promotion that have opened senior ranks to all qualified candidates regardless of gender, race, sexual orientation, or religion. Sadly, many private organizations remain much more rigid in job categorization and are often accused of politics and prejudice in the workplace. Public sector work units are often far smaller than many private organizations and no different than any workplace in appearance, energy, and professionalism.

A Chance to Develop "Portable" Skills

Developing portable skills—ones that you can take with you from job to job—is a recurrent theme in the Great Jobs series. These sorts of skills don't depend on a particular job vocabulary or knowledge of some economic sector. Nor are they relegated to certain geographic areas. They are job talents that one can apply in varying degrees to any job. Portable skills give you the flexibility to take on new jobs and challenges and qualify you to consider a wider range of employment.

Today's job market remains volatile. Downsizing and reductions in staffing continue to shift workers in and out of the job market. If you stay aware of trends in the workforce and develop those work skills that you can transfer from one job to another, you can look forward to a lengthy and productive work life. Public sector jobs provide excellent access to technology, the opportunity to enhance your computer expertise (a portable skill), and a heavy emphasis on training and professional development. Most important, these jobs require you to interact with a number of other public sector institutions as well as nonprofit organizations, trade and professional groups, law firms, contracting and consulting firms, research organizations, and international organizations and groups.

It is impossible to do justice to all your public sector employment possibilities in just one chapter. So, consider these pages the first chapter in your own book on public sector employment possibilities. As you'll see, a great deal of information is available directly from the government itself, which has set up websites to answer questions from those seeking a career in the public sector. In addition, the bibliography lists some wonderful references, including *The Complete Guide to Public Employment* and *The Book of U.S. Government Jobs*.

Federal Government

If someone asks you, "Who hires sociology majors?" the federal government should be your first response. It will also be the best answer to that question. The U.S. government has always been respectful and appreciative of the potential of liberal arts graduates, especially in the social sciences. The federal government is the largest single employer in the country. More than 1.8 million people work for Uncle Sam in more than one hundred government agencies, boards, bureaus, commissions, and departments. Many of these governmental units are directly focused on the social life, changes, and causes of human behavior. College degrees are held by 37 percent of the total federal workforce. Certain jobs require a general four-year degree, while others emphasize a particular major. A graduate or professional degree is necessary for some professional jobs.

Some of the departments hiring the largest number of college graduates (regardless of major) include the Veterans Administration, Housing and Urban Development, Defense, Agriculture, Interior, Commerce, Transportation, the Environmental Protection Agency, Education, Treasury, and Energy. College graduates may also find work in special government agencies such as the Peace Corps, National Institutes of Health, and the National Institute on Aging. There are more white collar, professional, and administrative positions in the federal government than there are in the economy overall. These jobs are also often much more relevant to your sociology degree.

Social Scientists Are in Top Demand

Another consideration in seeking public employment is the nature of government agency work and the qualifications the agencies desire in candidates for that work. Governments seek a greater number of employees who have an educational background in the social sciences than do nongovernmental agencies. It can be a bit of a challenge to determine exactly what specific qualifications the government is seeking. Luckily, the federal government's own websites and informational brochures can provide some of the answers.

For example, one government resource prepared by the OPM lists the federal jobs that are often filled by college graduates with appropriate college majors.[1] The list is not exhaustive, and a sociology major can find many additional opportunities. Some fields that might particularly appeal to sociology majors in fact call for the background provided by just about any major in college. These include:

- Administrative officer
- Civil rights analyst
- Contact representative
- Environmental protection
- General investigator
- Logistics management
- Management analyst
- Paralegal specialist
- Personnel occupations
- Public affairs
- Writing and editing

There are also career paths in the government that specifically call for sociology majors.

- General Accounting Office (GAO) evaluators
- Program analysts
- Social science aids and technicians
- Social scientists
- Social service aids and assistants
- Social service representatives
- Sociologists

Navigating the Federal Screening Process

Some people might claim that you would need to major in "Getting a Federal Job" in order to seek a position in the federal government. The fact is that while getting a job in government can be a complex process, there is no "gatekeeper" trying to keep you out of the system. Indeed, the federal government has taken extraordinary steps to use the Internet to inform people about how to find the right federal job, and has even made it possible to do all of your job searching as well as applying online. It still can be a disconcerting process, but when one remembers that the government is the largest employer in the country, it must not be impossible! Simply put, the federal application and screening process requires skill and care. That certainly may help to weed out those who are easily discouraged, have difficulty doing research, or find forms and documents an impossible challenge. The federal employment process probably does play a small part in self-selecting good candidates. All you have to learn is enough to make the system work for you.

Federal workers are classified into two major groups. First are those paid according to the General Schedule (GS), largely the white collar, professional, administrative, scientific, clerical, and technical employees. This is the category offering employment that most college graduates will find attractive. The other classification is trade and labor, which employs those who support the efforts of the armed forces. These individuals are paid under the Federal Wage System (WG).

Salaries in governmental jobs, except in some specific areas, tend to be higher than competitive private-sector jobs. This makes the government attractive as an employer, increases its pool of candidates, and allows it to skim the cream off the top, selecting the best and most qualified. A recently published General Schedule (GS) pay scale is included later in this chapter. Entry-level positions for most college graduates begin at the GS-5 or GS-7 level.

Applying for a Federal Job

The federal application process became dramatically easier about ten years ago but still demands more information than many private-sector employers require. Nevertheless, you can apply for most federal jobs with a résumé that you create or by filling out the Optional Application for Federal Employment (OF 612). While the federal government still demands more information than many private sector employers concerning your education, work experience, and personal background, the informational demands have been scaled down, and in many cases, personal questions are not requested until you are a finalist for the position.

If you decide to apply for a job with a résumé, it is very important that it cover all the information asked for in the OF 612. Even if you are not sure at this point if you are committed to applying for a federal job, it may be a useful exercise nonetheless to complete an OF 612. Doing so will give you an opportunity to organize and categorize your educational and work experience.

One of the most exciting developments is that the federal government's OPM has made it possible to apply for federal jobs online. The USAJOBS site, at usajobs.opm.gov, contains very detailed information on federal jobs, including listings and step-by-step descriptions of the process. At the USAJOBS site you can access their "Résumé Builder" to create a résumé to use when applying for federal jobs. You can also apply directly for the hundreds of jobs posted. It is still up to you to identify the exact job that you are applying for, but that's easily accomplished using the job search engine. In other words, you cannot simply fill out an online form and wait for Uncle Sam to contact you with your dream job! But with a little effort you can put yourself in the running for an interesting job almost anywhere on the planet.

After you have passed the first screening process you will still have other paperwork to complete. Before you can actually be hired, you will be asked to complete the Declaration of Federal Employment. This form determines your suitability for federal employment, and is largely concerned with personal questions of felonies, loan defaults, and so forth. Though you may be asked to complete this declaration form at any time, it is often requested of final applicants for a position. And depending on the nature of the job there may be additional steps toward securing employment, particularly if you are working in an area that affects national security. In addition, if you are male, older than eighteen, and born after December 31, 1959, you will also have to show that you have registered with the Selective Service System (or have an exemption).

The federal government and civil service jobs in general can provide solid employment prospects, but competition is keen. You will need to ensure that your résumé document is competitively professional, error-free, and as explicit about your experience and qualifications as you can make it. Government jobs can provide excellent, highly competitive incomes, superior working conditions, and, to many who are employed in this sector, an ambiance and atmosphere no different from any other sophisticated major employer. Your effort in the application process, however challenging, is well worth it.

Federal Departments and Agencies

Previously, governmental agencies known to hire large numbers of college graduates, regardless of major, were listed. Some of the larger federal agencies and departments that hire workers with an educational background specifically in sociology include the Department of Agriculture, the Substance Abuse and Mental Health Services Administration (Health and Human Services), the Drug Enforcement Administration (Justice), the Environmental Protection Agency, the U.S. Customs Service (Treasury), and the United States Information Agency. Federal mailing addresses and telephone numbers for personnel offices change frequently, so the most reliable way to find the current contact numbers is to go to the agencies' websites, which are updated frequently.

Department of Agriculture (USDA). This department and its divisions serve all Americans daily to improve farm income, to expand overseas markets for farm products, and to assure consumers of an adequate food supply at reasonable prices. The department works to safeguard the wholesomeness of our food supply through inspection of processing plants, and ensures food quality through voluntary food-grading services. By nutrition education, the USDA helps consumers choose nourishing foods and the most for their food dollar. It also provides the lower income groups with better diets through food assistance programs. The Department of Agriculture is a highly decentralized organization with a permanent workforce of approximately 95,000 employees in all states of the union and several foreign countries. It recruits B.S. and B.A. graduates in sociology for positions in personnel management and as management analysts.

For more information go to usda.gov.

Substance Abuse and Mental Health Services Administration (SAMHSA). This administration is part of the U.S. Department of Health and Human Services. SAMHSA is the lead federal agency in the national effort to control and treat alcohol and drug problems and to treat mental and emotional illnesses. The agency conducts clinical and biochemical research in its own laboratories and supports research by scientists who work in a variety of disciplines in universities, medical schools, and hospitals, as well as drug abuse and mental health treatment centers. In addition, SAMHSA provides support through a block grant that allocates federal funds to be managed by the states and to help them establish and operate alcohol, drug abuse, and mental health programs. The agency also distributes information to health professionals and the public. It employs approximately 550 individuals such as physicians, psychologists, sociologists, social workers, research scientists, and educators.

For more information go to samhsa.gov.

Drug Enforcement Administration (DEA). The DEA in the Department of Justice is the principal federal law enforcement agency involved in combating drug abuse. The agency hires both bachelor's and master's degree holders in sociology to work as intelligence research specialists at the GS 5, 7, and 9 levels. (GS-5 and GS-7 are generally pay levels reserved for recent college graduates with or without experience. GS-9 is most often used to recognize either an advanced degree and/or significant work history in the field.) The DEA was established to control narcotics and drug abuse more effectively through enforcement and prevention. In carrying out its mission, the DEA cooperates with other federal agencies and with foreign as well as state and local governments, private industry, and other organizations. Its objectives are to reach all levels of the source of supply and to seize the greatest possible quantity of illegal drugs before they reach the user. To achieve its mission, the DEA has stationed highly trained agents along the numerous routes of illicit traffic, both in the United States and in foreign countries.

For more information go to dea.gov.

Environmental Protection Agency (EPA). Nearly 18,000 people work for the EPA in numerous locations throughout the country. Sociology majors at both the undergraduate- and graduate-degree level are sought by the EPA for positions as environmental protection specialists. The mission of the EPA is to protect the health and welfare of the American people by preventing and cleaning up pollution hazards. The EPA is engaged in an all-out effort to:

• Restore America's waters
• Reduce air pollution
• Clean up hazardous waste sites
• Formulate a comprehensive approach to other environmental problems including the manufacture, use, and disposal of chemicals (pesticides and other potentially hazardous substances), radiation, and solid waste

The agency tries to accomplish its mission systematically by integrating its various activities of research, monitoring, standard setting, and enforcement. Overall, the EPA strives to formulate and implement policies that lead to a compatible balance between the often deleterious effects of human activities and the efforts of natural systems to support and nurture life.

To apply for a job at the EPA one must have computer access, as the only way to be considered for most positions is to go through the agency's own Internet-based system, ezhire@epa. Paper applications are not accepted except in cases of extreme hardship.

For more information, go to epa.gov.

U.S. Customs Service. More than 14,000 highly trained and dedicated employees make up the Department of the Treasury's U.S. Customs Service. This service hires sociology majors at the bachelor's and master's degree level for a large number of occupations, with most employees working in one of the 300 ports of entry along our land and sea borders.

The U.S. Customs Service provides the country with its second largest source of income, returning $22.1 billion to the treasury in 2001. Along with working to stop drug trafficking and money laundering, the Customs Service protects the American public as well as labor and business by enforcing trademark, copyright, and patent privileges. Modern computer technology and communications are used extensively to facilitate the processing and security screening of the more than 1.3 million passengers entering the United States by air, land, or sea each day. Merchandise processing is being streamlined through the use of sophisticated automation, and science and analytical research assist customs officers in their efforts to stop illegal and fraudulent activities. Increasing emphasis is being placed on the investigation of schemes that defraud the U.S. government of rightful revenue, on the illicit transportation of currency, and on export violations including the illegal shipment of arms and technology abroad.

For more information, go to customs.gov.

Office of Homeland Security. The Office of Homeland Security was established in 2001 to develop and coordinate a comprehensive national strategy to protect the United States from terrorist threats and attacks. The office works with federal, state, and local governments, collecting information and ensuring that national preparedness programs and activities are developed and regularly evaluated.

Although the Office of Homeland Security itself is not a major hiring organization, serving primarily as a site for coordinating the efforts of other government agencies, the federal OPM has stepped up efforts to recruit individuals for positions in all aspects of homeland readiness and security. These include positions with the Border Patrol, U.S. Capitol Police, the U.S. Coast Guard, the Federal Bureau of Investigation (FBI), the Federal Emergency Management Agency (FEMA), the Food and Drug Administration (FDA), and the Transportation Security Administration. Other agencies are also increasing their staffs in order to meet the new standards of security.

For more information about positions supporting homeland readiness and security, go to usajobs.opm.gov.

For more information about the Office of Homeland Security, go to whitehouse.gov.

Definition of the Career Path

Your advancement as a sociologist within your federal position will be a function of your time in the position and any advanced education you may undertake. For example, candidates for the GS-7 and above rank must have either professional experience or graduate education (or a combination of both) in addition to the basic requirements (undergraduate degree in sociology with some course work in sociological research methods). This professional experience or graduate work must be directly related to sociology.

In addition to the basic requirements, the following professional experience is required for grades GS-7 and above:

Grade	Minimum Professional Experience (years)
GS-7	1
GS-9	2
GS-11 and above	3

In addition to the experience and the basic requirements, the following educational requirements exist for grades GS-7 and above:

Grade	Minimum Educational Requirements
GS-7	One full academic year of graduate education
GS-9	Master's or equivalent degree or two full years of graduate education
GS-11	Doctoral degree (Ph.D. or equivalent) or three full years of graduate education

Entry-level career opportunities in the federal government are widely advertised, and detailed job specifications are available for all but the most classified occupations. Although the application process may initially appear to be challenging, the screening and interviewing processes are fair and impartial, and diversity is welcomed and encouraged. Entry-level positions are classified according to government pay grades and promotions, and advancement opportunities are clearly indicated. Unlike many civilian occupations, the career path in most governmental jobs can be well defined. During your interview process you should be prepared to discuss with representatives of the agency or department you are applying to the career path possibilities from your entry-level beginning.

Working Conditions

It's truly impossible to make any generalizations about where people work in the federal government. Truly any working situation in the private sector can be found in duplicate in the public sector, and indeed there are thousands of federal employees on loan to private sector employers as consultants. Federal employees work in offices, hospitals, laboratories, aircraft hangars, warehouses, shipyards, construction sites, or outdoors in national parks or forests, even on Arctic research stations! Some work in very structured environments, some in very relaxed work settings, while still others may be involved in hazardous or stressful conditions.

It is difficult and not particularly responsible to try to make generalizations about the largest employer in the United States. Certainly, it has been made clear in this section that the application process, even learning about job openings, is an indication of the size and complexity of the employer. But once hired, is it so different than any other job? Yes and no. The federal government shares many of the advantages and disadvantages of a very, very large employer. There is bureaucracy, red tape, some forced mobility, and some loss of personalization. There are also excellent salaries, benefits, career advancement, and training opportunities. Mobility may be an attraction for some. Many minorities have declared that the federal government offers them the most level playing field for success. The advantages of the federal system may be seen by some as disadvantages—the regularity and stability of government employment, for instance.

Many a federal employee will tell you that the working conditions of his or her job are no different from the private sector. Alternative work schedules, including flextime and compressed work schedules, are available to many. Some government agencies are even experimenting with flexible schedules and telecommuting to allow workers to work at home. Many larger federal sites have on-site day care for working parents. Most government jobs make fewer out-of-hours demands on their staff than private sector jobs do. Most federal agencies (more than 60 percent) have some type of Quality of Work Life or Employee Involvement program that encourages employee participation at all levels for the purposes of improving efficiency, productivity, and working conditions. Some issues of working conditions that surface in any conversation on federal employment include job security, bureaucracy, politics, and public opinion.

Job Security. Government jobs become more appealing during times of economic instability. They provide stability, as well as a sense of purpose. While the salaries in public-sector work are often lower than those in the private sector, the predictable schedule of promotions and raises, as well as the excellent benefits, make government jobs a logical choice for many. While there has been some elimination of government departments over time, the more recent picture is one of security and growth. Indeed, with 53 percent of federal employees becoming eligible for retirement in the next five years, there could be as many as 954,000 job openings by the middle of this decade.[2]

The stability and regularity of government salaries are seen by some as an advantage and by others as a distinct disadvantage. If the economy does well or if an individual employee excels dramatically in his or her job, the private sector can respond with increases in salary. This is not possible in a federal job.

Bureaucracy. Federal employment will take a long time to live down complaints of bureaucracy. The truth is, just as the federal government has streamlined and dramatically simplified its employment practices, it is paying equal attention to unnecessary paperwork, rules, and constraints in every other aspect of its business. Innovation, minimizing red tape, and risk taking are equally valued by the federal sector and private employers.

Politics. Without a doubt, the overall shape and drive of government is responsive to the political party in office. This response, however, is rather diffuse and slow. New administrations can bring about large-scale changes in government management, but many day-to-day decisions are not affected by political considerations. Federal employees are no more political than any other group of employees, though unlike their private-sector counterparts, they may pay more attention to news of the political process.

Public Opinion. In general the public has not had a very positive image of federal employees and the jobs they do. One reason lies in the fact that it is often "invisible" work. The federal sector's efforts don't have the visibility of the private sector—which uses mass media to single out star performers and successful organizations—and employees are apt not to be perceived as interesting or as active in their field. Because the relationship of the federal budget to income taxes is always a subject of public debate, federal employees are seen by some as a burden on the tax rate. On the other hand, recent events have made the public more open to seeing the benefits of having a strong, organized federal government, particularly when it comes to issues such as mobilizing for national defense.

Training and Qualifications

Let's examine the government classification of sociologist (GS-184) as a good example of what training and qualifications are expected of an entry-level federal employee in this field.

Description of the Work: Sociologists employ established sociological methods and techniques to perform work that relates to (1) the culture, structure, or functioning of groups, organizations, or social systems, (2) the relationships between groups, organizations, or social systems, (3) collective human behavior in social situations, and (4) the demographic characteristics and ecological patterning of communities and societies. The work requires a professional knowledge of sociology, sociological theory, and methods of social research. Sociologists also interpret research results, articulate the implications of research for policy, and administer programs making use of research results.

Basic Requirements of All Grades: Candidates for all positions must have successfully completed at least one of the following basic requirements.

- A four-year program in an accredited college or university leading to a bachelor's degree or higher that includes or is supplemented by at least 24 credit hours of sociology, with course work including the theory and methods of social research.
- Courses in an accredited college or university consisting of 24 semester hours in sociology, with course work including the theory and methods of social research, plus additional experience or education. This combination will total four years of education and experience and give the applicant a technical knowledge comparable to that described in the first point.

While the specifications for sociologist require a sociology degree, as previously noted, the OPM has categorized a number of jobs that are open to any qualified graduate with a four-year degree. This includes positions such as environmental protection specialist (GS-028), budget analyst (GS-560), archives specialist (GS-1421), administrative officer (GS-341), manpower developer (GS-142), and many, many others.

Even for those positions requiring a four-year degree, frequently, a generous range of degrees is acceptable. In Chapter 11, you read of numerous opportunities for using your degree in the personnel management function of private businesses and organizations. These same jobs exist in the federal government, as well. For example, the entire range of personnel officers (GS-200, including specialist level positions in personnel management, personnel staffing, salary and wage administration, employee relations, labor relations, and employee development) requires a four-year degree from an accredited college or university, the ability to communicate effectively both orally and in writing, analytical ability, and a general understanding of the system and methods and administrative machinery that accomplishes the work of any organization.

Earnings

Job security and competitive pay are among the top attractions for many seeking federal employment. There are eight predominant pay systems. Approximately half of the workforce is under the General Schedule (GS) pay scale, 20 percent are paid under the Postal Service rates, and about 10 percent are paid under the Prevailing Rate Schedule Wage Grade (WG) Classification. The additional pay systems include the Executive Schedule, Foreign Service, Nonappropriated Fund Instrumentalities scales, and Veterans Health Administration.

While the private sector offers higher salaries for some specialized positions, particularly in fields such as medicine, engineering, and computer technology, government salaries are still gauged to be competitive. One of the more welcome aspects of a government job is that pay raises, advancement, and promotion is determined by largely objective criteria, and your ability to grow in your career and be rewarded for that growth is explicitly outlined. Benefits and pension plans are competitive and, in some work situations, unique.

The most common federal pay scale you will encounter is the GS. You will frequently see positions listed with a GS pay-scale level, jobs for entry-level college graduates usually at GS-5 or GS-7. Promotion is usually two grades at once until GS-11; at that point, each promotion opportunity results in one grade at a time. Within each grade are steps; these within-grade increases occur based on time on the job. Most people start at Step 1 of their GS grade level. For some kinds of positions (especially those in short supply) there are higher salaries, and for some locations (Los Angeles, New York City, San Francisco) cost-of-living differentials are added to the base salary.

The chart on page 213 shows the GS Salaries for January 1, 2002.

Career Outlook

Federal employment is generally not as severely affected by cyclical fluctuations in the economy as is employment in many private sector industries such

SALARY TABLE 2002-GS
2002 GENERAL SCHEDULE
INCORPORATING A 3.6% GENERAL INCREASE
Effective January 2002

Annual Rates by Grade and Step

	1	2	3	4	5	6	7	8	9	10	Within Grade Increase Amounts
GS-1	$14,757	$15,249	$15,740	$16,228	$16,720	$17,009	$17,492	$17,981	$18,001	$18,456	VARIES
2	$16,592	$16,985	$17,535	$18,001	$18,201	$18,736	$19,271	$19,806	$20,341	$20,876	VARIES
3	$18,103	$18,706	$19,309	$19,912	$20,515	$21,118	$21,721	$22,324	$22,927	$23,530	$603
4	$20,322	$20,999	$21,676	$22,353	$23,030	$23,707	$24,384	$25,061	$25,738	$26,415	$677
5	$22,737	$23,495	$24,253	$25,011	$25,769	$26,527	$27,285	$28,043	$28,801	$29,559	$758
6	$25,344	$26,189	$27,034	$27,879	$28,724	$29,569	$30,414	$31,259	$32,104	$32,949	$845
7	$28,164	$29,103	$30,042	$30,981	$31,920	$32,859	$33,798	$34,737	$35,676	$36,615	$939
8	$31,191	$32,231	$33,271	$34,311	$35,351	$36,391	$37,431	$38,471	$39,511	$40,551	$1,040
9	$34,451	$35,599	$36,747	$37,895	$39,043	$40,191	$41,339	$42,487	$43,635	$44,783	$1,148
10	$37,939	$39,204	$40,469	$41,734	$42,999	$44,264	$45,529	$46,794	$48,059	$49,324	$1,265
11	$41,684	$43,073	$44,462	$45,851	$47,240	$48,629	$50,018	$51,407	$52,796	$54,185	$1,389
12	$49,959	$51,624	$53,289	$54,954	$56,619	$58,284	$59,949	$61,614	$63,279	$64,944	$1,665
13	$59,409	$61,389	$63,369	$65,349	$67,329	$69,309	$71,289	$73,269	$75,249	$77,229	$1,980
14	$70,205	$72,545	$74,885	$77,225	$79,565	$81,905	$84,245	$86,585	$88,925	$91,265	$2,340
15	$82,580	$85,333	$88,086	$90,839	$93,592	$96,345	$99,098	$101,851	$104,604	$107,357	$2,753

as construction and manufacturing. However, shifting national priorities and concerns can have a dramatic effect on staffing levels. Each presidential administration may have different public policy priorities that result in greater levels of federal employment in some programs and declines in others. Layoffs, called reductions in force, have occurred in the past; however, they are uncommon and generally affect relatively few workers. Some extraordinary circumstances, such as military engagement, will also affect the number of people hired by the federal government.

On the whole, however, employment in the federal government remains relatively stable over the course of time. It is a particularly appealing field for entry-level workers, especially because promotion to senior positions is generally done with existing staff. The opportunities for those hoping to enter the public forces at a more senior level will depend on whether they can bring to the table particular skills that are in short supply within the existing government ranks.

Although entry-level employment remains the best start to a federal career, it is good to remember that the government is a very competitive employer whose labor force by all standards is better educated and more technically astute with higher language and math skills than the workforce as a whole. In spite of the number of positions available to any four-year graduate, those individuals with scientific, computer, and other quantitative skills definitely have an edge over others.

A sociology major considering a governmental position can look at jobs that value his or her specific degree. However if you want to enhance your attractiveness as a job candidate for a federal position you might consider acquiring some additional and more technical skills while in college. Use your college time to take advantage of courses such as statistics or a research design course if available. These would make an impressive addition to your degree. Or try to enroll in some computer courses. Take more than the basic introduction course. Enroll in some systems design courses or some IT courses. Talk to a computer science advisor about what two or three courses would work well together for you as a nonmajor.

These are simply two possible options that will enhance your attractiveness to a federal hiring agency. Experience is also important. As you have noticed in the discussion of pay scales, if you can document some related experience you are not only more competitive but you are also entering the government workforce at a higher scale.

Strategy for Finding Federal Jobs

Before doing anything else, identify the federal job titles that are right for your combination of education and experience. Candidates for federal jobs must apply for specific job titles. At any given time the government is hiring for just about every position, so the best way to learn exactly what job titles you want to apply for is to look and see what positions are open. On the OPM's USAJOBS website, you can search for job openings (which contain detailed job descriptions) under a number of categories, including professional, entry-level professional, clerical and technician, and worker-trainee. Say you were to begin your search with entry-level professional positions. You would then be able to narrow it down by field, such as social science and welfare or medical and health. Another excellent source is the *Federal Jobs Digest*, which has an online component at jobsfed.com. The free database lists more than 10,000 federal jobs and is updated daily.

The OPM has moved toward a Web-based hiring process, and several agencies (such as the EPA) will only accept applications submitted online. It is expected that in the coming years this trend will only increase, hence it is in your interests to become familiar with the online application process. It is important to find out whether one is to apply through the OPM or directly with the particular agency. The careers section on federal Web pages will assist you in determining the proper route of application.

This process is considerably easier than the past practices of the federal hiring process. One must identify the position and submit an application that contains the particular job title and announcement number.

As might be expected, each job application will have different requirements, depending on the level, agency, and location. Thus it will not be possible to submit a one-size-fits-all application for government jobs, just as that would not be possible or practical in the private sector. Instead, pay close attention to the specific requests for information required for each position you are applying for.

Once your application has been processed through the preliminary stages, you will be required to have a formal job interview. There may also be examinations or tests to fulfill the skills requirements for any given position.

The end result—obtaining one of the many excellent government jobs for individuals with sociology degrees—more than justifies the means. Admittedly, the process includes a challenging and sometimes frustratingly detailed and complex set of applications, job postings, and hiring rules and regulations. It can become a job in itself just to master the various systems. Try to remember that the government, whether it be federal, state, or local, is made up of millions of people just like you. They are interested in your application. So if the going gets tough, and it probably will, ask for help.

Directly Contact the Department. Successful governmental job seekers have indicated one of the best ways to break through the bureaucracy is to personalize it. Even though the application process is increasingly computerized, this does not preclude speaking with personnel representatives in various agencies. You will also find that most of the individual agency websites of different government departments contain very informative sections on seeking a career with that agency. There you will find contact names and numbers, as well as helpful hints for creating a successful application.

Review All Federal Job Sources. The government job market is unlike any other. Consequently, your job-search strategies will be different as well. Your first task will be to make certain that you are seeing as many of the available job postings as you can. While the OPM's USAJOBS site is by far the largest listing of federal job openings, other sites can help you narrow your search or suggest other routes to follow. A persistent job seeker will check each of the relevant sources. You will become familiar with each source and determine how often new jobs are listed so that you can create a postings review schedule for yourself.

Try as many of the services that follow as your time and budget allow. One excellent place to start is with the Federal Jobs Digest Matching Service that will help shortcut the long process of identifying where you would find your best government job fit. The government job sites are free to use.

Federal Jobs Digest Matching Service
Federal Jobs Digest
220 White Plains Rd.
Tarrytown, NY 10591
(914) 366-0333
jobsfed.com

This service matches your background to federal requirements. You send in a copy of your résumé (either by E-mail or regular mail) and receive a list of job titles and grade levels for which you qualify. Federal job descriptions and qualification statements are provided for every job title that the service identifies for you. The fee is $35. Use the information to streamline your job search using the federal application channels.

Office of Personnel Management. The OPM is the source of employment and listings for many federal government positions, but with decentralization, many agencies and departments can hire independently. The OPM can offer counsel on these questions and remains the best source on the application process for government jobs in general. The USAJOBS website is usajobs.opm.gov. The OPM also runs an automated telephone system that allows you to access information on current job openings.

StudentJobs.Gov. StudentJobs.Gov is a joint project between the OPM and the U.S. Department of Education's Student Financial Assistance Office. Most federal agencies post their openings on this website, including positions that are available to you while you are still in college or graduate school. This resource also provides a "gateway" to agencies that are hiring.

Possible Employers

In the federal government, some specific agencies have indicated that they are interested in hiring workers with sociology degrees, while others express a more general need for four-year college graduates of all majors. Earlier in this chapter you found profiles of six federal agencies specifically interested in the sociology major. Those agencies include: Department of Agriculture, the SAMHSA (Health and Human Services), the DEA (justice), the EPA, the U.S. Customs Service (Treasury), and the United States Information Agency.

Agencies hiring the largest numbers of college graduates (any degree) include the Departments of Veterans Affairs, Housing and Urban Development (HUD), Defense, Agriculture, Interior, Commerce, Transportation, Education, and Energy. College graduates may also find work in special government agencies such as the Peace Corps, National Institutes of Health (NIH), and the National Institute on Aging. Each governmental unit has its own personnel department, and you would be best advised to directly contact the ones you would like to work for. The following is a list of several federal agencies that might be of interest to sociology majors. Be advised that federal government addresses change with remarkable frequency, so it is best to check on the website of a particular agency to get the correct and up-to-date contact information.

- Administration for Children and Families: acf.dhhs.gov
- Administration on Aging: aoa.dhhs.gov
- Bureau of Prisons: bop.gov
- Bureau of the Census: census.gov
- Centers for Disease Control and Prevention: cdc.gov
- Commission on Civil Rights: usccr.gov
- Department of Agriculture: usda.gov
- Department of Commerce: doc.gov
- Department of Defense: defenselink.mil

- Department of Education: ed.gov
- Department of Energy: energy.gov
- Department of Health and Human Services: os.dhhs.gov
- Department of Justice: usdoj.gov
- Department of State: state.gov
- Department of Transportation: dot.gov
- Department of Veterans Affairs: va.gov
- Drug Enforcement Administration: dea.gov
- Environmental Protection Agency: epa.gov
- National Institutes of Health: nih.gov
- Peace Corps: peacecorps.gov

Possible Job Titles

As you delve into the process of investigating government jobs, you will begin to create your own customized list of job titles for each of the three sectors of public employment. You'll be surprised and gratified at the range of job titles that your sociology degree qualifies you to fill. We've already talked about some of the possible jobs that the government considers appropriate for certain majors, but the truth is that there is truly almost no limit to your options once you step into the public sector. Here we present a few more teasers just to get you started thinking about the spectrum of choices before you.

Academic exchange specialist	Legislative aide
Customs inspector	Management analyst
Employee development specialist	Peace Corps volunteer
Human rights worker	Personnel management specialist
Intelligence research specialist	Position classification specialist
Labor and employee relations specialist	Program specialist
	Writer/editor

State and Local Government

Often, when people consider a job in government they overlook the rich source of options available at the state and local level. But it is at this level that some of the more engaging and fulfilling work is to be found, bringing your background in sociology to bear on the issues affecting your own community. For example, a large city government working to resuscitate its downtown area may desire someone with sociology experience to help develop trade and to market the attractiveness of housing possibilities in the center city. A state economic development office seeking industry to locate within their boundaries might develop a task force to identify potential workers who might attract new industry. The individual who brings a knowledge of sociology to these kinds of teams provides an irreplaceable service.

The need for workers with sociology skills has become much more pronounced at all levels of civil service employment, including states, cities, towns, and municipalities. Police officers in even midsized cities may find growing communities of people whose principal language is not English. These communities have a structure and value system that needs a sociology graduate's sensitivity and education to communicate to others who may not understand their neighbors.

State Government

With the exception of foreign policy and defense, state jobs mimic the federal level to a remarkable degree. Finding a job with state governments is similar to finding one with the federal government. Depending on the size of the state and the bureaucracy established, the system may be as complex and multitiered as the federal government. However, unlike the federal government there is apt to be a central personnel office (usually in the capitol) and branch personnel offices that list all state openings and can provide specifications sheets for each of these positions. These spec sheets list required qualifications and salary schedules and tell you whether or not a test is part of the application process.

State governments have become increasingly professionalized; consequently, competition for positions is keen and the candidates often exceptional. While local governments emphasize elementary and secondary education, health, and police and fire services, state governments emphasize higher education, health, highway, and correctional services.

Visit a state personnel office, learn how to file a formal application, read the current job posting, and then stay abreast of additional postings by fax, phone, or periodic visits. In some states, you can file one application and indicate the kinds of jobs you want to be considered for. Your application will become part of those applicant pools for a period of time.

If you know where you want to work in state government, visit that location, meet the people associated with the office, and express your interest.

Bring a résumé or arrange for an informational interview (see Chapter 4). However, a word of caution is due here. This is best done ahead of any formal job posting. To make such a visit after a job is announced would be disadvantageous for you and uncomfortable and anxiety provoking for personnel in the state office.

The state personnel office can be of great assistance in explaining the various state agencies and directing you to more information about the mission of each of them. Remember, their job is to secure the best qualified applicants for the state, so they're interested in raising your level of awareness and appreciation of state government.

Local Government

There are more than 80,000 government and public sector agencies throughout the United States, employing more than 10 million people. It not only fits your sociology degree in the kinds of jobs available, but also represents a promising employment market.

Many different local government institutions make up the crazy patchwork quilt of democracy in this country, and you will need to conduct your own research on the who, where, and what of each local governmental unit in order to understand them. Fortunately, most local government jobs are advertised and communicated to the general public.

Typically, you will be looking at five categories of employers in local government:

1. **Counties:** Used as a local unit of government throughout the country except in Connecticut, Rhode Island, and the District of Columbia.
2. **Municipalities:** Called cities, towns, villages, or boroughs, these urban areas incorporated within or sometimes separate from their resident county function as governmental units on their own.
3. **Townships:** A political subdivision of a county found in twenty states in the eastern and midwestern part of the country, they can be called towns, plantations, or locations, and are governed by elected boards.
4. **School Districts:** Existing both dependently and independently, these exist in an overwhelming majority of states (not Virginia, Maryland, North Carolina, Hawaii, Alaska, or the District of Columbia) to administer school systems.

5. **Special Districts:** Otherwise termed boards, authorities, or commissions, these government units often focus on only one service. They administer services such as cemeteries, water, sewage, fire protection, parks and recreation, flood control, highways, and libraries.

Nowhere will your curiosity, perseverance, and research skills serve you better than in your exploration of jobs in local governments. Unlike the federal and state systems, local governments conform to no overall system. Each is different, and informal aspects of the job search (talking directly to local officials) may be far more important here than the formal application process.

The composition, names of offices, and structure of these various governing organizations is idiosyncratic. The different structures have evolved over time, and the only similarities tend to be in the functions of local government. Typical functions include education, health care, highway maintenance, police, fire, parks and recreation, sewage, and water quality.

There is no one strategy for approaching this diversity of local government organizations. Some small towns' hiring practices are very informal, and a résumé, letter, and request for a formal interview might actually disqualify you. Other governmental organizations have job postings, application processes, and pay-scale systems that rival their federal and state counterparts.

You must assess each local government structure individually and decide on your best approach. Once again, share what you are looking for with people, ask lots of questions, and use local reference sources (such as the local library and their staff) to educate yourself on the kinds of jobs available, what it might take to fill them, and the type of application process used.

Strategy for Finding State and Local Jobs

Where are the jobs? As you've seen in the discussion on federal job sources, knowledge is power, and the federal government, for all its complexity, is manageable. State and local government jobs can be found through national, regional, and local sources. State and local government jobs are grouped together here because many of the sources combine these two categories. Your very best bet for state government jobs is the state employment office and its branches, which produce job listings and specification sheets for all state government positions. Your college career office may be on a mailing list for state job listings. Both state and local jobs are also advertised regionally in the want-ad section of the newspaper.

One of your easiest sources of job listings to access is the telephone directory. Many county, city, and state personnel offices maintain an employment hot line or employment information job line. And it should be no surprise that many local governments post information regarding job openings on their websites. Check the telephone book under the particular governmental unit and call the number. The following is another source to help uncover all of the state and local jobs.

The Municipal Yearbook
International City/County Management Association
777 N. Capitol St. NE
Washington, DC 20002-4201
(800) 745-8780.

This is not a job posting, but a comprehensive directory of municipal officials and organizations. It costs $84.95 plus $5 shipping and is published annually in May.

Paperwork Is Critical at the State and Local Level. The application and hiring process in public employment is often more heavily dependent, in the early stages, on the careful submission of paperwork. As a recent college graduate, you would have the advantage of on-campus recruiting, numerous job postings in your career office, and many posters and fliers from hiring organizations eager to interview new college graduates. Although public employment relies more heavily on application forms and résumés to initially screen their applicants, once the interview process is initiated there is little difference between public and private employment screening.

Knowing this, you should appreciate the importance of paying particular attention to the application forms and their completion. Make several copies of every form you receive and work up a rough draft of every application and form before submission. Many application forms demand frustratingly long responses in very small spaces, often requiring attaching additional sheets. You'll want to work out your responses on a copy of your original form before completing the finished product. Appearance is critical as is the thoroughness of your information.

Follow-Up. The people who staff offices in the public sector are no different from anyone else; they're just people. Once you've applied for a position and your paperwork is complete, don't be shy about telephoning, stopping in, or writing a brief note to inquire about your application or the hiring process for the position you are seeking. Applicants frequently say to me "But, I don't want to be a pest!" Unless someone specifically tells you that your contact is inappropriate or unnecessary, maintain a professionally active interest in the position you are seeking. It is just as important to follow up on your federal, state, or local government application as it is in the private sector. Make contact to verify that your materials were received, to demonstrate that you are actively involved in your job search, or simply to remind them of your qualifications and availability for employment. If you haven't yet visited the office or agency you would like to work for, and you are able to do so, now is the time to put a face with one of the many applications that these offices receive. Introduce yourself, check on the status of your application, and let them see your energy and enthusiasm.

The incorrect impression is that jobs in the government sector undergo a more impersonal, formalized screening process than a similar search in the private sector. Because of the highly structured classification of employees in government, most applicants believe that once you submit your application there is little you can do but wait out the process.

The reality is that for anyone who is responsible for a hiring decision, the ultimate goal is the same—the best person for the job. While public sector employment application processes and hiring conditions are certainly more codified than in the private sector, that does not mean you cannot put a face to your application or a voice to your name with a visit or a phone call.

Possible Employers

You will need some strategy to build your list of possible employers in the specific state or local government units you may be considering for your job search. State personnel offices may list state jobs, but you'll want to contact the hiring departments directly. For a local government search, you will need to build your own personal directory of the local hiring authorities. For a national search of local government jobs, consult *The Municipal Yearbook* for addresses and telephone numbers.

Be advised that many smaller municipalities will not and cannot afford to mail job listings. Offer to send some self-addressed, stamped envelopes if that is the objection. Some state offices will maintain limited mailing lists; others require you to visit a personnel office or satellite location in person to pick up job listings. Some maintain telephone job lines that list that week's vacancies in a recording, updated weekly. In your initial contact with any employment office ask about these options so that you can stay abreast of current offerings.

Possible Job Titles

The following are possible job titles you may find in state government jobs:

Administrative assistant	Personnel coordinator
Affirmative action worker	Program aid
Analyst	Program assistant
Assistant director	Program coordinator
Assistant manager	Program monitor
Inspector	Supervisor
Investigator	

The following job titles may be found at the local level:

Administrative analyst	Office manager
Administrative assistant	Planner
Corrections staffer	Program analyst
Counselor	Program planner
Investigator	Rehabilitation counselor
Inspector	Urban planner
Juvenile court worker	

Professional Associations

Professional associations are the best-kept secret of the job search. Raising the level of professional employment in their area of expertise is one of the goals of most of these organizations. No matter which occupation you choose to enter, at least one association will exist to serve your professional needs. Some of these associations will be able to assist you by providing possible leads for networking or actual job listings. Look for those groups that have membership directories or some type of job listing service. For the most part you will have to join an association to take full advantage of related services, but if you know which field you want to enter, consider it an investment in your future. If you're not sure what type of governmental work you want to seek, review the following list of government-related associations to get an idea of what's out there.

American Federation of State, County and Municipal Employees
1625 L St. NW
Washington, DC 20036
Members/Purpose: AFL-CIO
Publications: *AFSCME Leader, Public Employee*

American Foreign Service Association
2101 E St. NW
Washington, DC 20037
Members/Purpose: Associate membership is open to individuals and
  international organizations and corporations interested in foreign affairs,
  international trade, and economic policy.
Training: Conducts international conferences and symposia.
Publications: *Foreign Service Journal, Directory of Retired Members*

Association of Inspectors General
P.O. Box 94095
Baton Rouge, LA 70804
Members/Purpose: Consists of inspectors general and professional staff in
  their agencies, as well as other officials responsible for inspection and
  oversight with respect to public, not-for-profit, and independent sector
  organizations.
Publications: Newsletter

**Association of Management Analysts in State and
Local Government**
University of Pennsylvania
Fels Center of Government
3814 Walnut St.
Philadelphia, PA 19104
Members/Purpose: Management analysts from business and state and local
  government, professors, and heads of university public service institutes
  and state training institutes
Publications: Conference papers, directory of members and conferences
  attendees, *MASLIG Messenger*, workshop manual

Civil Service Employees Association
Box 125, Capitol Station
143 Washington Ave.
Albany, NY 12210

Members/Purpose: AFL-CIO. Members are state and local government employees from all public employee classifications.
Training: Conducts training and education programs
Publications: Newsletter, *Public Sector*

Federal Managers Association
1641 Prince St.
Alexandria, VA 22314-2818
Publications: *The Federal Manager, The Washington Report*

Government Finance Officers Association of U.S. and Canada
203 N. LaSalle St., Suite 2700
Chicago, IL 60601-1210
Members/Purpose: Finance officers from city, county, state, provincial, and federal governments, schools, and other special districts; retirement systems, colleges, universities, public accounting firms, financial institutions, and others in the United States and Canada interested in government finance.
Publications: *Bulletin, GAAFR Review*, newsletter, membership directory, *Public Investor, Government Finance Review*
Job Listings: See *Government Finance Officers Association Newsletter* for job listings.

International City/County Management Association
777 N. Capitol St. NE, Suite 500
Washington, DC 20002-4201
Members/Purpose: International professional and educational organization for appointed administrators and assistant administrators serving cities, counties, districts, and regions
Training: Operates ICMA Training Institute
Publications: *Municipal Yearbook*, newsletter, *Public Management*
Job Listings: *Job Opportunities Bulletin*

International Military Community Executives Association
1125 Duke St.
Alexandria, VA 22314-3513
Members/Purpose: Army, air force, marine, and coast guard personnel who manage military clubs, golf courses, and bowling centers.
Training: Conducts seminars on club management training
Publications: *MWR Today, IMCEA Annual Membership Directory*
Job Listings: Encourages recruitment activities

National Association of Black County Officials
440 First St. NW,
    Suite 500
Washington, DC 20001
Members/Purpose: Black county officials organized to provide program planning and management assistance to selected counties in the United States. Acts as a technical information exchange to develop resolutions to problems on the local and national levels.
Training: Conducts seminars
Publications: *County Compass* (quarterly), *County to County* (bimonthly)

National Association of Government Communicators
526 King St.,
    Suite 423
Alexandria, VA 22314
Members/Purpose: Government employees, retired persons, nongovernment affiliates, and students. Seeks to advance communications as an essential professional resource at every level of national, state, and local government.
Publications: *GC Magazine*
Job Listings: Maintains placement service

National Association of Government Employees
159 Burgin Pkwy.
Quincy, MA 02169
Members/Purpose: Union of civilian federal government employees with locals and members in military agencies, Internal Revenue Service, Post Office, Veterans Administration, General Services Administration, Federal Aviation Administration, and other federal agencies, as well as state and local agencies.
Training: Offers seminars
Publications: *The Fednews*

National Association of Governmental Labor Officials
44 N. Capitol St. NW,
    Suite 401
Washington, DC 20001
Members/Purpose: Elected and appointed heads of state labor departments. Seeks to assist labor officials in performing their duties and to improve employment conditions for American workers.
Publications: Membership directory, *NAGLO News*

National Association of Regional Councils
1700 K St. NW, Suite 1300
Washington, DC 20006
Members/Purpose: Interested in regionalism as an approach to meeting problems that cross local governmental boundaries, including economic development, transportation, environmental management, housing, services to the elderly, and rural development
Training: Annual convention with workshops and exhibits
Publications: *Directory of Regional Councils* (annual), *The Regionalist* (quarterly), *Regions* (bimonthly), and special reports

Society of Government Meeting Professionals
6 Clouser Rd.
Mechanicsburg, PA 17055
Members/Purpose: Individuals involved in planning government meetings on a full- or part-time basis; suppliers of services to government planners. Provides education in basic and advanced areas of meeting planning and facilities; professional contact with other government planners and suppliers knowledgeable in government contracting.
Publications: Membership directory, newsletter

Women Executives in State Government
1225 New York Ave. NW, Suite 350
Washington, DC 20005
Members/Purpose: Women executives employed in elected or appointed state government positions. Works to enhance members' skills in management, public policy development, government and business relations, and leadership.
Publications: Annual report, newsletter, membership directory
Job Listings: Operates job search assistance and referral service

Women in Municipal Government
National League of Cities
1301 Pennsylvania Ave. NW, No. 550
Washington, DC 20004
Members/Purpose: Women who are elected and appointed city officials including mayors, council members, and commissioners.
Publications: *Constituency and Member Group Report*, membership directory

13

Path 5: Social Research and Data Analysis

Picture yourself working as an entry-level researcher at an organization that is engaged in exploring drug use and related violence in the population of rural American teenagers. Your place of employment is funded by government and foundation grants; it has just received a grant from the SAMHA to gather information about which drugs are most readily available to teenagers outside of big cities, who is doing the selling, and where are narcotics being sold.

Even as simple as this research request is, it involves significant effort. Historical analysis of police logs and arrest records over many years with subjects categorized by age, family structure, educational history, juvenile justice records, and other categories will probably be required. All of this information will need to be entered into databases so that you can run correlations and analyses that will provide insight into the issues.

Your research might involve many nights as a participant observer, riding through dark roads in the backseat of a patrol car to observe drug trafficking at close hand. You may accompany police to drug houses, observe a bust, and watch suspects being arrested and handcuffed. Your study might involve actual interviews with criminal suspects and with members of the police force.

As you can see from this hypothetical scenario, a career in social research and data analysis can be one that involves a great deal of action. It is not dull, it is not a desk job, and it is not dry and dusty. It is highly social, can be very exciting, and has even been dangerous for some researchers. And it is vital to our understanding of social patterns.

In their efforts to understand different forms of social behavior, researchers use a variety of methods, procedures, and research strategies. Usually the research project begins with a definition of the problem and areas to be studied. Then all the different factors or variables must be identified and any relationships between variables expressed. Sometimes the relationship between two variables is only a generalization that must be studied to be proved empirically. Those generalizations of relationships are called *hypotheses*.

Research in sociology can be in the laboratory or in the field; it can be done by surveys or studies. Every research strategy has its advantages and disadvantages in terms of cost, time commitment, and the precision possible with any particular technique.

Research on family support programs is certainly worthwhile work, and the results of your research efforts may have broad implications. Although much social research has public approval, some may be more controversial. In addition, some methods may be seen as violating people's privacy.

Ethical issues are critical for the researcher in sociology because social research is about people's lives. Most gathering of data presents some ethical issues for the researcher, not only relating to the methods but sometimes about the implications of the findings. Frequently, controversy over social research has centered around the applications of the research as well as the means by which data are obtained. Those of you considering careers in applied research, especially in government and business, may have to confront ethical questions about the kinds of studies being undertaken and the uses to which the data are being put.

For those with an advanced degree, research careers in sociology generally come in a close second in popularity to teaching careers. In fact, if you've read Chapter 9, you understand that for those who go on to advanced degrees in sociology, teaching and research go hand in hand. Research is one of the common core career options suggested by the American Sociological Association for those holding at least a master's degree in sociology.

The research and data analysis careers discussed in this chapter are specifically those available in the private sector to the bachelor's degree candidate. Public agencies at the federal, state, and local level also provide a number of fine research jobs. For information on your job search in the federal, state, and local government sites, consult Chapter 12. Nonetheless, most of the applied research positions that will be discussed in this chapter are equally available in the public sector. For example, the position of legislative aide is frequently a research position, designing and executing studies for lawmakers or gathering and interpreting existing secondary data.

Industrial firms, research institutes, nonprofit agencies, and, of course, business are all big users of research services. Much of the research done by these organizations concerns people and how they behave. If the organization is large enough and the research department well-funded, you will find a level of professionalism that could well provide a springboard to further education and enhanced job opportunities.

For jobs in this career path you need to truly enjoy the research process and all that it entails; you need to enjoy problems and problem solving. In your own self-assessment process as outlined in Chapter 1 of this book, you may have realized that you enjoy challenges and are creative in not only seeing these challenges from different perspectives, but in solving them as well. That would be an important attribute to anyone contemplating a career in research or data analysis.

In addition to the problem solving and critical thinking required, writing is essential. Outlining research projects and expressing the relationships between variables, hypotheses, or findings requires an extensive vocabulary and a sense of style and nuance. "Elegant" is an adjective frequently used to describe not only the design of a research study but also the expression of the data in the written word. Writing facility will become even more critical as you seek to advance your career.

Technology, principally the computer and telecommunications capabilities, has accelerated not only the quantity and detail of information, but also the speed at which we can provide information to those needing it. Sociologists and those researching in sociology use the computer for just that reason. However, computers demand precision and quality. Anyone who has struggled to write even the most basic program can appreciate the painstakingly simple logic of the computer, which when accelerated and provided with multiple tasks and huge amounts of information, becomes truly awesome.

Though jobs require significant computer skills, the everyday world of the sociologist is most often uncertain, illogical, and highly qualitative. Computers and information processing, in general, introduce a strong bias toward producing and using information and criteria that may even contradict the realities they are intended to deal with.

Sociology provides so many different ways to look at the world and to rethink how we understand social life, change, and the cause and consequences of human behavior. It offers a range of research techniques from participant observation, experimental studies (both in and out of the laboratory), surveys, and field studies. These can be applied to any issue from street crime to mainstreaming and learning disabilities, to consumers' perceptions of competing products. The research function is an exciting discipline with enormous opportunities and a wide range of career paths.

Definition of the Career Path

One myth that dies hard is that research and data analysis positions are dead-end jobs. In fact, the reality is very different.

Let's take a typical example. Perhaps you leave college and take a position as research assistant with a small manufacturer in your state. You work hard (of course) and, after a few years of experience and some success, you are promoted to an associate position in the department. At this point, you would be in a particularly good position to move to another organization as a data analysis manager or database manager or, if the organization was large enough, to a position as associate or assistant director of research.

If changing organizations doesn't appeal to you, you might find opportunities for growth right at your doorstep. Perhaps you can provide your manufacturing firm with enough evidence of the impact of your research on sales, profitability, and consumer satisfaction to warrant a larger expenditure on research activities. You are given more space, more financial resources, and even, perhaps, eventually, the directorship of a new department—research! At about this time in your career, you may also be receiving strong signals from your professional colleagues or mentors that you need to continue your education to remain eligible for promotion.

Working Conditions

One of the great mistakes made about careers in research and data analysis is to think they are "behind the scenes" jobs or, even more incorrectly, desk jobs. Nothing could be farther from the truth. The variety and descriptions of the research and data analyst positions cited in this chapter should be your first indications that these are active, vital, involved positions that require energy, enthusiasm, curiosity, and, sometimes, good driving skills.

Researchers in sociology and sociologically related fields are not brought on board after a project is designed or up and running. They participate in the original thinking of any project and in every stage of project design and implementation.

Important aspects of research or data analyst positions with a bachelor's degree include:

- Collaboration
- Networking
- Customer service orientation

- Balancing multiple projects
- Supervision

Collaboration

Research is an enormous effort. Anyone working in research will tell you that even the simplest projects can consume many hours of work in planning, data gathering, and report writing. They will also tell you research is not just "done." Research is conducted for a purpose. Someone has asked a question or postulated a theory that needs evidence in order to formulate a response.

There are many roles involved in a research team. Some people on your team will design the research project, stipulating the data-gathering techniques; others will design the necessary instruments (surveys, experiments); and still others will collect the information that is passed on for others to organize and enter. Some team members will analyze that information and others will write the research findings. Yet another group may present those findings before an audience. Researchers and data analysts are an important and integral part of any project team and are included from the beginning stages of any project.

High-level involvement may come as a surprise to some who are unaware of the active role researchers and data analysts play, not only in providing support for planning needs but in helping to shape strategy. Knowledge of the organization's past experiences, successes, and failures and an ability to bring those experiences to bear on new efforts makes the information specialists important team players, and not just a behind-the-scenes resource.

Networking

Many misconceptions about researchers exist. One is that researchers are always solitary. Another is that researchers and analysts are "keepers" of information. Both of these ideas are incorrect. Research can be a very social process that relies on extensive networks of professional relationships that can help you secure the information you need quickly and efficiently. Researchers are not interested in hoarding what they learn but want to share it with others. Many researchers voluntarily send ideas, information, articles, and relevant materials along to individuals they know have an interest. Of course, owing to your own innate sense of organization as a researcher, you will build some files of your own. This may help you respond to frequent requests for the same kind of information. But you can never acquire all the information you need for a project ahead of time. The information specialist doesn't amass information and then distribute it as requested. You will have to generate the research you need for a project through your own efforts and the combined efforts of your contacts and whatever networks you can develop.

Networking can be a specific job demand, as in the position above, or it can be a skill you need to develop in order to secure the information you are seeking. In providing a historical analysis of window curtain treatments over the past ten years to determine trends in window dressing for a curtain manufacturer, you may first seek historical sales figures from the sales division and then rely on your computer department for processing and printing that data. You may do some research outside the organization on competitor sales and employ the services of a librarian or commercial data-retrieval firm. You may go to a library yourself to read and view advertisements in older magazines. You might get really creative and decide to watch videotapes of popular television shows to observe how window treatments were designed to reflect the model families of decades past. Very often your work is the product of cooperation among many individuals, and information specialists maintain elaborate and well-developed networks of contacts to provide them with the information they need.

Customer Service Orientation

Research and data analysis is a people business. So the researcher needs to respond to clients (customers) in a positive, service-oriented, and professional manner. Research and data analysis is crucial to many projects. So, get ready to be popular and busy! To have fun doing this, you need to understand that you are the specialist in information, and those seeking your help are your customers. They can't always appreciate the work behind their requests or even, sometimes, the feasibility of providing the information they want. You'll enjoy your job a great deal more if you can avoid getting angry or frustrated that people don't understand everything that's involved in what you do. Just remember, the woman or man who can provide on-target information when it's needed is going to be a vital member of any organization. You'll be even more prized if you can provide that information quickly and in a manner that people can appreciate and understand but not be burdened with all the technicalities involved in accessing it.

You may be surprised to hear speed mentioned in a research job. A common complaint of both researchers and data analysts is that "everybody wants it yesterday." Fortunately, many requests repeat themselves with stunning regularity, and the skillful resource professional will begin to build information packets to satisfy those traditional requests. But many searches are challenging and are prompted by a need to respond to some outside influence or market demand—quickly! If you begin with a clear and mutually agreed-upon definition of the materials and information requested, you have accomplished the most important element in rapid information provision. A good staff, the right technology, a strong memory, developed note-taking skills, and efficient records management and retrieval will all help you to get information seekers what they need as quickly as possible.

In an information management position, you have the opportunity to meet and help coworkers from every department and level of employment within your organization. You'll be called on frequently, not just for formal requests for information but for the simple questions, such as "How many workers did we have in 1923?" or "Where exactly in the city was our first showroom?" The information resource professional is very often (and wisely) brought in early in the planning stages of most projects so he/she has a full understanding of the information needs of all concerned parties. This helps the researcher to best consider how to accomplish the task.

Frequently, you'll get requests for information that you don't understand. The person making the request may be unused to dealing with an information specialist and not particularly adept at expressing informational needs. That's where your communication skills and customer service orientation come into play. Skillful questioning, a patient manner with good eye contact and attending behavior will encourage people to express exactly what they perceive to be their requests. Your questions and discussion will help clarify the request and bring your results closer to their original intentions.

Supervision

The official title of sociologist is reserved for those individuals with advanced degrees. This book attempts to expose the undergraduate degree holder to a variety of professional options that might be best termed working sociologist positions. Research, because of the critical nature of both the process and outcomes, is, in most cases, going to be done under the authority of someone with a master's or doctoral degree in sociology or a related field.

Supervision has marvelous advantages for the new college graduate. It allows you to learn and, therefore, to make mistakes without the full burden of responsibility. If your supervisor is a professional, it means a work situation with opportunities to learn and grow with the assurance that you are meeting generally recognized professional standards.

Because supervision involves hiring, evaluating, and training, your opportunity to observe a professional researcher/manager will provide countless examples of people management styles that you can consider in anticipation of one day being in the same situation.

The idea of a leadership role for yourself in the future is what often spurs a worker to seek the education and experience needed to take a research management or directorship role. If you work hard in your new position and learn as much as you can, you may find yourself frustrated that you cannot make more decisions on your own. It's a wake-up call that means it's time to move on in your career and take the necessary professional development steps to make it happen.

Training and Qualifications

Your sociology degree will be your foot in the door to some of the possible positions in research and data analysis. Nonetheless, it's one thing to have a degree, but quite another to know your research field well, especially at the entry level.

Employers don't care whether you have built your skills in a classroom setting, at a part-time job, while in an internship, or in a volunteer position. They just want to know that you'll be able to do the work they're hiring you to do. Having had experience using necessary skills will certainly set you apart from the group of people who simply say they think they can do the work.

Research and data analysis can involve great creativity, intuition, and educated guesswork. Those are hard to determine in the interview process and even harder to pin down and evaluate. There are several attributes that go into the skill package of a research or data analysis position, and though how they are prioritized might be the subject of intense debate, most would agree on the following basic list:

- Organization
- Attention to detail
- Teaching skills
- Social skills (networking/discretion)
- Curiosity (for general information)

Organization
Stop in at a busy researcher's office and somewhere, on a desk, on the wall, on the computer screen, you are likely to discover a tracking chart of all the various ongoing projects and their individual stages of completion. Seldom is there the luxury of having only one project; there are usually many projects. The atmosphere may not be exactly chaotic, but it won't remind you of a library, either. It's more like the newsroom of a major daily right before press time. You may well ask "Why not just work straight through on one assignment, finish it, and move on to the next?" The reason for this should give you significant insight into the nature of research work.

Frequently, the researcher or data analyst cannot immediately acquire the materials or data he or she needs and must seek the help of another information specialist to provide that. This may involve letters, fax transmissions, E-mail, or telephone calls to anywhere in the world. Delays may occur, as these individuals have their own agenda, and they, in turn, may need to seek out additional information. Keeping track of these requests and the projects they relate to can be a task in itself. It even has a name—*traffic management*.

A library provides an excellent illustration of the need for organization. It also serves as an analogy for the work and role of the information specialist in any organization. A library, especially a large collection, is almost useless without the order imposed on it by indexing, cataloging, shelving, and retrieval systems. The newest in online catalogs provides the user with a book's location and availability. Without the system created by librarians (who can also function as researchers or data analysts), a library would be chaos and of very little use to us despite its potential.

But librarians do more than just order and shelve their collections. They create systems for sharing material between collections. Interlibrary loans are a good example of the librarian's ability to provide what he or she doesn't have by establishing sharing networks with those that do. Newer consortia of libraries often share databases and allow us to search the catalogs of other collections for material or references we may require.

In a nutshell, the job of the researcher or data analyst is to connect the information seeker with the desired information. It sounds simple. But it is a complex task, one demanding all of the sociology graduate's skills to perform efficiently, quickly, and at low cost.

Every part of your job in research and data interpretation cries out for organization. Organizing your resources, time, and priorities to fulfill the information requests you receive will make constant and ever-increasing demands on your organizational ability. How frustrating and wasteful to be asked for something you've done before and yet can no longer locate, necessitating an entire repeat search. Organization is a requisite for anyone entering this field.

Attention to Detail

The researcher or data analyst wants to provide exactly the information clients request. "Almost" or "close" isn't good enough for the professional. If someone wants to know how many teenage girls pierce their ears, facts about ear piercing in women eighteen to twenty-five years old isn't going to fit the bill. You'll need to dig deeper and find statistics on an age population of thirteen to nineteen years old to satisfy this request. The specialist is precise about facts for two reasons. First, clients are going to make decisions based on the information provided to them by the information resource. Second, these decisions will ultimately have an effect on the viability of the organization and its ability to stay in business and keep you, the research specialist, employed.

Social Skills

Listening, questioning, and determining needs are vital skills. The researcher or data analyst is interacting with people constantly to best ascertain information needs. Your possession of strong interpersonal skills will help you work quicker and smarter. To communicate successfully with a variety of people, you will need an easy-to-understand vocabulary and, sometimes, visual aids.

Working conditions will involve lots of partnerships and cooperation with others in a variety of fields. Your networks of contacts will be vital, and your day will include much telephone and computer work and probably a fair amount of written correspondence. The importance of good written and oral communication skills can't be emphasized enough.

Confidentiality is another important skill required in social research and data analysis. In research on topics such as the safe-sex practices of gay men, a new line of children's dolls based on a much-loved storybook character, or the indictment of a major political figure, one should easily discern the importance of confidentiality.

With top-level access to privileged information in any organization and first look privileges at potentially sensitive or powerful findings, it is essential the information specialist be trusted and valued for his or her confidentiality and discretion.

Earnings

To get a handle on the possible earnings range or spread for an entry-level information specialist, you'll need to look at these positions (by whatever job title) across the full spectrum of possible employment sites (nonprofit, business/industry, education, libraries, and so forth). Government position salaries average in the low- to mid-20s for bachelor's degree holders with minimum experience. College and university positions (database management, non–library science library positions) range somewhat higher up to the low 30s. Research assistants in business and industry with good software skills average $28,000 in their first position. A research position, for example, with a major magazine that requires surveys, statistical analysis, and other techniques—to develop profiles of the magazine's actual and potential readership that will attract advertisers and better position the content of the magazine—generally pays in the high 20s.

If you bring to your first position some specific information-management experience, better-than-average computer skills, and strong documentation of these abilities, you can expect your entry-level salary to more closely approximate the high end of a stated range. For stated entry-level salaries, you may be able to negotiate as much as 10 percent more with exceptional experience.

Career Outlook

In determining the future needs for social research and data analysis, you will immediately encounter a research challenge of your own. For example, let's look at one specific job title, that of market research analyst. These individuals—who most often work in business and industry—are charged with seeking growth opportunities for their firms by tracking new and growing markets, suggesting the de-marketing of no-longer viable products, recommending product changes to correspond to new needs and uses, and developing initiatives to respond to competition in the marketplace.

Because the competitive marketplace is increasingly volatile and the global market a reality, information sourcing and data analysis have become crucial aspects of marketing strategy. Jobs in this business sector for researchers and data analysts will grow faster than average over the next ten years. On the other hand, these positions demand that the sociology graduate arrive at business and industry's doorstep with a correspondingly complete set of skills. The very same business climate that demands researchers and data analysts stay competitive demands competitive qualifications of their applicants.

In academics, a large part of the research workload is undertaken by graduate students and faculty. In an environment that prizes the graduate degree, it is a challenge for a new job candidate with a bachelor's degree to find a spot. Nevertheless, as the job ads cited in this chapter demonstrate, with diligence you can find an entry-level research position and use your experience, and perhaps a benefit package that may include tuition benefits to advance your education and qualifications. Positions in academia are expected to grow at an average rate over the next ten years.

In the human service field itself, research and data analyst positions are often embedded within other job titles and, consequently, hard to identify and track. Because of the numbers of college graduates entering the helping professions at every degree level, it is expected that even with the anticipated growth in agencies and organizations dealing with social issues, supply will exceed demand and growth will be average or slightly slower than average over the next ten years.

You would not want to design a career strategy based on supply and demand. After all, these estimates are based on aggregate numbers, and you are looking for just one job. Nevertheless, it's a good idea to have your eyes wide open about job probabilities in whatever field you ultimately choose. But, regardless of what the experts say about your chances, if you are truly interested in a particular area and have a résumé that will get you in the door for an interview, by all means go for it.

The underlying point in any discussion of job outlook is the issues of competitiveness and the fit between your particular combination of skills and attributes and those the employer is seeking. To ensure the brightest outlook possible for your career in social research and data analysis, not just for your first job but for your continued employment in a changing market, remember one thing: use your present situation to acquire as many skills as possible. This book, and others in the Great Jobs series, has stressed the need to have as many portable skills as possible. Portable skills go with you from job to job.

If you're lucky enough to still be in college when you read this, take advantage of the suggestions in this chapter and tap into your college's computer services and learn as much as you can. Meet all of your sociology professors and learn about their career histories and their research interests. Get their views on the job market. Meet and talk, in person or by telephone, to as many alumni as you can who are working in sociology related careers to hear their views on the best job preparation and hiring needs in their fields. Do an internship, if at all possible, that focuses on research or data analysis—even if the content area is outside sociology. Your experience with research methods or software systems is more portable than the topic of the research.

Once on the job, use this same advice. Meet and get to know your colleagues. Find out what their research interests may be. Take advantage of all your benefits. Attend professional development workshops, seminars, and conferences if you can. If your employer provides some sort of educational benefit, use it. Take courses that will not only make you a more valuable employee right now, but in the future, as well.

Though it may be a challenge to sum up the career outlook for all the possible research and data analyst opportunities available to you at graduation, it is no exaggeration to say that the career outlook is brightest for those who know and take full advantage of their current opportunities.

Strategy for Finding the Jobs

Perhaps the best test of your research potential would be to leave this section out of the chapter! Research positions and data analyst jobs are prevalent but widely dispersed across the employment spectrum. A good-sized organization, for example, might only have one researcher and one data analyst, or the two jobs might be combined. Locating these positions is difficult because they could be in the marketing, personnel, customer relations, or computer services department. You can enhance your job prospects by incorporating the considerations described in this section into your efforts.

Networking is essential for understanding the breadth of occupational opportunities available to you and for hearing firsthand about working conditions and hiring considerations. A college is perhaps the best place to start networking because you have an immediate network of alumni who share the common bond of your alma mater. There should be many graduates in sociology who have gone ahead of you to careers such as the one you seek. Be certain to check with your career office about connecting with these alumni.

The tremendous variety of research positions available in many different settings argues strongly for making some decisions that focus your search. It would be difficult to master the specific vocabulary, concerns, and issues of any one area if each week you were interviewing everywhere from cancer research facilities to doll manufacturers. Use your reading, networking with faculty and alumni, and information interviewing to help you sharpen your focus on one, two, or three of the job areas listed later in this chapter.

One networking technique—informational interviewing—has gotten some very bad press lately. Too many career experts have suggested job candidates use the pretense of an informational interview to present themselves as candidates for a job. At the same time that this duplicitous strategy began to be used with increasing frequency, managers in organizations were doing more work with fewer resources. They were less inclined to offer job seekers any kind of an interview, much less an informational interview.

Things have eased a bit in organizations and there is an appreciation that informational interviewing helps to raise the overall knowledge and education of the job seeker. The more aware the job seeker, the better the employment candidate. Everyone who hires understands he or she must play a part to raise the general employability of the market.

Those seeking informational interviews have become more candid, as well. They now know to frankly express where they are in their job search and what they hope to accomplish in the informational interview. They put their cards on the table and nobody's time is wasted.

Another new twist on the informational interviewing is using your own alumni network. Most colleges maintain networks of alumni, some specifically for career information. Talk to your alumni director, explain the kinds of alumni you want to talk with and why, and see if he or she can help.

Once you have an opportunity to sit down and talk with a professional researcher or data analyst, ask about how he or she hires for entry-level jobs. What education background and qualifications are being sought. After you talk with these professionals, you'll have a better sense of the kinds of information specialties that seem to match your interests and talents.

Informational interviewing will help you gather more information about jobs and work environments. For example, library work is often thought of as being solitary and in a very quiet setting. Talk with a professional to uncover the realities. Library staff members do have fun, and teamwork is critical to their success. Advertising is often thought of by students as a busy, hectic, and unconventional industry. Information specialists working in this industry may find themselves very busy indeed, but the work is often not as glamorous as some believe it is. No matter what type of work or work setting you are considering, find out what it's really like. Talk with other entry-level employees as well as seasoned veterans to get the complete picture, so you can better judge for yourself whether that setting would be a good place to work.

Focus Your Search

To begin building a career as an information specialists, you will have to—at a fairly early stage in your career—make a decision about how you want to specialize. You will certainly be able to gain an entry-level position with a bachelor's degree, but to see career growth in an information specialty you will probably need an advanced degree. If library work interests you, for example, you would be able to obtain several types of library jobs with a bachelor's degree in sociology, but if you hope to work as a librarian, a master's degree in library science will be required. If you are interested in organizing the information gathered by a large corporation, an advanced degree in information systems management or a more general master's in business administration would be needed to move into upper levels of management.

So how do you begin to decide what to specialize in? Part-time work, summer jobs, and internships are all employment opportunities you can use while you're in school. They can give you experience in various environments to see what they're like, what type of people work in each setting, and to gain a deeper understanding of the nature of the work.

Peterson's Internships is a fine resource for finding internship opportunities on an ongoing basis. The Peterson's directory contains research positions in human services, education, parks and recreation, business, law and criminal justice, and most business and nonprofit organizations.

Though most internships are unpaid, if you can afford to take an internship, it often breaks the cycle of "no experience—no job." You'll come away from the internship with solid research experience, references from professional researchers, and a network of new acquaintances to support you in your job search upon graduation.

If you have already graduated, you may want to consider temporary or term employment opportunities. Recent statistics indicate that about 28 percent of the new positions created in the first twenty-eight months of the current recovery were temporary positions. This kind of employment can be useful if you want to experience several types of jobs before you make a commitment to specialize in one area or field. Temp agencies operate in nearly every geographic location, and some of them specialize in the type of placement they make (paralegal, systems management, and so forth).

Possible Job Titles

The variety and confusion of job titles should indicate several important things to the job searcher:

- **The field of information specialization remains largely undefined, at least in job titles.** Certainly, those who employ people to act as information specialists have not yet agreed on a common terminology. The lack of a definitive job title may also indicate individual job roles vary equally as much. People working in informational services still organize themselves by content area and not by their more general role as information networkers.
- **The lack of a common job title requires you to read and carefully understand the job description for which you are applying.** It is in these job duties and responsibility delineations that you will come to appreciate the focus and emphasis in that particular position and

whether it meets not only your expectations of the job of an information specialist, but if you have the particular skill package the employer is seeking.

Data analyst	Research director
Labor force and manpower	Social science analyst
Policy analyst	Social survey director
Population analyst	Statistical analyst
Principal investigator	Survey research technician

Professional Associations

In the following, you will find a wide range of organizations that will be able to provide additional data about particular information specialties. Review the "Members/Purpose" section for each organization and decide whether the organization pertains to your interests. Membership in one may well be worth the investment in terms of networking opportunities, job listings, or placement services. Remember, some organizations will provide limited career information at no charge, but if you want to receive publications that often include job listings, you must actually join the organization. Many, however, have greatly reduced membership dues for full-time students.

American Consultants League
30466 Prince William St.
Princess Anne, MD 21853
Members/Purpose: Full- and part-time consultants in varied fields of expertise
Training: Offers a home study program
Publications: *Consulting Intelligence*

American Library Association
50 East Huron St.
Chicago, IL 60611
Members/Purpose: Librarians, libraries, trustees, friends of libraries, and others interested in the responsibilities of libraries in the educational, social, and cultural needs of society

Publications: *ALA Handbook of Organization and Membership Directory, ALA Washington Newsletter, American Libraries, Library Systems Newsletter, Library Technology Reports*
Job Listings: Offers placement services; see *American Libraries* for listings

**American Society for
Information Science**
8720 Georgia Ave., Suite 501
Silver Spring, MD 20910-3602
Members/Purpose: Information specialists, scientists, librarians, administrators, social scientists, and others interested in the use, organization, storage, retrieval, evaluation, and dissemination of recorded specialized information
Training: Conducts continuing education programs and professional development workshops
Publications: *Annual Review of Information Science and Technology, Bulletin,* handbook and directory, *Jobline, Journal of the American Society for Information Sciences, Proceedings*
Job Listings: Maintains placement service; see *Jobline.*

**Association of
American Publishers**
71 Fifth Ave.
New York, NY 10003-3004
Members/Purpose: Trade association representing producers of hardbound and softbound general, educational, trade, reference, religious, scientific, technical, and medical books; instructional materials; classroom periodicals; maps, globes, tests, and software
Training: Conducts seminars and workshops on various publishing topics, including rights and permissions sales, and educational publishing
Publications: *AAP Exhibits Directory, AAP Monthly Report, Green Book of College Publishing, International Fairs Calendar*

International Guild of Professional Consultants
5003 Red Bug Lake Rd., Suite 403
Winter Springs, FL 32708
Members/Purpose: Supporting the educational and communication needs of consultants throughout the world
Publications: *Powerlines* (bimonthly), *IPGC Report*

National Science Foundation
4201 Wilson Blvd.
Arlington, VA 22230
Members/Purpose: Independent agency in the executive branch concerned primarily with the support of basic and applied research and education in the sciences and engineering. Funds scientific research in many areas including social science research.
Publications: Annual report, *Antarctic Journal of the U.S.*, *Bulletin*, guide to programs, *Science Indicators*
Job Listings: Contact the personnel office for information.

Society for Nonprofit Organizations
6314 Odana Rd., Suite 1
Madison, WI 53719-1141
Members/Purpose: Executive directors, staff, board members, volunteers, and other professionals who serve nonprofit organizations
Training: Sponsors seminars and workshops on nonprofit management and leadership
Publications: *National Directory of Service and Product Providers to Non-Profit Organizations, Nonprofit World: The National Nonprofit Leadership and Management Journal*, resource center catalog.
Job Listings: Suggests job seekers review *Community Jobs*

Special Libraries Association
1700 18th St. NW
Washington, DC 20009-2514
Members/Purpose: International association of information professionals who work in special libraries serving business, research, government, universities, newspapers, museums, and institutions that use or produce specialized information
Training: Conducts continuing education courses
Publications: *Information Outlook, Who's Who in Special Libraries*
Job Listings: Provides employment services; see publication called *Jobline*

Notes

Chapter 9

1. *In Pursuit of the Ph.D.*, by William G. Bowen and Neil L. Rudenstine, Princeton University Press, 1992.
2. Elapsed time to degree: number of years between entry to graduate school and the awarding of the Ph.D.
3. *Occupational Outlook Handbook*, 2002–2003. Bureau of Labor Statistics, U.S. Department of Labor. Electronic edition.
4. *The NEA 2001 Almanac of Higher Education.* National Education Association.
5. *Occupational Outlook Handbook*, 2002–2003. Bureau of Labor Statistics, U.S. Department of Labor. Electronic edition.

Chapter 10

1. "The Growth of Youth Gang Problems in the United States: 1970–1998." Office of Juvenile Justice and Delinquency, U.S. Department of Justice, April 2001.
2. *The World Almanac and Book of Facts: 2001.* Electronic edition.
3. *The World Almanac and Book of Facts: 2001.* Electronic edition.
4. *New York Times Magazine*, December 18, 1994, p. 30.
5. "Economic Perspectives in Alcoholism Research, Alcohol Alert No. 51." National Institute of Alcohol Abuse and Alcoholism, 2001.
6. *The World Almanac and Book of Facts: 2001.* Electronic edition.
7. Ibid.
8. "The Numbers Count." National Institute of Health Publication No. 01-4584.
9. "A Profile of Older Americans: 2000." Administration on Aging (AOA), U.S. Department of Health and Human Services.

Chapter 11

1. *HR* Magazine Online, Society for Human Resource Management, shrm.org.

Chapter 12

1. From the Office of Personnel Management USA JOBS website: usajobs.opm.gov.
2. *U.S. News and World Report*, February 18, 2002.

Index